Tracks West – New Mexico:

The True Cost of Civil War

by

Elizabeth Wall Rogers

ACKNOWLEDGMENTS

Many years ago, I read *The Robber Barons* by Matthew Josephson. The first edition included a short history of Stephen B. Elkins. At the time I lived in Elkins, West Virginia. I was curious since Elkins practiced as an attorney in New Mexico and spoke Spanish. My father grew up in Cuba as an American. Like Elkins, he adopted a second culture. Later, another edition of the book was printed. It did not include Elkins. It appeared there was some dispute about his status as a "Robber Baron." I vowed to research the subject until my questions were answered.

This project has taken over twenty-five years. I thank the judges of the U. S. Court of Appeals, 4th Circuit in Richmond, Virginia in 1992 who accepted the recommendation of Judge James Sprouse of West Virginia. They encouraged my project.

More recently there has been support from the Library of Virginia, then the Osher Group at the University of Richmond. The assistance of the University's Technology Help Desk and Technology Lab have been critical to the book's completion. I especially thank Anastasia Salnikova.

Table of Contents

Preface 2
Chapter One: Occupy the Gold Fields 1
Chapter Two: Colonel James H. Carleton 17
Chapter Three: Remove Rebels and Indians 50
Chapter Four: Mines vs. Reservations 71
Chapter Five: The Ute Reservation 97
Chapter Six: International Interest 114
Chapter Seven: A Navajo Crisis 140
Chapter Eight: A Telling Census 153
Chapter Nine: Politics and Indian Investigations 191
Chapter Ten: Michael Steck 223
Chapter Eleven: The Utes Revolt 243
Chapter Twelve: An Election Scandal 280
Chapter Thirteen: Empty Promises 318
Chapter Fourteen: Selling Two Grants for A Railroad . 343
Chapter Fifteen: "New Mexico All Right" 378
Chapter Sixteen: Politics, Riots and Railroads 401
Chapter Seventeen: Steve Elkins 442
Chapter Eighteen: The Snake Sheds Its Skin 471
Chapter Nineteen: The Financial Wizard 517
Chapter Twenty: Comanches and the Texas Cattle Trade
.... 546
Chapter Twenty-One: The Treasure 573
Chapter Twenty-Two: Smoke Signals 597

Preface

In 1861, when New Mexico was invaded by Confederate Texans, the nation was virtually bankrupt. A plan was adopted in Washington to have Union soldiers in the West mine for gold while protecting the life and property of citizens and new settlers. The treatment of hostile Indians who defended their hunting grounds became a matter of discretion on the part of the Army commander entering and crossing Indian country. He would not normally initiate an attack but would certainly mount a defense. Punishment for continuous Indian raids on stock and other property in newly settled areas was considered "chastisement."

The Treaty of Guadalupe-Hidalgo was the settlement of the Mexican War. Its resolution protected the land grant claims of many Mexicans who lived within the confines of American New Mexico. The Mexican and

Spanish land grants did not have formal boundaries. Their descriptions indicated many were over 100,000 acres. Their deeds or patents were covered by documents held in the Santa Fe archives. The 36th Congress of the United States provided an act to confirm these land claims of former Mexican citizens for lands granted under Mexican rule.

The Gadsden Purchase was made in June 1854 when Mexico agreed to sell its lands on the treaty's border for $10,000,000. That land, 29,670 square miles, was part of what became Arizona in 1864. It also accommodated the building of a railroad along the two nation's borders. It attempted to settle conflicts which arose after the Guadalupe-Hidalgo resolution.

The Colorado Territory's southern border was established February 1861. The new boundary line cost New Mexico most of Los Conejos country. The decision was not popular with the New Mexico Assembly, but no direct confrontation with Congress was sought. The New Mexico Territory had fought to maintain its own southern boundary against previous encroachments by Texas. That boundary had been in dispute over the location of the Rio Grande.[1] In 1864, New Mexico and Arizona were divided by the 109° meridian.[2]

The 1787 Northwest Ordinance was first designed for the development of Ohio, at the time a territory of the United States. It was the model for New Mexico's Organic Act that established the Territory, gave it temporary boundaries, and provided for territorial government. Humane treatment of Indians was advised, but there was no specific means of enforcement. It was a kind of internal colonial system and a bill of rights rolled into one act.[3] It

---

[1] Keleher, William A., *Turmoil in New Mexico*, Book One, Chap. Six, "General Kearny Comes to Santa Fe," p. 126, fn. 48.
[2] Colton, Ray C., *The Civil War in the Western Territories*, Chap. 8, "Political Developments," p. 203.
[3] Lamar, Howard R., *The Far Southwest, 1846-1912: A Territorial History*; Univ. of New Mexico Press, Albuquerque, 1966 (Revised Edition). Introduction, p. 6.

supported public education with land and denied slavery, demanding just treatment of the Indian population.

The Ordinance anticipated that government would evolve through several stages, first with appointed officials, next with local self-government, and finally, with a minimum of 60,000 population eligible to vote, capable of electing a legislature and a member of Congress. In this last stage, the territory could form a Constitution and choose statehood. The document kept the fine balance between the rights of the individual and the requirements of Empire.

Chapter One: Occupy the Gold Fields

July 1861 – October 1861

It was July 21, 1861. Rumors of Confederate invasion on New Mexico's southern district spread across the territory with the speed of a prairie fire. Most regular Union troops were secretly withdrawn for duty in the East. Sensing their absence, hostile tribes preyed on vulnerable white settlements and ranches.

The area's Indian agents had every reason for alarm. The Territory was about 235,000 square miles and defended by only 2,466 trained soldiers. Fort Craig and Fort Union, separated by over 175 miles, contained the greatest number of regular Union troops.[4]

John Greiner, Indian agent at Santa Fe, wrote to his colleague, Apache agent Michael Steck at Mesilla's Fort Fillmore, near the Texas – New Mexico border.

Dear Doctor [Steck]:
[He describes his office and the safe he guards there. It weighs 4200 lbs.] . . . but I have not a cent in it nor is it probable that I shall ever have unless they make me a sub treasurer and send the money out here to pay off with instead of drafts.

I have had several pleasant interviews with the Governor – talked with

---

[4] Colton, Ray C., *The Civil War in the Western Territories;* University of Oklahoma Press, Norman, 1959, p. 13.

him freely and fully upon the condition of the Placer mines and think that leasing them out at $6,000 a year which he has done especially as the leases [sic – leasers] appear to have all the knowledge and skill to ensure their full development. They are getting out gold in enough quantity to ensure their entire success. [The two agents and other local authorities have interests in the area mines.]

[He reports on learning Ceran St. Vrain, Kit Carson, and J. Francisco Chaves accepted positions as officers in New Mexico's 1st Regiment. Dr. Steck's request to be named the territory's Indian Superintendent was recently refused. Greiner continues in a humorous vein to cheer him up.]

What are you doing down there [at Mesilla] among the Secessionists of Arizona? Some say that you are part and parcel of the sutler's[5] establishment at Fort Fillmore. Others that you are about resigning and going home! You certainly are not green enough for that. Another story is that you are still more foolish than that if possible and are about fighting some fellers there, as you have been seen practicing with pistols day and night for weeks past. How is it? You surely are not demented! Some say that Fort Fillmore is to be taken by the Secessionists. Others agree that Fort Bliss will be captured by our troops and the 500 Secessionists among you kicked

---

[5] The Army post's store. See *Pioneers of the Mesilla Valley*, Paxton Price. Biography of Colonel Samuel John Jones, p.118. ". . . . Jones had secured the appointment of sutler of nearby Fort Fillmore. The sutler sold food, liquor, and other necessities to soldiers. These men were often sponsored by city merchandizers, or patrons.

like thunder! How is it? Write by return mail and give me all the news.

When will you come up here? Yours ever,

John Greiner[6]

John Greiner first came to New Mexico in 1851 from Ohio. He was a former printer who joined President Harrison's campaign in 1840. A popular temperance orator, he also wrote election songs. Before he was appointed New Mexico's Indian agent, he was Ohio's state librarian. Following the Indian agency assignment, he was territorial governor in 1852. In Santa Fe, he was Receiver of the United States land office in 1861.[7]

The rumors of attack, of course, proved all too true. On June 23, 1861, New Mexico's Fort

---

[6] Letters of John Greiner, NM Territorial, General Records of the Office of the Secretary . . . . Letters sent relating to employees of the Treasury Department and its bureaus, 1857-78. 56.2.1 (Textual Records: Name and subject indexes. Also, 56.3.1 Correspondence. Textual Records. Correspondence, 1841-1917.)

[7] Appleton's Encyclopedia of American Biography.

Fillmore commander resigned to join the Confederacy – along with six leading officers of the California district. Many forts had to be assigned new commanders.

On July 23, 1861, Colonel John R. Baylor, and his 400 to 700 Texas Confederate Rangers, struck New Mexico's Fort Fillmore and occupied the nearby town of Mesilla.[8] The town had recently declared itself the seat of Confederate government in the territory of Arizona. The morale of the fort's 380 men was poor and its commander, Major Isaac Lynde, was newly appointed.

The Union abandoned the fort, and the Union troops were caught on route to Fort Selden. They were without adequate water and forced to surrender. Baylor occupied Mesilla and Fort Fillmore. He declared the Territory of Arizona, including all that

---

[8] Colton, Ray C., *The Civil War in the Western Territories*, Chap. 2, "Confederate Invasion,"; pp. 13-25.

portion of New Mexico south of the thirty-fourth parallel, north latitude, extending from Texas to California, a part of the Confederate States of America. He awaited reinforcements from Texas led by General H. H. Sibley to mount a full-scale attack on northern New Mexico.

The Union Army in the East commanded the full attention of the Lincoln administration until August. Orders from Washington were then issued to General E. V. Sumner. Many California officers resigned their commissions to serve the south where their homes were located. Colonel Edward S. Canby was appointed in charge of New Mexico in June.

At nearly the same time as the Rebel attack on Fort Fillmore a messenger from Indian country on the west delivered news to Colonel Canby. It was as forbidding as the enemy on the southern border. The rider reported a scene of horror at Fort Fauntleroy in

Navajo territory. It would burn itself into the collective souls of the Navajo people, leaving a bitterness against the Americans not soon to be forgotten.

Fort Fauntleroy was the westernmost fort in New Mexico. For several years it was the practice at the fort to supply the Navajos with rations of meat, flour, and other provisions on a fixed day each month. It was expected that the tribe would refrain from raids on white settlements as a sign of gratitude. These rations excited the Navajos and drew families who traveled far to attend. Some tribal members walked, others came on horseback to see the fort and the soldiers as well as get their provisions. Horse races were put on for the day's entertainment, to be enjoyed and participated in by both soldiers and tribe members. It was customary for the Indians to race their horses against the soldiers' horses. The Navajos considered horse racing more than a sport. They gambled extravagantly. The Indians brought trinkets and blankets to trade for tobacco and whiskey.[9]

The races were held outside the fort. Inside, bets were laid. The day was beautiful, the scent of fall, cedar, and piñon filled the air.

Among the soldiers, some bet their horses, the rest, money. The Indians were wild with excitement this day because one of their tribe, a six-foot-four Navajo, Pistol Bullet, had bet his horse against the post surgeon's quarter horse. Lieutenant Ortiz would ride the quarter horse.

It was mid-afternoon when the final race between Pistol Bullet and Ortiz began. The start went well, but within seconds the Navajo and his horse had trouble. Everyone rushed to see the problem. Pistol Bullet's horse's rein had been recently cut with a knife. The Indian had lost control. Lieutenant Ortiz continued around the track.

---

[9] Keleher, William A., *Turmoil in New Mexico,* Book Four, The Long Walk, Chap. Two, "Then the Navajos," p. 298.

The Navajos surrounded the judges, also fort soldiers. The Navajos claimed they were tricked. They insisted the race must be run again. The judges held to their decision. Pistol Bullet's defective bridle was just a bit of hard luck for the Indians. An interpreter announced the judges' decision. The Indians rushed for their bets inside the fort. The officer of the day ordered the gates closed.

Inside the fort Ortiz and the quarter horse were paraded while soldiers beat drums, played musical instruments, and celebrated wildly.

Outside, an apparently drunken Indian rushed the gates to get inside. Sentry Morales fired on him point-blank. The Navajos on the outside were frightened they might also be shot. They turned to run for open country. They pulled their women and children behind them. The soldiers pursued the fleeing Navajos, using their rifles and bayonets. The Indians left behind their dead and wounded.

Amid the chaos, one soldier was seen shooting and seriously wounding a squaw and killing her two children. An officer, a witness to this wanton outrage, arrested the soldier and disarmed him. Lieutenant Ortiz, of the winning horse, threatened Captain Hoydt with a cocked pistol. Hoydt was forced to let the murderer go. Immediately afterward, Hoydt reported Ortiz to the commanding officer. Hoydt was told Ortiz was in the right. The commanding officer then forced a sergeant to fire on the Indians who were in range, and to continue to do so until all were gone.[10]

The commanding officer was later reported to be Manuel Chavez. He was faced with a court martial, but the trial was delayed and finally never held. The Union men now had two enemies: Confederates and Navajos. The Confederates in Texas were still occupying the southern district.

---

[10] Ibid, Book Four, "Then the Navajos," p. 299.

Colonel Canby foresaw four major hurdles to New Mexico's defense: lack of money, acts of treason, a shortage of men, and raiding Indians. He first suspended the writ of habeas corpus. There would be no unauthorized arrests or annoyances to peaceable citizens. The only arrests to be made would be at the order of the superior commander of each district. These would be in cases of persons threatening the public safety. He considered that although a great many citizens in the southern district were Confederate sympathizers, none would commit treason or endanger others.

Colonel Canby then wrote the Paymaster General in Washington. He must provide his troops with clothing, food, and arms for the Territory's defense. Citizens sensed the public's vulnerability.[11] He had met with the chief

---

[11] Ibid, Book Two, Chap. One, "The Confederates Invade New Mexico," p. 155.

quartermaster and chief commissary officer and determined to float a loan which would be capitalized by the Territory's business community. Canby, and his financial officers wrote promissory notes to these merchants and capitalists that the money would be repaid in Treasury notes at 7.3 per cent interest from the date of the loan. If anything failed, he was personally pledged for the interest.[12]

On August 8, 1861, the Lincoln administration and Congress passed the Confiscation Act which permitted the Union to seize Confederate property. In New Mexico, Territorial Secretary W. F. M. Arny, an ardent abolitionist, was interested in punishing the supporters of Confederate invaders.[13] The western war is clearly a war to control the valuable minerals of Colorado and New Mexico.

---

[12] Ibid.
[13] Murphy, Lawrence R., *Frontier Crusader: W. F. M. Arny*, Chap. 7, "Secretary of the New Mexico Territory," p. 117.

On September 7, 1861, John Greiner wrote Treasury Secretary Salmon Chase, a fellow Republican friend from Ohio. He asked for an advancement of funds. As he requested, the amount would be drawn from his [Greiner's] salary. It would be used to send Dr. Steck back East to safety. Money was extremely scarce in the Territory and the only bank was the Federal Depository. The Federal bank was a place of safekeeping and served as the source of the Union soldiers' pay. Greiner asked for $625, his salary for the period of January 1, 1862 to March 31, 1862.[14] The outcome of the transaction is not known. However, through the efforts of Steck's brother-in-law, the doctor was made post sutler for the Seventh Regiment of General Meade's brigade in the Army of the Potomac.[15] It is likely Chase's influence was also brought to bear.

---

[14] Letter of John Greiner to Salmon Chase, 9/7/1861. Letters sent relating to employees of the Treasury Dept. and its Bureaus, 1857-78, Textual Records: Name and Subject Indexes.

On September 8, Colonel Canby requested Colorado Governor Gilpin to send four to six companies as reinforcements. The dispatches did not go through immediately.

Months went by while Union forces were gathered on the California coast. General E. V. Sumner was the Pacific's Commander-in-Chief for Colonel Canby. Newly appointed in June 1861, Canby sought at once to combine and coordinate the many distant military installations.

Governor Connelly wrote Washington about the Navajo Indians and their aggressive conduct on October 26, 1861. He proposed the sword or starvation.[16]

In December General Wright, replacing General Sumner, ordered Colonel James H. Carleton to command 1500 troops and reinforce Canby's

---

[15] PHD Dissertation of Paul A. Lester, "Michael Steck and New Mexico Indian Affairs, 1852-1865," Univ. of Oklahoma, 1986, p. 178.
[16] Ibid., Book Two, Chap. One, "Baylor, Sibley and Canby," p. 156.

army. Carleton had been an officer since the Mexican War, remaining in the area, but based in California. Recently he was a dragoon commander on the Utah border.[17] He previously served for two years in New Mexico and was familiar with its peculiarities. The settlers were mostly native Mexicans. The native population was predominantly Indian. Spanish was the common language. It was a Union territory, but peonage, a form of slavery, was practiced there.

---

[17] Dragoons were mounted infantry of a cavalry regiment who fought on foot.

Chapter Two: Colonel James H. Carleton

January 1862 – July 1862

Colonel Carleton was known as a stern disciplinarian, uncompromising, tenacious, and ambitious. His attention to detail was evident in his personal dress and grooming. Tall and broad-shouldered, his brows and jaw formidable, his steel-grey eyes appeared as deadly as arrowheads. He was a familiar figure in southern New Mexico. He was assigned to New Mexico after the Mexican War.[18]

---

[18]Hunt, Aurora, *Major General James Henry Carleton,* 1814-1873, *Western Frontier Dragoon*, "The Battle of Buena Vista."

His wife, Sophia Garland Wolfe Carleton, owned twelve buildings, corrals, and other improvements in Albuquerque where Army provisions and equipment were stored.[19] His family resided in California, but he had spent at least two years as an officer in the Territory since 1849.

Carleton's primary officer was Lieutenant Colonel Joseph R. West who was given charge of companies E, G and H of the 1st California Infantry. He was assigned to relieve the garrison at Fort Yuma. West was to control traffic on the Colorado River until the troop crossing was complete.

Months went by while Union forces were gathered on the coast. Troops from the Sacramento area were recruited and began training at Fort Latham to be sent to Fort Yuma for New Mexico's service. The troops who trained for the assignment shortly became known as the California Column.

---

[19] Keleher, William A., *Turmoil in New Mexico*, Book Four, Chap. Eight, "Carleton on the Defensive," p. 458, fn. 146, pp. 507-508.

In Colorado, express messengers brought dispatches from General Canby in New Mexico requesting mounted troops on September 8, 1861. They were needed at Santa Fe at once to defend against approaching Texas troops. Two companies were recruited and sent to Fort Garland in September.[20] In mid-winter they were sent to Fort Craig and Fort Union.

During the early months of 1862 New Mexico awaited rescue by further forces from Colorado. At Denver, Governor Gilpin received Canby's reinforcement request at Camp Weld by February 10. He turned to John Slough, a Denver attorney and sometime miner, who was commissioned a Colonel. Sam Tappan was commissioned a Lieutenant Colonel and sent to Fort Wise, 200 miles below Denver in the southeastern

---

[20] Colton, Ray C., *The Civil War in the Western Territories*, Chap. Two, "Confederate Invasion," p. 20.

territory, to lead troops stationed there. They would meet near Pueblo in early March. Slough recruited two companies, 950 of his fellow miners and frontiersmen.

There were seven other companies under Major John M. Chivington at Camp Weld. They would combine at Fort Union by March 10 for further supplies. Colonel Slough took command at Fort Union with a battalion of U. S. Fifth Infantry, one detachment of cavalry, a single company of New Mexico volunteers, a four-gun battery, four mountain howitzers, accounting for his artillery support. The total rescue force would be 1,342 men. Operations were finally beginning to move forward toward Raton Pass and the rescue of New Mexico.[21]

Only two companies were mounted to scout, the rest of over a thousand men had marched the

---

[21] Ibid., Chap. Three, "Colorado to the Rescue," PP. 42-48.

entire freezing distance on foot in the roughest terrain. Those who came from Denver had made the 400-mile journey in thirteen days.

As they climbed the pass in bitter winter conditions, they were met by a courier who told them of the Union defeat at Valverde near Albuquerque. It was believed the Confederates were not aware of the reinforcements and were preparing to leave Santa Fe and attack Fort Union.

On February 8, 1862, Carleton wrote to Captain McMullen, Commander of Volunteers First Infantry at Camp Latham. "Order Second Lieutenant Rynerson (if he has accepted his appointment) to temporary duty with it."[22]

Will Rynerson was unusually tall, reputedly seven feet. He was from Kentucky, but he attended Franklin College in Illinois.[23] He read some law

---

[22] OR, War of the Rebellion, *Operations on the Pacific Coast*, Chap. LXIL, p. 852.
[23] Roberts, Gary L., *Death Comes for the Chief Justice;* University

while prospecting for gold in California.[24] Attaining rank in the state militia, he also served as deputy clerk of Amador County.[25] No other notice would be taken of him until the column would arrive at Fort Fillmore, New Mexico.

Gold and silver mining in New Mexico and its Arizona district were of primary interest to the California officers who developed the plan to reinforce Colonel Canby's troops. There is no doubt the same interest was shared in Washington when Carleton's forces were assigned. The appointment of Carleton's brother-in-law, Nathaniel Pishon, from sergeant to the captaincy of Company D, First California Cavalry, is a case in point.[26] Pishon and his company were among Carleton's advance

---

Press of Colorado, Niwot, 1990, p.57.
[24] Poldervaart, Arie W.; *Black Robed Justice*; Arno Press, New York, 1976, Ch. 7, p. 71.
[25] *New Mexico Historical Review,* LII:1, 1978; "Carleton's California Column: A Chapter in New Mexico's Mining History", Darlis Miller.
[26] Masich, Andrew E., *The Civil War in Arizona*; Chap. 1, "Column from California," p. 16.

soldiers who would later attempt rescue of one of Carleton's favored officers. Carleton had a special mission for Pishon and his men, but the assignment would be temporarily on hold.

When the Californians learned of the Union loss at Valverde just south of Fort Craig, more troops were added.[27] Carleton would march with a total of 2,350 men. On March 22 at Fort Yuma, the Gila River was flooding from heavy rains and the Colorado River was unable to carry the flood waters in its banks. The troops waited. Nearly all the houses in Colorado City were washed away. Carleton received a message that Sibley had defeated General Canby at Valverde near Fort Craig.

Carleton wrote to the Department in San Francisco for further assistance. The response came quickly. Five hundred more troops were sent. He had

---

[27] Colton; Ray C., *The Civil War in the Western Territories*, Chap. 2, "Confederate Invasion," p. 28. (Feb. 1862)

two hundred wagons, his own regiment, First Infantry, First Cavalry, five companies, and Colonel Shinn's battery. The Fifth Infantry California Volunteers would remain at Fort Yuma to back up the troops if needed. They could soon prevent a Confederate invasion of California and remove the enemy from Arizona and New Mexico.[28] They could also prevent a Confederate advance to the gold fields of Colorado.[29]

Colonel Carleton carefully guarded the secrecy of his mission. When Carleton and Major Edwin Rigg, another high-ranking officer, arrived at Fort Yuma for duty in New Mexico, they sent out spies to Tucson. The spies used the Sonoran route to avoid notice. They carried a secret code. The key to the code was locked at Fort Yuma.[30] The later

---

[28] Masich, Andrew E., *The Civil War in Arizona*, Chap. 1, "Column from California," p. 13.
[29] Colton, Ray C., *The Civil War in the Western Territories,* Chap. 2, "Confederate Invasion," p. 41.
[30] Masich, Andrew E., *The Civil War in Arizona,* Chap. 1, p. 30.

reports given by these spies were evidently erroneous, or at least misleading. A soldier gave a news account relating that five or six hundred Rebels were already reported at Tucson.[31] They were awaiting reinforcements. Ditches were dug, and earthworks thrown up. The rooftops of the houses held supports for muskets.

At Fort Yuma on March 6, Carleton sent his most trusted officer from his former dragoon company, Captain William McCleave, to the Pima Villages across the Colorado River.[32]

Carleton had one individual in mind for capture or hanging, left for his friend to serve as his avenger.

"There is one Elias Brevoort, of Santa Fe, a spy and a traitor. Let him be where he may, in the vicinity of Tucson; when caught, and if he be found

---

[31] Ibid, Chap. 6, "California Column Soldier Correspondents to the San Francisco *Daily* Alta, p. 166.
[32] Ibid., Chap. 1, "Column from California," p. 18.

guilty of playing the spy or traitor, let him be hung as speedily as possible."[33]

McCleave signaled to him with his forefinger across his neck.

Elias Brevoort was a former owner of the now-named Mowry Mine. He was also a mail contractor with Judge Joab Houghton. They received $16,750 yearly for the contract and held it since 1854. The contract was to deliver the mail once monthly to twelve towns between Santa Fe and San Antonio, Texas.

Other events interceded. It was finally decided that of the forty men McCleave took, only eight should serve as scouts and accompany him to White's mill. They would check on subsistence stores stocked away for the army's arrival. McCleave was lured into a trap.[34] He and his eight

---

[33] Keleher, William A., *Turmoil in New Mexico*, Book Three, Chap. Two, "On to the Rio Grande," p. 235.
[34] Colton, Ray C., *The Civil War in the Western Territories*; Chap. 5,

men were forced to surrender on March 20. Following their capture, McCleave and his scouts were taken to Confederate headquarters at Fort Fillmore, New Mexico.

In northern New Mexico, a lieutenant and twenty cavalry men found and captured several Rebel soldiers. The Union troops were above Fort Union, New Mexico. It was two a.m. on March 26, near Pigeon's ranch and the entrance to Glorieta Pass. The discovery revealed the presence of the enemy. Colonel Slough was alerted and began to prepare his men for battle. Two battles were fought beginning at dawn on the 26th at Apache Pass, and again at Glorieta Pass on the 28th. On the last date, Colonel Chivington's 400 men were sent to scout the area for Confederate reinforcements. They found none, but discovered the location of the supply train.

"Confederates in Retreat," p. 102.

They stormed the train. Someone escaped their raid and warned the 1100 Rebel forces.

The troops fought two day-long battles to a draw, but when the Confederates learned their supply train was destroyed, they sent up a flag of truce. The Generals leading the troops, brothers-in-law, were not present at the battles.[35] General Canby, at Santa Fe, did not issue an order to surrender. The Confederates began a retreat to Santa Fe to reach additional supplies.

At Santa Fe, Indian stores meant to last the tribes for the duration of the year were either found or released. Retreating Texans began their return home. One other battle occurred at Peralta as the Confederates sought plunder on the route to the Texas border.

---

[35] Ibid., Chap. 3, p. 86.

Colonel Joseph R. West commanded the 180-mile desert trek across the desolate basin and sandy dunes of the Colorado desert. Once at Fort Yuma, from February 17 to March 5, the command received the expedition's supplies in drenching rains. There was much concern for Confederate treachery. Despite extensive flooding, the supplies were safely stored.

When the California troops arrived, they were subjected to continuous drilling. In March Colonel Carleton consolidated his forces and sent them across the Colorado River. They reached the Pima Villages on April 30. The march ahead of 2,000 men began in earnest in early June. The troop units were staggered in groups of one hundred to preserve water.

Carleton appointed Captain William P. Calloway of Company I, First California Infantry to take command of the advance.[36] Two hundred seventy-two men represented both infantry and cavalry. They included the cavalry companies of Captains McCleave and Pishon of the First Cavalry. Lieutenant James Barrett commanded the absent McCleave's company. Second Lieutenant Jeremiah Phelan led a detachment of unattached recruits who would manage two mule-packed mountain howitzers and later join them.[37]

    The march was grueling, the desert phase often taken by night. They traveled on an alkaline road. The dust was up to six inches deep, its clouds rising two or three feet above the men's heads. The noon-day heat was once 119 degrees when they rested in the shade of a brush house.[38]

---

[36] Masich, Andrew E., *The Civil War in Arizona*, Chap. 2, "Arizona," p. 35.
[37] Ibid., pp. 35-36.
[38] Ibid., Chap. 7, "Arizona Dispatches, 1862," p. 178.

The General hinted the plan was to chastise the Tonto Apaches.[39] The information was generated to mislead Confederate spies. His real mission was to destroy Confederate forces and declare New Mexico Union territory. He would provisionally declare Arizona a U. S. territory and impose martial law. In the process, all Rebel properties would be confiscated, mainly mines. The troops were warned to avoid a fight with the Indians.

The most damaging occurrence of the Yuma-to-Tucson march was the loss of flour and hay stored for the army by the Pima Indians. A platoon of the Rebel's mounted rangers was sent along the Gila River to burn haystacks. Before the Union's arrival, they fired the hay at six stations. The Rebel unit that captured McCleave and his men returned the rest of the army's stores to the Indians. The advance guard led by Captain Calloway arrived at the Pima Villages on April 12. This was the point where the

---

[39] Ibid, Chap. 2, "Arizona," p. 37.

stage road left the Gila River for Tucson. Calloway was forced to repurchase the captured wheat.

General Carleton received his commission on the approach to Tucson.[40] He was told a ten-man Rebel post guarded Picacho Pass forty-five miles northwest of Tucson. There were two routes to Fort Thorn, the destination. Picacho Pass was the shorter one. The enemy intended to watch the road for the advancing Union Army. Still hoping to rescue McCleave and his men, Carleton sent Captain Calloway to cut off the route.[41]

Two detachments were assigned to surround the Rebel camp. The second detachment of ten men left first with Lieutenant Barrett in charge. They came upon a chaparral where Captain Hunter's Rebel pickets were playing cards at the base of Picacho Peak. Barrett's surprise led him to fire his pistol and demand surrender. Inside were Captain Hunter, a sergeant, and nine privates. The Rebels

---

[40] Ibid, p. 48.

were prepared. A volley of shots caught Barrett's men in their saddles.

Barrett was struck in the first volley. Only one of his men escaped to warn the first detachment of the deadly skirmish. They arrived in time to capture three Rebels, but Barrett and three of his men were killed and three wounded. Hunter and six of his nine men escaped.[42]

The Union dead were buried, and the scouts returned to the Army to join the advance on Tucson. Captain William Calloway's vanguard of 272 men now contained two mountain howitzers. He ordered a retreat to Stanwix Station, one hundred miles away. They met Lieutenant Colonel West and his detachment, returning to the Pima Villages. A permanent fortification was built and named Fort Barrett for the fallen officer. It would become a trading post for wheat and forage the Indians could supply.

---

[42] [42] Ibid, p.39.
Colton, Ray C., *The Civil War in the Western Territories,* Chap. 6, "California to the Rio Grande," p. 104

On May 14, the advance guard left Fort Barrett and traveled to old Fort Breckenridge. The U. S. flag was raised, and the "Star Spangled Banner" played. They continued to Tucson. On May 20, the California Advance Guard established a camp outside of Tucson. Colonel West was then ordered to leave Tucson to inspect Fort Buchanan.[43] Captain William McMullen would command Tucson.

General Carleton reached Tucson on June 7, 1862. The enemy had left the town. Most of the residents departed with the Rebels. Only chickens, dogs, and a few stragglers met the advance guard. Word was sent to Carleton that the way was clear. The General's promotion arrived just before reaching Tucson. He had planned a fanfare, including formalities. Following a ten-gun salute, on June 17, General Carleton declared martial law, and himself Arizona's military Governor. The next day, 1st

---

[43] Masich, Andrew E., *The Civil War in Arizona,* Chap. 3, "Campaigning," p. 58. Carleton blamed Col. West for food shortages and a rift developed between them. Soldiers had to be sent to far-flung post to have adequate provisions.

Lieutenant Benjamin F. Cutler was made military Secretary of State. Less than 500 people of the previous 1500 remained to view the spectacle.[44]

After reporting to California headquarters, the General began a program to install law and order to the new seat of government.[45] He arrested and imprisoned nine men and applied a graduated tax to businesses. A military pass system accounted for the comings and goings of all citizens entering or leaving town. A supply depot was established to aid other territorial forts. Licenses and a monthly fee were required of gambling houses. The money was to be deposited in a hospital fund for the sick and wounded of the California Column.

On June 8 Colonel West was placed in command of the District of Arizona.[46] Carleton sent him to inspect Fort Buchanan. His visit revealed the fort had been destroyed.

---

[44] Ibid., Chap. 2, "Arizona," p. 46; Chap. 7, "Arizona Dispatches," p. 206.
[45] Ibid., pp. 48-49
[46] Ibid., Chap. 3, "Campaigning," p. 58.

The site was consecrated with a flag raising and the scouts returned to Tucson.

Several days after the Column's arrival, a letter was received from T. Scheuner, metallurgist at the Mowry Mine near the territory's border with Mexico. Scheuner accused Sylvester Mowry of the Mowry Silver Mines of complicity in selling percussion caps and other war materials to the enemy. Mowry announced that he would be governor of the Territory in six months. He boasted of his ability to whip one hundred Northern troops. Another Arizona citizen provided information of the same nature about the mine owner.

Carleton sent Lieutenant Colonel E. E. Eyre with a detachment of troops to arrest Mowry. On June 13 Mowry was seized. An army board of officers under Lieutenant Colonel West was convened. The officers found Mowry guilty of all charges. Mowry, and other prisoners, were taken to Fort Yuma for imprisonment.[47] Mowry's mine was impounded. Carleton instructed Colonel West to bring all provisions of the mine to Tucson. These would help feed the hungry troops.

Since the outset of their journey, officials expected that Governor Pesquiera of Mexico's Sonoran state, would be able and agreeable to provide food for the troops. The General made a special offer to remove an earlier immigration ban on Mexicans wanting to cross the border to work in the mines on the lower Colorado River.[48] However, the difficulty of being at war with the French, as well as the poor crop return that year, halted the request.[49]

Money, or goods for barter, could not be had. The General asked the army to ship ten thousand yards of manta (cheap cotton cloth) and five thousand pounds of other "gifts" to be traded with the Indians for grain and fodder.

---

[47] Colton, Ray C., *The Civil War in the Western Territories*, Chap. 6, "California to the Rio Grande," pp. 109-110. Also, Masich, Andrew E., *The Civil War in Arizona,* Chap. 2, "Arizona," p. 49.
[48] Masich Andrew, *The Civil War in Arizona*, Chap. 5, "Border Patrol and Mustering Out," p. 120.
[49] Ibid, Chap. 2, p. 45, Chap. 3, p. 57, Chap. 4, p. 105.

Neither the Indian contractors or the Arizona white people and merchandizers trusted the army. California's economy was based on gold. The army dealt in scrip, or paper. Paper money was discounted as much as 60% during the war. General Wright, who followed General Sumner in mid-1862, earnestly tried to have the army pay California troops in hard currency. Citizens disliked government scrip, but specie was in short supply.[50] Those who carried coin were the most likely targets for robbery and murder.

General Carleton waited in Tucson until the entire column arrived to send his vanguard forward. He made certain his men and the town were supplied with adequate food and forage. On June 15 he sent his trusted express rider, John Jones, with Sergeant William Wheeler and a guide named Chaves, to get a message to General Canby that the Column was nearby.

---

[50] Ibid, Chap. 3, p. 59; Chap. 4, p. 96. Specie was gold or silver coin. Scrip was paper money discounted 60%.

Carleton exercised great caution in concealing the covert message on Jones' body, providing a second message easier to locate. Although Jones and his companions were apprehended, Jones alone escaped. The others were later found mutilated. After 200 miles traveling alone, Jones was then caught by Confederates, and jailed at Mesilla. A loyal Union townsman, John Lemon, provided Jones with a horse for his escape. The real message was secure and reached Canby. Lemon was nearly hanged.[51]

Lieutenant Colonel Edward Eyre was sent with his 140-man First California Cavalry out of Tucson. The detachment faced a harrowing 300-mile road trip in the summer heat with water only available at thirty-five to sixty-mile distances. They left on June 21 and arrived at Apache Pass on the old Overland Mail stage route on June 25. At noon four shots were heard, a likely Indian approach signal. The shots came from the area where their horses

---

[51] Colton, Ray C., *The Civil War in the Western Territories*, Chap. 6, "California to the Rio Grande," p. 111, fn. 27.

grazed under guard. Almost immediately, armed Indians appeared carrying a white flag.[52]

The detachment commander, Eyre, rode out to meet the party, hoisting his flag of truce. The chief was Cochise who left his 100 men to talk peace with Eyre. He offered a gift of pemmican and attempted a parley. The chief promised that neither the soldiers nor animals would be harmed. He requested food and tobacco which was given him. He further asked that they meet at sunset.

When Eyres' returned to his troops, he learned three men were missing. A search was conducted, and their bodies found. They had been stripped, their clothing and guns removed. A horse had also been stolen. They had defied orders and strayed from the troops. One officer in the command vehemently protested Eyres' decision not to engage the Indians, but Eyre followed Carleton's command.[53] The dead were buried, and the troops

---

[52] Masich, Andrew E., *The Civil War in Arizona*, Chap. 2, "Arizona," pp. 51-52. Also, Colton, p. 111.
[53] Ibid.

continued. When the men pitched their tents for the night, several shots were fired into the camp by Indians. One shot struck Surgeon Kittridge, wounding him. Another shot and killed a horse. However, there was no retaliation.

On July 23, 1862, Major David Fergusson was placed in command of the district of western Arizona at Tucson, encompassing the region between Fort Yuma and Fort Bowie.[54] Major Fergusson had formerly been chief commissary for the Californians.

Carleton held Colonel West responsible for the food shortage in the district. He replaced West with Fergusson and sent West to scout for food among the farmers along the Texas border. West was also to utilize the former Confederate flour mill at Franklin, Texas, owned by Simeon Hart. There were many lives dependent on finding food. Even the civilians at the Pinos Altos mining camp

---

[54] Ibid.

twenty miles from Mesilla were isolated and starving, threatened by Apaches.

One month after Lieutenant Colonel Eyres' experience with Cochise's 100-man party, on July 16, Captain Thomas L. Roberts' command was ambushed by Apaches. Cochise and Mangus Colorado led the Indian party. The army traveled through Apache Pass with one infantry company, one cavalry detachment, and two mountain howitzers. The Indians were strewn among the boulders on the mountainsides. A four-hour fight ensued while the army maneuvered the howitzers in place. This was the Indians' first, and fatal, experience with heavy artillery, a rude awakening.[55]

Many Indians were killed by the howitzers and the rest quickly withdrew. Afterward, at Carleton's command, Major Theodore Coult and a company of the Fifth California Infantry built a post at the Pass to discourage the

---

[55] Colton, Ray C., *The Civil War in the Western Territories*, Chap. 6, pp. 114-115.

Apaches. The Roberts' infantry command later marched fifty-four miles in thirty hours, under a burning sun with dust all about them, and almost without water. They had only one meal in twenty-four hours, a remarkable accomplishment.[56]

On the route to the Rio Grande, the General and his company found the bodies of nine miners from Pinos Altos. They had been murdered and mutilated. One man's body was tied to a stake and burned. Again, they buried bodies. The unfortunate party had attempted to escape. Certain of their origin, Carleton realized the desecration belonged to Mangus Colorado and his band. The Chief continually raided the attempts to mine at the property he claimed for his tribe. Soon after the burial, Carleton sent out his scouts with dispatches for General Canby.

The danger of the Apache attack led Carleton to establish a post named Fort Bowie to protect the Butterfield

---

[56] Ibid, Chap. 7, "Arizona Dispatches: 1862," pp. 248-249.

Stage and any Americans crossing Apache Pass. Although the mail was canceled due to Apache attacks, Carleton designated an elite corps of vedettes[57] and reestablished mail deliveries on the southern route.[58]

The Column's vanguard arrived at the Rio Grande on August 2. Carleton sent a letter by courier to General Canby at Santa Fe reporting on the status of his command, and his company's expected arrival. He reached Fort Thorne and the booming guns of welcome on August 1. 1862.[59] He expressed appreciation for his troops and by letter asked General Canby for permission to inspect several forts in north Texas before taking command at Santa Fe. General Canby advised him to use his own judgment in the disposition of troops in Arizona and New Mexico. The Confederates had retreated. Carleton assumed

---

[57] Vedettes were sentries positioned beyond an army's outposts to observe the movements of the enemy.
[58] Masich, Andrew E., *The Civil War in Arizona,* Chapter 2, p. 52. Vedettes were messengers chosen for their speed, reliability, and signal communication skills.
[59] Keleher, William A., *Turmoil in New Mexico,* Book Three, Chap.2., "On to the Rio Grande," p. 254.

Canby's command and martial law. The cavalry was ferried across the river in flat bottomed boats and the General made his way toward Texas.

Carleton left for Las Cruces, forty-five miles south of Fort Thorn. He was surprised to find the advance guard, a squadron of cavalry under Lieutenant Colonel Eyre, preceded him. They had raised the Stars and Stripes and celebrated July 4th with loud cheers when they reached the destination, never too late to celebrate the national holiday.[60]

In September General Carleton commanded the District of Arizona, a stretch of land from the Colorado River to the Rio Grande. Major Theodore Coult commanded the sub-district of Western Arizona to drive out the remainder of General Sibley's Confederate troops. When Carleton arrived in Santa Fe, General Canby complained of food shortages.

---

[60] Ibid., p. 251.

"Your troops will eat up the few existing food supplies," he told Carleton.

Carleton answered, "I don't intend to "embarrass you to keep my troops supplied. We did not cross the continent thus far 'to split hairs' over how the several departments ought to be supplied."[61]

Shortly after the California Column arrived at Mesilla a letter was found in the wastebasket of Fort Fillmore's Quartermaster's Office. It was from Confederate Colonel John R. Baylor who reported the success of his July 25, 1861, attack on the fort. He boasted that Major Lynde's command was composed of 700 men and his own forces at the surrender were less than 200.

Upon Sibley's retreat to Fort Bliss, Texas, he delivered a valedictory address in which he acknowledged the aid of wealthy New Mexicans. Drafts, redeemable in gold, given the Confederates, amounted to $200,000.[62]

---
[61]Ibid., p. 254, fn. 65.
[62] Ibid., Book Two, Chap. One, "The Confederates Invade New Mexico," p. 203, fn. 38.

Thousands in greenbacks and gold had been taken from the safe at Fort Fillmore.

Now, Colonel Baylor and General Sibley were gone. Their replacement was the seven-foot tall Second Lieutenant Will Rynerson. His advancement was already noticeable when he attained the rank of Captain in 1863.

In December of 1862 Sylvester Mowry, released from prison at Fort Yuma, filed a damage claim in the amount of $1,029,000 for the loss of his Patagonia mine property. He named Carleton and other officers involved in his arrest in the suit. He was well-connected and known in New York City. In 1863 the city's newspapers carried articles sympathetic to his efforts at restoration of his property.

New Mexican civilians, caught in the conflict, were able to resume their daily routines in the autumn. Indian raids increased during the upheaval surrounding Civil War. Secretary Arny attempted to establish his powers of office when Governor Connelly's health issues caused him to leave the territory for treatment in the east.[63]

---

[63] Murphy, Lawrence R., *Frontier Crusader: W. F. M. Arny*, Chap. 7, "Secretary of the New Mexico Territory," pp. 116-117.

Chapter Three: Remove Rebels and Indians
April 1861 – March 1863

In Washington, on April 23, 1861, there were less than 200 employees in the War Department. Money and personnel were needed to negotiate contracts for the instruments of war. Uniforms, blankets, horses, medical supplies, food, and more were needed. Secretary Chase devised a scheme for raising money to stay ahead of the war's constant financial drain.

A bill to produce greenbacks had to pass Congress with the new banking bill.[64] Secretary Chase had a solution. Consulting with his financial advisor, Jay Cooke, a plan was activated at once to avoid being delayed by Congressional argument. Secretary of the Treasury Chase presented the plan to the Lincoln Cabinet. Millions of dollars would be dispensed to "trusted individuals to negotiate and sign contracts that would mobilize the military."[65] The Cabinet gave its unanimous consent. Privately, the western soldiers' mining was endorsed as well.

In New Mexico, Joab Houghton was U. S. District Attorney in a Grand Jury trial before Circuit Judge Joseph G. Knapp of the 3rd District at Mesilla on August 17, 1862. Houghton would attempt to enforce the recently passed 2nd Confiscation Act.[66] Southern collaborators were indicted

---

[64] Goodwin, Doris K., *Team of Rivals*, Chap. 17, "We Are in the Depths," p. 461.
[65] Ibid., Chap. 13, "The Ball Has Opened," p. 366.
[66] *New Mexico Historical Review*, Vol. IV, No. 4, October 1928, "The Exploitation of Treason," p. 138. Also Miller, Darlis and Wilson,

for treason. Those named were largely prominent New Mexicans from the Southern district at Mesilla. The town had declared itself the Confederate capital of Arizona.

The money contributed by wealthy New Mexicans to the Confederates became known after General Sibley's retreat speech at Fort Bliss.[67] Few were present for the trial. All but two of the charged were originally Easterners. They had left the Territory with the escaping Confederate Army in March. Jose Manuel Gallegos, a former Congressman, served as jury foreman. Houghton was not a trained attorney, and the trial was bungled. It was continued for a later term when the accused would likely return to their homes.

Territorial Secretary Arny was behind Marshal Cutler's property seizures to punish the supporters of

---

Norman, Ibid, 55:4 1980, "The Resignation of Judge Joseph G. Knapp," p. 335. Poldevaart, Arie W., *Black Robed Justice,* Chap. 6, "When Benedict Was Chief," pp.60-63.

[67] Keleher, William A., *Turmoil in New Mexico*, Book Two, "Confederates Invade New Mexico," Chap. Two, "From Valverde to Apache Canyon," p. 190.

Confederate invaders. An ardent abolitionist, he often spoke out for the six hundred Indians being held as slaves in the Territory. He also sought the means to compel masters to collect servants' incomes and finally cancel the slaves' debts.[68]

The resolution of the Territory's Indian stand-off lay with the Superintendent of Indian Affairs. Two men competed for the position: Michael Steck and James Collins. Except for the Governor, it was the highest paid federal office in the Territory. Arizona and its martial law remained in General Carleton's district, but he was a part of the plan to make it a separate territory.

General Carleton's whole mission was to back up General Canby, clear the Rebels from Arizona, confirm the presence of gold in substantial quantities, and report the activities of unruly Indians. Now savages would be removed, and roads prepared for prospectors.[69] Although

---
[68] Murphy, Lawrence R., *Frontier Crusader – William F. M. Arny,* Chap. 7, "Secretary of the New Mexico Territory," p. 118.
[69] Keleher, William A., *Turmoil in New Mexico,* Book Four, The Long

Mowry's mine was confiscated, and he was imprisoned, he was a former U. S. Army officer. There had been no previous indication that Carleton would confiscate other local properties. The Second Confiscation Act also specifically named the properties to be taken as those belonging to absent owners who supported the South. Some of the men charged remained in the local area.

The expense of feeding and supplying Carleton's men certainly exceeded the amounts available to him to manage a force of over 2000 soldiers.

Judge Joseph G. Knapp was named to the southern district of New Mexico by President Lincoln in early 1861. His district was the largest in New Mexico. Its seat was in Mesilla, at the time the second largest town in the Territory. Only forty miles from the border of Mexico and Texas, it was a lively spot. Franklin, Texas was a larger town just over the border. Citizens moved freely between the two

---

Walk, p. 293. Letters of James H. Carleton, 4/27/63, letter to Sam Jones.

locations. The Texans and Mesillans' together owned many of the largest businesses in the area.

Hugh Stephenson, a silver mine owner, and Simeon Hart, a flour mill owner, were two of the prominent local area men who contributed to the Confederate cause in the Territory during the occupation.[70] Two Armijo brothers of New Mexico were wealthy grant owners who figured importantly in local freighting and mercantile firms. All four left the area with the southern Confederates.

When General Carleton imposed confiscations on Rebel properties of both present and absent men there was a general unfavorable reaction. Even though many friends overlooked each other's political leanings, all believed that confiscations were illegal and usurped citizens' rights to their property, or just compensation for it. Judge Knapp was of the same opinion. In the Judge's case, he spoke out on the matter and made himself unpopular with General

---

[70] Ibid., Book Two, Chap. One, The Confederates Invade New Mexico, "Baylor, Sibley and Canby," p. 192, fn. 4.

Carleton. The General's declaration of martial law allowed him to override the local civil courts and impose fines, or confiscations, on the Territory's citizens.

By the time of Supreme Court hearings in Santa Fe, Carleton had added a passport law which was interpreted to include Judge Knapp. The passport law was to keep Confederate spies out of the Territory. Knapp refused to honor the "law" in his own case, saying that he was appointed by the U. S. President and such a trust could not be violated by a military ruling.

In the fall of 1862, New York City's newspapers took an interest in the arrest of Sylvester Mowry in Arizona's Apache country. When he was released from the prison at Fort Yuma, he protested his treatment in charges and in letters to New York City newspapers. He had appealed to Congress for Arizona's territorial status in 1857. He conducted himself in a colorful manner. His case attained celebrity standing. A West Point graduate from a prominent Rhode Island family, his silver mine was a model business of its kind with a proven market abroad. The recent accusations of fraud in the New Mexican office of the Quartermaster were taken quite seriously. The public was angry at the misuse of public monies.[71] Mowry's pleas for justice were met with sympathy by a broad range of New Yorkers.

Among those interested in Arizona's successful mines was the President himself. His part in assigning officials to set up government and function as a new Territory must be assumed.

There had been early attempts to make a treaty with the Apaches that would allow an eastern company to mine in peace in the region. A treaty was imminent from 1858 to 1860. The company involved former California custom house officials at San Francisco and Eastern financiers. The easterners and former California government officials had

---

[71] Santa Fe *New Mexican*, 3/5/64, "Imputation of Fraud in the Quartermaster and Commissary Department", p.2.

spent a great deal of time researching the Gadsden Purchase area and its surrounding countryside to substantiate reports of copper, gold, and silver in paying quantities.[72] The eastern company was primarily concerned with railroad interests.

A surveying engineer in charge of the Gadsden Purchase's boundary line linked these quasi-government interests and the railroad company's proposed financing agents. Dr. Steck, the Apache agent in the southern district, served as a facilitator for the easterners and the Apaches.[73] Steck was a trusted friend of Chief Mangus and the southern Apaches. Allowing the Apaches negotiation rights was likely anathema to most ordinary Americans of the era.

In late summer 1862, General Carleton was anxious to turn the public's focus away from confiscated property

---

[72] Lamar, Howard R., *The Far Southwest;* Part Four, Chap. 16, "Arizona: No Man's Land," pp. 362-368 and 380.
[73] Ibid., p. 364. From 1856 through 1858 Dr. Steck was Indian Agent to the southern district's Apache Indians. See Keleher, *Turmoil in New Mexico*, Book One, Chap. Seven, "General Kearny Comes to Santa Fe," p. 96.

to an issue which he could remedy. The recent attacks by Apaches alarmed the public and threatened business. The Mescalero Apaches defended the Pinos Altos Mines as their own territory. Valuable businessmen like Sam Jones, Mesilla attorney, had interests in the Pinos Altos mines. Carleton was determined to control these valuable mines for the Union.

General Carleton began his Apache campaign on September 22, 1862, when he notified Washington of his plans. He summarized his reasons for waging war. His intention was to transplant the Navajo tribe to the Bosque Redondo. It would serve as a "spacious tribal reformatory" far from their homeland hiding places, he later stated.[74] He would place Kit Carson in command. Carson spoke against the campaign at first, warning that there were many more Navajo than the 5000 Carleton anticipated.[75]

---

[74] Ibid., p. 310.
[75] Keleher, William A., *Turmoil in New Mexico;* Book Four, The Long Walk, "First the Apaches," p. 279.

Indian agent Lorenzo Labadi provided a reliable account of Mescalero Apache depredations for Superintendent James L. Collins on September 25, 1862. He described how in August alone the tribe killed forty men and six children. They had been continuously hostile for months without interference from the military. They kidnapped children, stripped them, and left them to find their way back. They robbed every kind of livestock. A year before, eighty Mexicans went into Apache country and pursued their stolen property. They returned with four Indian children and forty horses and mules. Labadi turned the Indian children over to the Fort Union commander.[76]

On September 22, 1862, Governor Connelly issued a proclamation calling for reorganization of the Territorial militia by October 15.[77] A reluctant Kit Carson was persuaded to join them. He was sent almost immediately to Mimbres Apache country at Fort Stanton. The fort was in

---

[76] Ibid., pp. 281-284.
[77] Ibid., p. 282.

shambles. Most of its salvageable materials had been hauled away by scavengers. It had been abandoned on August 2.

On October 10, 1862, Superintendent Collins wrote to the Commissioner of Indian Affairs based on Labadi's report and other sources. He stated that the only permanent remedy was for the government to colonize the Indians. He believed reservations were needed and should be located at once. Governor Connelly then likewise published a proclamation on October 15, to initiate a campaign against the Apaches and Navajos.[78]

Carleton ordered Carson's Volunteers to begin the campaign against the Mescaleros. His mounted troops were to fan out down two rivers. At the mouth of the Penasco they would find plenty of Mescaleros. He ordered Carson to kill the Indian men. Those willing to surrender could be taken to the Bosque Redondo reservation.[79] Carson's men

---

[78] Ibid., p. 284-285.
[79] Ibid., p. 286 and p. 309.

covered terrain within a radius of one-hundred miles of Fort Stanton. Captains McCleave and Pishon took several companies from Fort Franklin, Texas. They were to cooperate with Carson but be independent of him.

On November 2, 1862, Colonel J. R. West wrote Captain Ben Cutler in Santa Fe, General Carleton's Assistant Adjutant-General. He asked that the General send an "expedition against the Indians in the vicinity of the Pinos Altos Mines. He said these mines were "were growing in importance daily. Were they relieved from the danger of Indian outrages they would rapidly develop." [80]

The Navajos also murdered many persons during the year. They terrorized ranches and villages in Bernalillo, Albuquerque, Los Padillos, and other river settlements, driving off hundreds of cattle. They stole 1,610 sheep within sight of Fort Craig.[81]

---

[80] OR, Records of the War of the Rebellion, California Adjutant General's Office, Chap. LXIL, "Operations on the Pacific Coast," p. 200.
[81] Keleher, William A., *Turmoil in New Mexico: 1846-1868*, Book Four, The Long Walk, Chap. Two, "Then the Navajos," pp. 296-297.

General Carleton ordered General West in Mesilla to begin a campaign against the Gila Apaches in the Gila [River] area in southwestern New Mexico. Carleton stressed to West the country must be "opened up" since it contained an enormous quantity of precious metals.

"Ask for no quarter, and give none," Carleton told him. "There must be no peace, or conference, with any Indians living on any of the tributaries of the Mimbres, or the headwaters of the Gila, down as far as Fort Stanton until they are completely subdued.[82]"

West was to track down the Gila Apaches and attack them whenever and wherever they appeared. Carleton's concern turned to the chiefs.

In December of 1862, the seventy-year-old Mescalero chief, Mangus Colorado, was lured into one of the Army's posts commanded by Colonel West. He went

---

[82] Ibid, Book Four, The Long Walk, Chap. One, "First the Apaches," p. 288.

there voluntarily and agreed to "deliver himself and a band of Apaches to the Army control."

Mangus was confined in the guardhouse and awakened when a soldier threw something at him. The soldiers reportedly prodded his feet with heated bayonets. He raised up to see what disturbed him and was shot repeatedly and killed. His tribe nearly worshipped him. After Mangus' death, the soldiers took his scalp, then severed his head, boiled the flesh and exhibited the skull as a badge of honor.[83]

The next day the lodge of the dead chief was attacked. Afterward, his scalp, and the scalps of his wife and daughter, were worn as ornaments. Judge Joseph Knapp of the southern district called Carleton's Apache extermination a "black flag" policy. The Apaches, from December 1862, were filled with revenge and fought with a seldom seen malevolence. The Civil War was now the

---

[83] Masich, Andrew E., *The Civil War in Arizona*, Chap. 4, "Occupation Duty," p. 90-92.

Union against local tribes, Navajos and Apaches, as well as the invading Confederates.

In December Carson's troops were directed to kill all Indian men of the Mescalero tribe without compunction. The women and children would be taken to Fort Stanton to be fed until other orders were issued.[84]

James Collins was New Mexico's Indian Superintendent for many years. He was long a resident of the Territory since its earliest days under Mexican rule. In late 1862, he had been editor of the Santa Fe *Weekly Gazette* for nearly as long. He was as confident as he was outspoken. His hair was grey and could not match Acting-Governor and Secretary Arny who was red-haired and as fiery in his dialogue as his complexion. Nevertheless, Collins stood tall before the twenty members of the Legislature who stared at him accusingly.

---

[84] Keleher, William A., *Turmoil in New Mexico*, Book Four, The Long Walk, Chap. One, "First the Apaches," p. 286.

The legislators listened attentively to Secretary Arny as he delivered the December 2 annual executive report. They requested an investigation of Superintendent Collins and his responsibilities in protecting Indian stores between April 17 and May 4, after the Battle of Glorieta. The public complained grievously of increased Indian raids over the summer months. They believed Collins' policies invited Indian reprisals.

Several legislators rose to report the comments of troubled citizens. Superintendent Collins protested each report. He answered each critic, then returned to his seat. The harangue continued as legislators reminded Collins that he was believed to have willingly sacrificed the Indians' food and supplies during the Confederate escape from the Battle of Glorieta to refuge at Santa Fe. Their supply wagons were destroyed by Colonel Chivington and his men. The Superintendent called the accusers "malicious and dishonorable." Finally, after each legislator's testimony, he conceded to appear for hearings under certain conditions. The hearings were set for January 17, 1863.[85]

The conditions demanded by Collins were that he could submit a list of witnesses in his defense, taken under oath, written down, and his attorneys could cross-examine the accusers. He would be represented at the hearings by two leading Santa Fe attorneys: Richard H. Tompkins and Merrill Ashurst.

On the appointed day, argument began at once over compelling witnesses' attendance. Were those from outside the district compelled to appear? Someone finally called for an adjournment. The lawyers reconvened the next Monday. The Republicans moved to suppress the requested hearings during a recess. The Legislature promptly passed resolutions condemning Collins' administration of Indian affairs. He was charged with fraud. It was proposed that a

---

[85] Murphy, Lawrence R., *Frontier Crusader: W. F. M. Arny*, Chap. 7, "Secretary of the New Mexico Territory," pp. 120-121.

"more suitable, capable, and honest person be appointed to replace him."

Secretary Arny was interested in Collins' position and did little to counter Collins' misfortune. Arny voiced a personal plea for support to Senator Samuel C. Pomeroy, a friend and former political cohort from his years in Kansas. However, in Washington, Collins had a strong defender in Territorial Delegate John Watts, another Democrat activist and long-time friend.

The legislature's anti-Collins memorials were sent to the President, Interior Commissioner J. P. Upshur, and Indian Commissioner, William P. Dole. Secretary Arny appealed to Pomeroy to be recommended for Collins' position. A power struggle was set in motion.[86] Not long after the dust-up it was learned that Secretary Upshur decided it was politically expedient to name another candidate to the office.

---

[86] Ibid.

At the same time, Judge Knapp of Mesilla was arrested for traveling without a passport. In January 1863 he was placed in the guardhouse at Santa Fe where he was also required to serve in the Supreme Court session.

Michael Steck was serving the Army in the East in March 1863. When he learned of the opportunity to file for the Indian Superintendent position, he did so at once. Dr. Steck did not know of the Indian war in New Mexico. By January 3, 1863, General Carleton was no longer concerned with a possible reinvasion of Confederates from Texas.

Colonel West had killed many Gila Apaches in the late fall of 1862. The superiority of the Army's weapons quickly overwhelmed the remaining southern Apaches. By February 1, 1863, the General and soldiers of the California Column were involved in a dual enterprise – fighting Apache Indians and mining for gold.[87]

---

[87] Keleher, William A., *Turmoil in New Mexico*, Book Three, The Long Walk, "Baylor, Governor of Arizona," p. 338.

Chapter Four: Mines vs. Reservations

January 1863 – January 1864

In January 1863 General Carleton visited Pinos Altos, the cherished mining district in the southwestern region of New Mexico. It was the area the Apaches had fought to control. He reported that gold could be seen with the naked eye.

One month later, he wrote General Lorenzo Thomas in Washington, "I have sent four companies of California Volunteers to garrison Fort West in the Pinos Altos gold region." He also initiated a furlough system to give the soldiers an opportunity to prospect and mine for gold.[88]

Carleton sent Apaches to the Bosque Redondo from primarily southern New Mexico tribes, the Gila, Mescalero, and Mimbres Apaches. The reservation was located on the fringe of the Llano Estacado, the Staked Plains of the Territory. On the other side of the Plains were the Comanche, Arapaho, and Kiowa tribes in the northern Texas panhandle. These tribes also grazed their cattle on the grama grass there. The plains were natural grazing ground for buffalo and had been officially ruled "Indian country."[89] The Bosque site had been initially promised to the Apaches for a reservation since it was in their traditional country. Unlike the Navajo, there was arable land and water for the much smaller tribe.

The Pecos River ran through the reservation area which was forty square miles. The recently built Fort

---
[88] Ibid., p. 338.
[89] Roberts, Gary L., *Death Comes to the Chief Justice*, Chap. 2, "The Zealot and the Politicians," p. 41.

Sumner stood in the center. The site was isolated from the white settlements although cattlemen from San Miguel County on the north, and the town of Las Vegas, grazed their cattle on the Plains.

Carson received Carleton's posts at Fort Stanton almost daily. He was directed to hunt down and kill all male Mescaleros who resisted. The Indians were mostly armed with only bows and arrows. A week after Carson's troops arrived at Fort Stanton, they had killed thirty-two Mescaleros, including two important chiefs, Jose Largo, and the elder Manuelito.[90] A few weeks later, he assembled five hundred men, women, and children. The prisoners were sent to Fort Sumner on the Pecos River.

In June of 1863, New Mexico's Chief Justice of the Supreme Court, Kirby Benedict, left the bench and joined a party of prospectors bound for Arizona. He had received a gold nugget from Captain Joseph Walker near the head of

---

[90] Keleher, William A., *Turmoil in New Mexico*, Book Four, Chap. One, "First the Apaches," p. 291 and Chap. Seven, "Dr. Michael Steck," pp. 416-417.

Lynx Creek in eastern Arizona. Arizona was then a county of New Mexico.

At once, General Carleton had a plan which he reported to General Thomas, his superior in Washington. He planned to send four companies of California Volunteers to garrison Fort West in the Pinos Altos gold region. One fourth of the command at a time would have one month's furlough to work in the gold mines on their own account.[91]

By mid-summer 1863 the Army's Apache war was over. General West had been ordered to burn the fields around the Apaches to starve out the ones who would not surrender. However, the Apaches continued to attack the mines at Pinos Altos until they were temporarily abandoned.

Dr. Steck, before the war and Apache Indian agent at the time, agreed with Carleton that the Apaches should

---

[91] Ibid., p.338

be located at the Bosque Redondo reservation on the Pecos River. Steck was not in New Mexico when Carleton determined to place the Navajos on the same reservation with the Apaches. Steck was hired as Indian Superintendent by Commissioner Dole on May 19, 1863.[92] When Steck learned of the new plan, he opposed it. He argued that there was not enough land for the Apaches and Navajos to produce crops for the total Indians in the two tribes. The situation was complicated by the fact that the tribes did not speak the same language.[93]

The Navajos realized the army was engaged in fighting the southern Apaches early in the year. They, or segments of the tribe, took advantage of the opportunity to conduct raids along the Rio Grande, from near Santa Fe on the north to Socorro on the south. They ransacked ranches

---

[92] Lester, Paul A., "Michael Steck and New Mexico Indian Affairs, 1857-1865," Dissertation for PHD, Univ. of Oklahoma, 1986, p. 178.
[93] Keleher, William A., *Turmoil in New Mexico.*, Book Four, Chap. Two, "Then the Navajos," p. 310.

near Bernalillo, Los Padillas, and other river settlements. They drove off hundreds of heads of livestock.

Carleton asked Colonel J. Francisco Chaves to call the Navajo chiefs together for a council at Fort Wingate in the early summer. They must get their people to come to terms and submit to the Bosque Redondo reservation or be killed. Their deadline was July 20. After that there would be no talking.[94] The Navajo chiefs protested that a great number of their people were peaceful. Carleton responded that there was no way to distinguish the bad Indians from the good and his decision to move the tribe remained in force.

The 1st Regiment, New Mexico Volunteers, commanded by Colonel Kit Carson, was getting ready to move against the tribe. The Rio Abajo *Press* in Albuquerque carried an editorial that reminded everyone that in 1859 the Navajos were told what would happen if

---

[94] Ibid, p. 303.

they did not behave. They were warned they would be hunted like wolves from mountain to mountain. The tribal leaders answered that they could not control their youth.[95]

Carson commanded 476 mounted men and 260-foot soldiers. There were twenty-seven officers. Carson requested permission to use the Ute Indians who would be paid in horses and sheep captured. A supply depot was established at Fort Canby. When the fight was in earnest, one of Carson's officers destroyed fields of wheat and corn. A single Indian scout killed the officer. When Carleton learned of it, he ordered "shoot to kill" and "lying in wait" tactics to Colonel Rigg and Captain Samuel Archer.

It was April 14, 1863, when Carson's regiment left for Canyon de Chelly and Navajo country. A few officers were California Column men. They gathered for final instructions twenty miles south of Albuquerque.

---

[95] Ibid.

On May 10, 1863, Carleton wrote to General Halleck in Washington that evidence of veins and deposits of precious metals led him to reestablish Fort Stanton where a hundred families had gone and opened farms, also locating gold there. At Fort West a fourth of the command prospected. He wrote of the need for a road from Fort Craig to the Gila River.

He told Halleck, "You will see by the enclosed notes what signs of mineral wealth are already discovered. If only I had one more good regiment of California Infantry . . . composed of practical miners."[96]

On June 22, 1863, Carleton wrote his old friend, Joseph R. Walker at the Walker Mines in Arizona. He was starting the war against the Navajo. He expected people would soon be rushing to the gold fields.[97] That same day the General sent Captain Nathaniel J. Pishon to take New Mexico's Surveyor General, John A. Clark, to

---

[96] Ibid., Chap. 3, "Baylor, Governor of Arizona," p. 339.
[97] Ibid., p. 340.

the gold fields.[98] He asked Pishon to bring back specimens for the War Department. Pishon should record each man's time and the amount of gold each obtained for his labor in that time. He was told to watch out for the best location a post might be built in the heart of gold country. The General then provided the men with a guide.

After Pishon and Clark left for the Arizona gold fields, Carleton confidently wrote high-ranking officials in Washington of the reality of the gold fields, ". . . . a tangible El Dorado, that has gold that can be weighed by the steelyards - gold that does not vanish when the finder is awake.[99]

The General did not stop with his efforts to alert the authorities of the wealth in New Mexico and Arizona. He by-passed military channels and wrote Postmaster General Montgomery Blair, Secretary of Treasury Salmon P. Chase, and General Halleck of the recent discoveries. When

---

[98] Ibid., p. 341-342.
[99] Ibid., p. 343.

Pishon returned, he brought samples the General ordered. Carleton promptly mailed some of these to Secretary Chase and invited him to present the largest gold nugget to the President. His letter to Halleck said, "It will gratify the President to know that Providence is blessing our country, even though it chasteneth."[100]

Carleton's campaign policy was to shoot all male Navajo Indians who resisted his troops. Haste was clearly a part of the plan in effect that summer. By November of the year a party of authorities would arrive in New Mexico. Articles in the Santa Fe *New Mexican* in the last months of 1863 indicate the official opinion of the need to settle the areas populated by wild Indians.[101] One article read, Arizona officials "would arrive to supply a link, in the great chain of governments, now spanning the continent, from the Atlantic to the Pacific."[102]

---

[100] Ibid., p. 345.
[101] Santa Fe *New Mexican*, 11/21/63, p. 2, cols. 2-3 and 12/24/1863, p. 1, col. 3, "Secretary Chase."
[102] Ibid., 11/21/63, "Arizona Arrivals," p. 1, col. 3.

The Santa Fe *New Mexican* had taken a decidedly Republican stance in singling out Secretary of the Treasury, Salmon P. Chase for praise. Secretary Chase's financial policy was to employ public land and Union soldiers to support the nation's economy during war. The new Arizona government would exploit the public land's wealth of precious metals. There would be privileges granted in certain quarters to those who would enable the mining. The same would apply to southern New Mexico.

Large quantities of gold, silver, and copper were in both Arizona and New Mexico. The gold and silver were being sent from New Mexico to California weekly or monthly, then processed and shipped from the San Francisco Mint to New York and Philadelphia to support the war. The Pinos Altos area in southern New Mexico was one proven area, the other in central Arizona where the army was building Fort Whipple for the new official site of government. The town of Prescott would shortly be developed there.[103]

The troops left Los Pinos on July 7, 1863. They were at Fort Wingate on July 14, and at Fort Defiance on July 20. Ute scouts arrived at Fort Defiance on July 20. They were willing to serve Carson who gave them rations, arms and ammunition. The Utes and Navajos were traditional enemies. Carson had requested the Utes, and Carleton asked for permission to use them. The Utes wanted to take women and children for compensation, but officials denied the request. He would pay twenty dollars for each good horse and a dollar for each sheep captured and delivered to the Quartermaster.[104]

The Navajo captives would be sent to Santa Fe. Once there, the Superintendent of Indian Affairs would make proper disposition of them. The Ute scouts

---

[103] Hunt, Aurora, *The Army of the Pacific*, "On Duty in Arizona," pp. 135-137.
[104] Keleher, William A., *Turmoil in New Mexico*, Book Four, Chap. 2, "Then the Navajos," p. 306.

discovered that the Zuni Pueblo people were harboring some Navajos. When Carleton learned of it, he promised to seize six of the principal men of the Pueblo to hold as hostages until all the Navajos in nearby villages had turned themselves in. If any Anglo men were injured, he would destroy the Zuni village.[105] Carson selected a supply depot twenty-one-miles west of old Fort Defiance. It was named Fort Canby and became his headquarters.[106]

On July 24, Carson reported the Navajos had planted grain and the wheat crop was promising. The corn did not look healthy. He was ordered to hasten the Navajo's submission by starving them. The Navajos had no surplus supplies of grain or food, and the day of surrender would be shortened by cutting down and destroying all wheat and corn in Navajo country.

On July 25, Carson ordered all the grain on the Rio de Pueblo, a Colorado River Creek, to be cut down. Major

---

[105] Ibid., p.308.
[106] Ibid., pp. 307.

Cummings was ordered to bring in 75,000 pounds of wheat and a large amount of corn to serve as fodder for the animals in the winter. The wheat was chopped down and carried to Carson's camp. The Navajo retaliated. They raided Carson's camp at night and stole his favorite horse. Three weeks later the Indians killed Major Cummings. Another officer was sent with ten men to destroy many more acres.

On August 3, Carleton began a dragnet to capture the Navajo. Starvation, lie-in-wait, and shoot-to-kill, were tactics Carleton used by August 4, 1863.[107]

On August 6, Captain Pfeiffer and ten soldiers destroyed ten acres of corn. Another fifteen acres of wheat and 120 acres of corn were destroyed in the Canyon de Chelly country on August 19. Canyon de Chelly served as the Navajo people's stronghold. There they felt safe among the caves high above the canyon floor.

---

[107] Ibid, p. 312-313.

A definite campaign strategy was formed by September 1, 1863. The Bosque would serve as a "reformatory for Indians."[108] The Navajo would be held there and grow a variety of crops which would support a great many people. Carleton advised the War Department of his program on September 6, 1863. He also reported that fifty-one Navajo Indians, men, women, and children, joined the 425 Mescalero Apaches at the Bosque to be held there as prisoners. Carleton believed that he could colonize the Navajo and Apaches together at the Bosque Redondo and added the same to the War Department in his report.[109]

In December 1863, Kit Carson was ordered to take his troops into the heart of Navajo country, Canyon de Chelly. He left Fort Canby on January 6 and took 475 soldiers to attack the fortress-like canyon. His troops killed 23 Navajos, wounding many others. Thirty-four prisoners were taken with 200 sheep. The prisoners were starving and

---

[108] Ibid, p. 310.
[109] Ibid., p. 310.

in rags. Carson sent out messengers that the Navajo had until ten o'clock the next morning to surrender. He promised they would be fed and protected. They would not be punished. He sent seventy-five men into the canyon to explore it and destroy all the peach trees and dwellings of the Indians.[110]

By January 25, 1864, Carson reported that 500 Navajo prisoners were at Fort Canby and another thousand were on their way to surrender. By the first of March, Chief Herrera and 2,400 Navajo prisoners were held at Fort Canby waiting to start for the Bosque Redondo.[111]

General Carleton wrote General Thomas in Washington on February 7, 1864, that the Canyon de Chelly campaign was an "unparalleled success."[112] He recommended favorable notice for Colonel Carson for the hardship he and his troops suffered in the freezing weather.

---

[110] Ibid., pp. 315-316.
[111] Ibid., pp. 315-319.
[112] Ibid, p. 318.

The letters describing the gold fields and the successful Indian drives were evidently taken quite seriously. The arrival of the officials for Arizona in November 1863 confirmed Washington's agreement. In fact, the first officials arrived at Fort Whipple by January 22.

The escort for the Arizona officials arriving at Santa Fe on November 21, 1863, was led by Captain Butcher of the 11th Missouri Cavalry. Soon after the party temporarily settled to await the final train, the local escort arrived. It was led by Colonel J. F. Chaves. His Missouri and New Mexico troops would lead the Arizonans to Albuquerque and on to Fort Whipple, Arizona. The Missouri 11th Cavalry would return to Fort Leavenworth on the Denver route from Santa Fe.

The remainder of the new arrivals came several days later. They were detained by heavy snows. Their wagons were nearly lost on the route near Las Vegas in San Miguel County, New Mexico.

The Aguirre train had ten mule-drawn wagons, each holding 10,000 pounds of weight, merchandise to be delivered at Santa Fe. The travelers rode in ambulances, carriages outfitted for comfortable sleeping. In daytime two seats faced each other so that six people could be easily seated together. Among the other passengers were two young men and a family of five, with a cook. A friend of the Aguirres, Dory Jones, and the train's hired cook, drove the provision wagon.

Epifanio Aguirre and his wife were newlyweds who had traveled in the east for nearly a year before returning to his family home in southern New Mexico at Las Cruces near Mesilla. They had their three-month-old baby and a nursemaid with them.[113] Mary Aguirre was the daughter of Westport merchant, Joab Bernard. A Bernard family friend, Steve Elkins, another traveler, served as a teamster. The

---

[113] Moynihan, Ruth B., Susan Armitage, and Christine Fischer Dichamp, Eds. *So Much to Be Done, Women Settlers on the Mining and Ranching Frontier,* Part III, "It was all A Wonder to Me," Mary Bernard Aguirre, pp. 245-254.

escort which joined them at Fort Leavenworth was a welcome sight for the passengers. They left Missouri immediately after the Quantrill renegades took revenge on the Kansas Jayhawkers. The Missouri men burnt the town of Lawrence and murdered most of the male citizens. Danger was everywhere.

Secretary William F. M. Arny arrived in the same carriage as Reverend Read, a part of the Aguirre train. He brought home $200,000 dollars for territorial salaries. The U. S. Marshal for the new Arizona Territory and the Superintendent of Indian Affairs left directly for the Arizona government site. One of the new officials in the Aguirre train was previously a missionary in Arizona, Reverend H. W. Read. He was recently employed in the Treasury Department.[114] He would be Postmaster at Tucson.

---

[114] Keleher, William A., *Turmoil in New Mexico*, Book Four, Chap. Three, "Baylor, Governor of Arizona," p. 335.

The decision to have the Arizona party arrive in late November was to familiarize them with the operation of the legislature. Instead, the Arizonans took notes and determined to move forward immediately.

A great deal of the excitement surrounding the easterners' visit was focused on Secretary Arny and his Treasury Department deposit. It was placed in the Federal Depository under John Greiner, Receiver. The year before the salaries were issued in drafts and were difficult to collect.

Arny obtained them as greenbacks, collectible at par. Because of Arny's success at the Treasury Department, the Federal employees were assured of their salaries and Arny was hailed as a hero.[115]

By the December 19 issue of the *New Mexican*, the tone and attitude of the newspaper toward Secretary Arny changed. William Manderfield, the paper's editor, noted in

---

[115] Santa Fe *New Mexican*, 11/23/63, "Two Hundred Thousand Dollars," p. 2, col. 2.

a short front-page item that Secretary Arny had "given out that he was a secret agent, charged by all the departments at Washington, to observe the conduct and give information of all the departments in New Mexico." The editor did not believe that "the government had established a system of secret spies throughout the country."[116]

Another article of the same issue wrote of Treasury Secretary Chase. Editor Manderfield attributed much of the financial success of the U. S. to Secretary Chase's influence. He concluded that, "The chains of Rocky Mountains, will, when thoroughly worked, furnish the means to pay the national debt. No minister of finance, has ever stood, more prominently distinguished for financial ability and success, than does Mr. Chase, at the close of the year 1863, and in the third year of war.[117]

The Arizonans were entertained at two receptions and introduced to a great deal of customs of the locale. The

---
[116] Ibid., 12/19/63, "How Is It," p. 1, col. 3.
[117] Ibid., 12/24/63, "Secretary Chase," p. 1, col. 4.

need to learn Spanish was critical for social acceptance. Several men carried their grammars in their coat pockets. Elkins had begun studying the language daily on his trip west.

Governor Goodwin and Secretary McCormick promised Editor Manderfield that they would maintain correspondence to assure New Mexicans of their progress. Colonel Chaves' destination for the party was the mines at Lynx Creek where Fort Whipple was under construction.

The route to Albuquerque descended gradually to a desert landscape. At Albuquerque they were entertained for several days. The expected government mules for the river crossing had not arrived. Colonel Chaves urged Aguirre to lend his mules to the task. The waters were surging from heavy snow in the Sangre de Cristo mountains.

The party walked toward a boat ramp beside a flat-bed barge. There were few tow boats on the Rio Grande. The wagons and carriages would be loaded, and the mules tied to the outer logs to fend for themselves in the raging water.

Epifanio delayed. He feared for his valuable mule teams. If they survived the surging waters, how would they be returned, and when? How much would he be paid for crossing, the long journey and back? He told the Colonel their value was ninety dollars each.

The officer insisted none would be lost. His soldiers would protect them, bring them to the banks with floats if necessary. If, by chance, any were lost on the journey, he would send to Fort Union for any replacements. Privately, Steve Elkins urged a written guarantee.

Epifanio provided a notebook and pen for the document. Chaves wrote the expense would be borne by the government, providing the date as one month ahead. He signed for the guarantee.

They left the riverbank to the laborers hired for transport. There were many jobs to be done. The work of transporting the party across the Rio Grande consumed many hours. That evening their camp lights could be seen at nightfall.

The next morning, when Steve stepped away from the tent compound, he was met by the Colonel at the corral gate. It was barely light, but there was no mistaking the man who approached him forcefully.

The man wanted to know who he was.

His direct manner surprised Steve. He answered that he was a former teacher in Missouri and was anxious to learn the language. He was trained as an attorney and might want to open an office in New Mexico.

The man seemed to ease a bit. He suggested that if he wanted to learn the language, he needed to stay in the business area. He should apply at Fort Fillmore to be close to his friends. A clerk was needed there. Spanish wasn't required for the position.

Steve was cautious. He had heard the officer was pompous and self-serving. Chaves had taken the job he was sent to do. However, the man would resent his presence. It wasn't intended for him to challenge a Mexican leader. There was little else he could do to earn his keep. There were no schools and little money circulating that he could see. He had heard of Chaves before leaving Missouri. He was the most educated of all the young Mexican and American men here. He was too impertinent and presumptuous. He would not make much of a friend for anyone. Certainly not someone who might be a match for his own ambitions.

The Aguirres left Albuquerque for Las Cruces with Steve. They were thrilled he had taken them up on their offer to stay with them in Las Cruces. He had provided them with many welcome stories on the route west. The companionship of their jovial friend was a welcome diversion from the tedium of such a long journey across the frigid plains.

Chapter Five: The Ute Reservation

September 1863 – February 1864

A Congressional election was at stake in September 1863. New Mexico's Congressman, Francisco Perea, a masquerading Republican, was pitted against Jose Gallegos, the Republican, a defrocked priest, also a former Congressional Delegate. Perea was accompanied by John Watts, usually associated with Democrats while in New Mexico. Secretary Arny was absent from the Territory when Governor Connelly, a Democrat, counted the votes and declared Perea the winner.

While Arny was in Washington, the Santa Fe *New Mexican* endorsed Perea and named many prominent men who allegedly supported him.[118] The reservation matter and Carleton's insistent policies concerning the Navajo people were not referenced. Gallegos was previously elected to Congress and was popular with the Mexican people. His popular appeal was no match for the support of four major Territorial businessmen. Perea's constituents were Colonel St. Vrain, Don Jose Martinez, Charles Beaubien, and Pedro Sanchez. At the time, the *New Mexican*'s editor was someone other than William Manderfield. The press may have been highjacked between editors Charles Leib, Charles Clever, and Manderfield to affect the election.

---

[118] *The New Mexican*, August 22, 1863, p. 1, col. 2. *The New Mexican* was not the normal title of the Republican newspaper. There was not an editor attributed with the publication of this date. The banner states it "Volume I."

Questions arose over the Socorro County outcome. The county's ballots were displayed for six days, then were seized and burned. Local officials provided the Governor with a record of the votes cast. However, Connelly substituted the record for actual ballots and declared Perea elected by a large majority.[119]

On Arny's return to New Mexico, he and Gallegos contested the election decision. The two parties were divided over Indian policy. The *Gazette* favored Carleton's management of the Bosque Redondo. Daily reports continued to arrive of crop failure and starvation. These facts supported Secretary Arny and his Republican faction which opposed the Bosque Redondo site as a suitable location for the Navajo.[120]

The challenge to the election continued into April 1864. Secretary Arny's request for additional time to present evidence of ballot tampering was finally denied by

---

[119] Murphy, Lawrence R., *Frontier Crusader: W. F. M. Arny*, Chap. 7, p. 124.
[120] Ibid, pp. 442-443.

Congress and Perea would remain New Mexico's Delegate until 1865.

In mid-summer, Steve was asked to mediate between two community leaders to avoid a duel. Sam Jones, Mesilla's leading attorney, had stood before the local court in July and called John Lemon, Mesilla's mayor, a charlatan, and General Carleton's toady. Lemon accused Jones of slander and demanded a public retraction. Steve was asked to intervene, having made friends with Jones who was known for his quick temper. Sam was not easily persuaded, but finally agreed to post his apology in several popular venues along the main street of town. The two men later met and publicly shook hands, bringing much relief to the court's followers. Sam was a former friend of Steve's father, Philip, at the time a Confederate officer.

It was August when the Democrats held their nominating meeting for county representatives to the legislature. No Republican meetings for nominations had ever been held. Steve had not declared himself Republican, but everyone knew he had been a Union officer. He decided to attend the meeting and see what might happen.

House members were determined by county population. Each county only had one legislative Senator. One House member would be named for Dona Ana County. The forum was open to the crowd for nominations. Steve's name came up at once for House member. When the vote was called, he was elected unanimously. Pedro Melendres, a Democrat whose father had held the Senate position, was elected to succeed his father.

Shortly after the Year's End holidays the Santa Fe and Albuquerque papers took up the subject of attorney admissions to practice law in the Territory. The members of the bar were required to undergo examination by Chief Justice Kirby Benedict before licensing. The *Rio Abajo Press* revealed that the Chief Justice had admitted persons to practice in his court "as a friendly compliment" which the editor noted "displays a reckless disregard for the honor of the Bar."[121] The Santa Fe *New Mexican* confirmed the same and advised the public of the names of the attorneys who were able to take their cases to the Supreme Court.[122] It would have been a surprise to the new arrivals that only six men were qualified in a territory of nearly 90,000 people.

Steve began work at Fort Fillmore for Captain Will Rynerson who spent much time at the Pinos Altos mines. He also traveled to a new fort site on the eastern plains. Steve's job was writing letters and reports. After working there for nearly two months the Captain told him he could no longer use him. Steve inquired of the reason. He was told he had misspelled "Arizona." The real reason seemed to be that he was suspect in some way, but it was useless to pursue it. Both men were considered attorneys, but Steve had the superior qualifications.

---

[121] *Rio Abajo Press*, 1/26/64, p. 1, col. 2.
[122] Santa Fe *New Mexican*, 2/6/64, p. 2, col. 1.

Sam Jones, his father's friend, was the most successful attorney in Mesilla. Sam was an unapologetic Confederate sympathizer. He was from Westport, Missouri where he had been a Postmaster. He also co-owned a mine at Pinos Altos with several local businessmen. When he heard of Steve's firing, he offered him a job as his clerk.

Steve had been cleaning ditches as a community service. It was much needed since so many men left the area with the Confederates. Jones wanted someone energetic who invited respect, his actions admirable. The clerk position was ideal since Steve intended to work his way into a lawyer's office eventually. His language skills were nearing a level where he could represent a client in court. There were several people whom he must meet to extend the scope of his future career in New Mexico. First and foremost was Michael Steck, Joab Bernard's friend and the new Indian Superintendent.

Steve learned more from Joab Bernard of the new Indian Superintendent. The two men were friends. When Indian Affairs Commissioner Dole appointed Dr. Steck, his position was yet to be confirmed by Congress. Dr. Steck was in Philadelphia in February and wrote his deputy, W. B. Baker, he would soon be leaving Washington for Santa Fe. He had been authorized to order ebony canes with President Lincoln's name engraved on them.[123] The canes signified the Pueblo governors' titles to land they sought in the form of patents. The patents would soon be issued. All that the Aguirres and Steve heard of Dr. Steck was favorable. Joab alone knew of the political intrigues which formed the backstage of American New Mexico. He had forewarned Steve of a few of them.

Steck practiced medicine for six years in his home state of Pennsylvania. He left for the West in 1851. He originally planned to travel West with his brother Jacob,

---

[123] *NMHR,* Dailey, Martha LaCroix, April 1994, "Symbolism and Significance of the Lincoln Canes for the Pueblos of New Mexico," pp. 127-144.

who subsequently died in Louisiana. Steck then traveled with a group of Masons. This was a brotherhood of men who were encouraged to go west to settle the new territories in the recently discovered mineral regions.

The doctor made his way to California but was dissatisfied with what he found there. He returned to New Mexico where his medical services were needed. He was a contract surgeon with the army in Socorro, New Mexico for two years. He next received a federal appointment as an Indian agent. By 1863, he spoke Spanish and several Indian languages. He served the Ute, or Utah, and Apache tribes until he unofficially replaced James Collins as Indian Superintendent in 1863.[124]

Steck was asked to begin his service at once. Anticipating further controversy, on October 23, 1863, John Greiner again wrote a letter on Steck's behalf to Secretary

---

[124] Keleher, William A., *Turmoil in New* Mexico, Book Four, The Long Walk, Collins' testimony, p. 300; and Steck ref. Chap. 7, p. 410 says Steck took office on July 17, 1863. See Dissertations of Martha L. Dailey and Paul Lester.

Chase. Steck needed all the influence possible to overcome the Democrats' protests in Congress on Collins' behalf. Collins edited the Democrat newspaper, the *Gazette*. He requested Chase interview Steck. The doctor was a firm abolitionist, unafraid to declare himself as such, and "dared to avow his unflinching support of the administration." As such he had incurred the wrath of the Copperheads.[125] The appeal added support to Steck's appointment.[126]

At Conejos, in southern Colorado, Dr. Steck, as Indian Superintendent, had been at the treaty negotiations between the United States and the Ute Indians in October 1863. President Lincoln sent his secretary, John Nicolay, to Conejos as his representative. Michael Steck was the Ute agent in 1853 and was chosen to accompany him. The

---

[125] Letters of John Greiner, NM Territorial, General Records of the Office of the Secretary . . . Letters sent relating to employees of the Treasury Department and its bureaus, 1857-78. 56.2.1 (Textual Records: Name and subject indexes. Also, 56.3.1 Correspondence. Textual Records. Correspondence, 1841-1917.)
[126] *Rio Abajo Weekly Press*, 2/26/64, p. 2, col. 1.

meeting lasted one week. Nicolay presented the Ute leaders with silver medals to commemorate the occasion.

Dr. Steck's goal in 1863 was to make good on a promise to the Pueblo governors. He would deliver the patents confirming the Spanish grants to the existing nineteen Pueblos. There were originally thirty-five distinct Spanish land grants to the Pueblo Indians totaling 700,000 acres. Steck applied to the Land Office for the patents. He also suggested that the President of the United States issue commemorative canes for the occasion.[127] The Pueblo governors had cherished similar canes given them by the Spanish governor at Santa Fe in the early 1800s as symbols of authority.[128]

The Conejos Ute Conference Dr. Steck attended with John Nicolay was conducted to define the domains of the Ute bands. It was in southern Colorado, in territory

---

[127] *New Mexico Historical Review*, Vol. 69, 2, "Symbolism and Significance of the Lincoln Canes for the Pueblos of New Mexico," pp 130, 134, and 138.
[128] Ibid., p. 129.

once a part of New Mexico. The Utes were spread over northern New Mexico and even found in Mora County. They were assigned a reservation there in March 1862. It was the only Indian reservation in the Territory at the time.

When Secretary Arny arrived in New Mexico in 1861, he was to serve as Indian agent to the Utes and Jicarilla Apaches at Taos. Kit Carson held the assignment until the war broke out and he was called to duty with the Volunteers. Officials in Washington decided it was best to locate the Utes and Jicarilla Apaches away from Taos. Eventually an agreement was reached with Lucien Maxwell to place the combined tribe on the vast property Maxwell managed for his father-in-law, Carlos Beaubien.

Maxwell farmed the largest ranch in the Territory. His exploits were renowned, his daring vaunted, and his wealth exaggerated. His fame was mostly among men whose lives were necessarily more routine, their travels less adventurous. He and his friend Kit Carson had driven several thousand sheep to California on two occasions in the 1850s, returning home with more money than could be hidden in an attic chest. In fact, he never bothered to hide his wealth. His bedroom dresser was reputed to have drawers filled with gold, silver, and greenbacks. He was friend, ally, and companion to men like John Fremont whose expeditions made pathways through the Rocky Mountains and the Sierra Nevada. There would be railroads to follow these men's trails.

Lucien Maxwell had survived nearly every kind of raid, robberies on the trail, and challenges in many a barroom or hostelry. On one occasion, when on a Fremont expedition with friendly Cheyenne Indians, Maxwell's hunting party spotted some dark-looking objects among the hills on their left. Presumed to be buffalo coming to the Platte for water, Maxwell turned to see the Cheyennes "whipping up furiously" behind him. He then turned once more to see the objects were Indians "coming at speed."

Fremont turned his men toward a clump of timber several miles distant. The men's weary mounts were no match for the Indians who quickly faced them.

On the hills above two or three hundred accompanying Indians appeared. The natives dropped toward them. There was no escape. The river was behind the trees. Just as Maxwell was about to fire on the lead Indian, he recognized him. He had traded with him recently. He shouted in their language, "You're a fool, God damn you, don't you know me?" The warrior recognized his own language from a white man and swerved suddenly. He turned about, offered his hand to Fremont, struck his fist to his chest, and identified himself as "Arapaho!" Maxwell had lived among them as a trader a year or two before. The near battle became a reunion and a buffalo feast.[129]

On several occasions Maxwell, and others including Kit Carson, traveled to California driving many herds of

---

[129] Murphy, Lawrence R., *Lucien Bonaparte Maxwell*, Chap. 2, "Apprenticeship in the West," p. 44.

sheep to feed the burgeoning population of the late 1840s and 1850s. It was reported that Maxwell earned between $20,000 and $50,000 from one expedition.[130]

For nearly five years Lucien's neighbor, Kit Carson, managed the reservation at Taos. The Army then used the site at Rayado where Lucien's ranch was first located. They decided to move the Indians to a more remote location. In March 1862, Maxwell offered a lease to them of 1280 acres in the Ponil Canyon for $20 per year.[131] They were then approximately forty miles from Taos. Maxwell also supplied flour and beef to the Indians as a government contractor. This site was the only reservation in New Mexico other than the Bosque Redondo in 1863. The two reservations were nearly 200 miles apart, but both were in eastern New Mexico.

---

[130] Ibid., Chap. 4, p. 96
[131] Murphy, Lawrence R., *Philmont*, Chap. VI, "Lucien B. Maxwell: Empire Builder," p. 74. Also, Murphy, Lawrence, , *Lucien Bonaparte Maxwell: Napoleon of the Southwest*, Chap. 6, "The Cimarron Indian Agency," p. 123. Murphy, Lawrence R., *Frontier Crusader – William F. M. Arny*, Chap. 6, "A Novice in the Indian Service," p. 111.

In February 1864 Lucien Maxwell's father-in-law, Charles Beaubien, died at Taos. The Beaubien-Miranda Land Grant was divided among a group of people, primarily Beaubien's heirs. Luz Maxwell was his daughter. Maxwell had bought a thousand acres from Beaubien for his ranch home. He had managed Beaubien's businesses in the elder man's years.[132] Not long after the death, Lucien began to buy out the remaining interests in the grant. He was an energetic and aggressive businessman and rancher.

The Indian reservation on the Beaubien-Miranda property had to be supplied with meat and flour. Maxwell provided both – for a price. The government did not always pay regularly. There were times when the weather and pests such as corn worms destroyed the crops. Maxwell was caught in the middle. When not fed, the hungry Indians would rob the nearby ranches. The government was blind to such emergencies. The Indians could starve.

---

[132] Pearson, Jim Berry, *The Maxwell Land Grant*, Chap. One, "Lucien Maxwell, Big Land Owner," pp. 11-14.

Lucien Maxwell was not reared to allow Indians to starve. His grandfather was a prominent official in Illinois and a respected Indian agent. Indian representatives were often visitors at their home. Maxwell was a member of an elite corps of early mountain men. He was grateful to the Indians who taught him how to master the wilderness and survive. He held all Indian tribes as people worthy of respect.

Chapter Six: International Interest
January 1864 – August 1864

The unique and successful plan of Secretary Chase to float bonds among wealthy citizens to support the war was the talk of the financial world. In Santa Fe, it had shaped the opinions of Editor Manderfield. The Treasury Secretary circulated a pamphlet which suggested the national debt was a blessing and the generation that fought the war should not have to pay for it. The link between Arizona's gold supply and the national Treasury was not public knowledge. Nor was the mining being pursued by soldiers at Pinos Altos and in the southern Organ Mountains.

By December 1863 Treasury Secretary Chase was able to report that nearly $400,000,000 worth of five-twenty bonds had been sold to finance the Civil War. It attracted the notice of William Blackmore, a British attorney and financier, and member of a distinguished British banking house in Liverpool.

Blackmore considered a similar plan which might attract Brits to such a bond issue, or one even larger, in England. This kind of investment could appeal to a middle-class group of English investors and speculators. He might be able to propose a loan of five hundred million dollars. It would be raised through the sale of gold bonds secured by land in the public domain.[133] European purchasers of these securities could choose repayment in gold with interest at

---

[133] Brayer, Herbert O., *The Spanish-Mexican Land Grants,* 1863-1878, Vol. I, "Novitiate, 1827-1868," pp. 40-45.

five per cent yearly or select public land set aside for repayment of the loan.

Blackmore's uncle, his mentor and a noted financier, applauded the plan. Blackmore arranged at once to travel to the U. S. and present the plan to Congressmen, Senators, and Treasury Secretary Chase. He requested letters of introduction from notable American financiers such as Brown Brothers & Company, merchant bankers of New York City. It was suggested that he satisfy the concerns of security-minded European investors. If necessary, they could seek congressional incorporation of a company which would secure subscriptions to the bond issue whose government obligations could be converted or finally discharged.

Blackmore arrived in the U. S. in December 1863. Although the plan was heralded wherever Blackmore went, and he was even heard by Secretary Chase and President Lincoln, the plan was ultimately rejected. The cost of the land would be less for foreigners than what United States citizens would have to pay to purchase the same lands.[134]

In December 1863, J. Ross Browne, a renowned sketch artist, and Charles Poston, an energetic Arizona promoter, set off on an expedition of the newly proposed territory. The two men left from Oakland, California by way of a steamer to Fort Yuma. Once there, they set out for the Pima and Maricopa Indian villages across the Colorado River in Arizona.

By May of 1864, they reached the Mowry Mine. Mowry had been discharged from imprisonment at Fort Yuma on November 8, 1862.[135] It was announced by the *New York World and Journal of Commerce* in February that Mowry's property was restored.[136] Browne believed the information when he visited. However, by July there were indications to the contrary.[137]

---
[134] Ibid, p. 45.
[135] *Arizona and the West*, Altshuler, Constance, "The Case of Sylvester Mowry: The Charge of Treason," pp. 63-82.
[136] Santa Fe *New Mexican*, 7/27/64, from the *New York World and Journal of Commerce,* "General James H. Carleton," p. 2, col. 1.

When Browne and Poston visited, the mine was operational and productive, yielding a high grade of silver. The reduction process in one day's work yielded twenty tons of silver paying $1200 and $480 of lead. Expenses were only $400. The calculations were made by a respected metallurgist on the site. Browne said of the property, "At the time of our visit [May 4] this property was in the hands of the Deputy-Marshal of New Mexico, who held it on behalf of the United States . . . . and the mine seized under the Confiscation Act."[138]

Some months later Browne and Poston learned that John B. Mills, Mowry Mine Superintendent for Sylvester Mowry, and Edwin Stevens, his replacement, were murdered by Indians on December 29, 1863. Mills was twenty-three and had come to Arizona with the U. S. Boundary Commission before employment at the mine.

---

[137] Ibid., 7/29/64, p. 2, col. 3, " . . . . Mowry interest sold on July 18 to Marshal Cutler [purchaser.] Price paid, $4000.
[138] Browne, J. R., *Adventures in Apache Country,* Chap. XXI, "The Mowry Mine," p. 208. Also, 4/30/1864, p. 2, col. 1, "General Carleton and the New York *World.*"

The two were traveling from Santa Cruz to the mine on the morning of the incident.[139] They were found riddled with arrows in a nearby field.

The New Mexico Mining Company renewed its activity in July 1864. John Greiner returned to Santa Fe in July from Ohio to manage the mines. He also resumed his position as Receiver for the Land Office and U. S. Government Disburser. The mining company, often called "The Placers", announced that it intended to reopen the mines with "vigour."[140]

On March 1, 1861, Congress had approved the company's land grant and survey for 69,458.33 acres.[141] The company leasing the Placers in northern New Mexico in 1861 was managed by Samuel Ellison, District Court Clerk. It was he who John Greiner spoke of in his letter to Michael Steck in May 1861. The mine was active for

---

[139] Ibid., p. 196
[140] Ibid., p.66.
[141] *New Mexico Historical Review*, XLVII, John Townley, "New Mexico Mining Company," 1971, p. 64.

eleven months. Ellison worked three shifts at the mine and mill and averaged $750 per day in gross output before the Confederates arrived.[142]

The Pinos Altos area was in an established county, legally organized and settled. Its cache of wealth would be impossible to conceal. It would require "a pact of silence" to keep from having a gold rush like the one of 1849 in California's Sacramento Valley. The first order of business for the Treasury Department was to develop a strategy to maintain that silence. It must secretly connect the soldiers' mining claims to investors who could finance the equipment needed to develop the mines into legitimate companies. The process involved incorporating companies for mining production. Claims must be formally made in the Territorial Secretary's office.

Unlike the Mowry Mine in the Arizona district, these mines must transport their ores to the California mint

---

[142] Ibid., pp. 65-66.

for shipment. The Mowry Mine shipped its ore by way of Matamoros on the Mexican coast. The mint at California processed gold and shipped it to New York.

When the Arizona officials arrived to establish the new territory, New Mexico's size was reduced to 124,450 square miles. In 1850, the boundary between New Mexico and Texas was fixed on the 103° meridian. In 1861, the U.S. Boundary Commission announced a new boundary between New Mexico and southern Colorado, approved February 28, 1861.

The original plan for the transcontinental railroad was through New Mexico along the Arizona and Mexico border. The plan was being reconsidered in 1863. Its route along the 35th parallel would deliver large quantities of ores to eastern cities and ports. Transported goods would supply the Indian reservations needing food, clothing, wood, and tools. In this period, such goods were only available by wagon train at great time and expense.

In 1863, the railroads ended in western Missouri. Newspaper editors could see the critical need for railroads if for no other reason than delivering food and timber to populous cities. Settlement of the western U. S. and the prairies had been sought by several administrations since the 1830s. Transportation, more than any other factor, held emigration back. A railroad was still needed to make the puzzle work.

The railroads' locations were based on many factors, but population distribution was a major consideration. There were five towns in New Mexico during the Civil War with a population of over one thousand: Santa Fe, Mesilla, Albuquerque, Las Vegas, and Taos. The territory's total population was 93,516 in 1860. In 1849, an estimated forty thousand people were native Indians.[143]

---

[143] Keleher, Wm. A., *Turmoil In New Mexico,* Book One, General Kearny Comes to Santa Fe, Chap. Five, "New Mexico's Wild Indians," p. 44 and Chap. Six, "Martial Law," p. 386.

In January and February 1864, *The New Mexican* and *The Albuquerque Rio Abajo Weekly Press*, the latter edited by Hezekiah S. Johnson, carried articles on New Mexico's railroad interests. An issue of the Rio Abajo *Press* on February 18, 1864 cited "a late number of the *Topeka Tribune*" relative to *The Atchison, Topeka, & Santa Fe Railroad Company*. The directors of the company included a name familiar to New Mexicans, W. F. M. Arny of Santa Fe. Among the stockholders were Simon Delgado, Jose Manuel Gallegos, L. B. Maxwell, and Diego Archuleta of New Mexico. Governor John M. Goodwin and Secretary R. C. McCormick of Arizona as well as John Greiner and W. B. Baker of Santa Fe, the last few included shortly afterward.[144]

The company had reorganized and secured a tentative land grant to the state's border with Colorado and New Mexico. They would have to construct the road to

---

[144] *Rio Abajo Weekly Press*, 2/16/64, "Our Railroad Interests," col. 1.

New Mexico's eastern boundary by a certain deadline. This railroad surely held promise for the Territory.

Colonel Joseph West, former Receiver at the Mowry mine, commanded the southern district of New Mexico and was responsible for feeding the troops. He occupied Hart's Mill at Franklin, Texas for its flour supply and surrounding pasturage. There was also ample room to house the troops. It was soon apparent that the Column's additional reinforcements severely taxed his resources.

Major Fergusson, in charge at Tucson, had to send his men to far-flung posts throughout the district when the food stores ran out. Local farmers along the Texas border were pressured to provide for the army. West came into conflict with Carleton when the farm produce did not prove adequate.[145] Poor transportation took part of the blame.

The Indian Department agreed in 1863 to manage the Apaches at the Bosque Redondo reservation. Agent

---

[145] Hunt, Aurora, *The Army of the Pacific, 1860-1866,* "On Duty in Arizona," pp. 134-135. Also, Masich, Andrew E., *The Civil War in Arizona,* Chap. 3, "Campaigning," p. 58.

Lorenzo Labadi acted as their manager, guided them in the care of their stock, and instructed them in the use of tools to plant their crops. They planted wheat, corn, and beans in the spring. When large numbers of Navajos arrived, they crossed the Pecos River to maintain their crops some distance from the Apaches, their traditional enemy.

Before long, the officers began to allow the Navajo to gather the Apaches' crops. Labadi complained that the Apaches' crops were stolen. Carleton countered that Labadi fed his own private stock on the reservation's land. Steck complained and was banned from the reservation. Labadi was also soon forbidden to serve the Apaches.[146]

At court in July 1863, Judge Knapp announced he would not continue further business until Carleton rescinded his passport order. Judge Knapp was forced to carry a passport although he was a Presidential appointee. The General subjected Judge Knapp to every possible

---

[146] *The Southwestern Historical Quarterly*, 8/17/1970, "The Steck-Carleton Controversy," pp. 193-194.

insult. Knapp had called Carleton's rule despotic and stated it in open court. Other officials and attorneys registered complaints against the General. These were presented to the Governor's office. Knapp was three times arrested and placed in the guardhouse by Carleton's subordinates.

Even with his passport, the judge was required to report to each military post between Santa Fe and Mesilla. Shortly afterward, he was once more arrested while traveling without identity papers.

Judge Knapp, frustrated by the refusal of military authorities to honor his position, had handbills printed by *The Denver News*. These were distributed in Mesilla, Albuquerque, and Santa Fe. Knapp wrote General Halleck in Washington. Halleck was then prompted to write General Carleton "of the line of demarcation between military rule and the civil courts. . . . In matters of debt, trespass, etc., between persons not in the military service . . . you have no jurisdiction over such cases." He added that the Secretary of War directed him to remind Carleton of the limits of his authority.[147]

As a result, Judge Knapp convened the Dona Ana Grand Jury in special session in Mesilla on June 10, 1864, and instructed the jury on its responsibilities. In effect, the report recited the Mesilla Valley citizens' grievances during the Civil War years.[148] Primarily, citizens regarded the failure of the Union army to protect them against the Confederate intruders in 1861, which Carleton would not acknowledge. He sought retribution on the southern district and used certain citizen's properties for the army's profit. After the grand jury met and its results were published in *The New Mexican*, citizens throughout the Territory favored the southern district's case.

Although Judge Knapp sought an interview with President Lincoln and traveled to Washington between July and September, he met John Watts at the President's door.

---
[147] Keleher, William A., *Turmoil in New Mexico*, Book Four, The Long Walk, Chap. Six, "Martial Law," p. 402.
[148] Ibid, p. 403 and Santa Fe *New Mexican*, 7/1/1864, p. 2.

Watts handed him his resignation papers. Knapp returned to New Mexico where he was celebrated as a hero. A fandango was held in his honor. Judge Knapp told the people of his district that he would remain as a citizen and reveal the military's, and Carleton's abuses.

Steve Elkins had begun a law practice of his own and was gaining clients rapidly. If events moved in the direction of a practice in Santa Fe, he would take the first opportunity.

Accusations were hurled between the Indian and War Departments. Dr. Steck became an active partisan. At the same time, General Carleton's acts continued to be criticized by Judge Knapp.[149] The judge protested martial law and the enforcement of passes.

On December 23, 1863, the judge wrote General West at Mesilla that "although horse thieves and Indians were not obliged to carry military passes, he had been

---

[149] *New Mexico Historical Review*, Vol. 5:4, 1980, "Judge Joseph Knapp," Darlis A. Miller and Norman L. Wilson, Jr., pp. 335-344.

prevented from going to Santa Fe without one."[150] He had criticized Carleton's policies in open court.[151] Knapp had notified military authorities to no avail.[152] The experience made Knapp Carleton's most vocal critic regarding civil rights.

In February 1864, at the same time General West was relieved of his command in the southern district, William Gilpin was notified in Colorado of Charles Beaubien's death. Gilpin made his way south to Taos. There, he paid Beaubien's widow the promised $15,000 for title to the one-million-acre Sangre de Cristo Grant. The ex-governor bought out the remaining interests and arranged with a mining expert to explore the land's potential. A crew of ten men accepted the assignment.[153] The Sangre de Cristo land grant adjoined the Beaubien-Miranda grant in

---

[150] Keleher, William A., *Turmoil in New Mexico,* "The Long Walk", Chap.6, "Martial Law," p. 441.
[151] Ibid., p. 335.
[152] Ibid., December 1863 Knapp notified military authorities he would not tolerate the indignity of a passport requirement for a federal judge.
[153] Santa Fe *New Mexican, 2/6/64*, p. 2, col. 1. Also, H. O. Brayer, *The Spanish-Mexican Land Grants,* pp.60-66. p. 193, fn. 46 and Howard Lamar, *The Far Southwest, 1846-1912,* pp. 124-126.

New Mexico. Each grant stretched into the other's territory to some degree.

By March 1, 1864, the Bosque Redondo had not been formally established as an Apache reservation. The Navajo were not yet assigned a reservation. However, 425 Apaches already occupied the new site on the Pecos.

By March 5, 1864, the Navajo war sent around 3,500 Indians to the Bosque Redondo. The Santa Fe *New Mexican* praised General Carleton for delivering peace and security to the Territory.[154] At the same time, a cloud hung over the horizon. In one local news item, it was noted that *The New York World* and *Journal of Commerce* had published several articles accusing the New Mexico Quartermaster's and Commissary Departments of fraud. Major John C. McFerran, Chief Quartermaster, was implicated.[155] *The New Mexican* acknowledged the New

---

[154] Ibid., 3/5/64, p. 2, "General James H. Carleton".
[155] Ibid., 3/5/64, "Imputation of Fraud in the Quartermaster's and Commissary Department," p.2, col. 1. Also, *New Mexican* of 4/30/1864, "Gen. Carleton and the New York *World,* p. 2, col. 1.

York newspaper's accusation but defended McFerran as an officer of known integrity in the Territory.

New Mexicans became more attentive to the conduct of the military. In March, when General Carleton announced the Navajo war ended, people were relieved. However, a new issue arose at once. Carleton was ready to turn the care of the Navajo over to the Indian Department. The prisoners had to be fed and clothed. They lived in dugouts for lack of enough wood and their rations were inadequate. The Indian Department declared that the War Department was responsible since the decision to fight the Navajo and leave them destitute in a Union prison had been of their own doing. The War Department alone had the money to care for them.

General Carleton, former Superintendent Collins, and Kit Carson conferred on how to care for the Navajo at the reservation. It was decided to handle the matter in two letters. Collins wrote General Carleton that at the rate of

Navajo surrender, four to five thousand Indians would be on the reservation by May. The Navajo had received no "gifts" from the government for the last two years since an unfortunate incident at Fort Fauntleroy. They had no clothing. Collins suggested, for the sake of economy, their rations should be only flour, corn meal, corn, and fresh beef or mutton. They would also need salt. Many New Mexicans thought they should be compensated for the land taken from them as well as stock and other useful articles for their way of life.

Carleton sent Collins to Washington with his letter, endorsed by Colonel Carson, to General Lorenzo Thomas.[156] The matter was urgent. Carleton stated that the U. S. now had an Indian country larger than Ohio since the Navajo were subjugated. He needed approval of an Indian policy. He also asked for 4,000 head of butcher cattle, for clothing for the women and children, and for agricultural

---

[156] Keleher, William A., *Turmoil in New Mexico*, The Long Walk, Chap.Five, "At the Bosque Redondo," pp. 370-374.

implements to "insure crops." An assistant supervisor was needed at the Bosque to keep accounts and manage business affairs. He suggested a law should be passed to provide for reorganization of Indian management.[157]

James Collins left in April and would not return to New Mexico until September.[158] It was in this period that General Carleton assumed Collins' role as *Gazette* editor. During this time Carleton supported General McClellan for President over Abraham Lincoln.[159] An Army officer could not be involved in political matters. It was contrary to military law.

The Navajos were no longer hostile, Carleton believed. He wrote Major Henry Wallen, commanding officer at Fort Sumner on March 11, 1864. Consulting with Carson, Governor Connelly, and Quartermaster McFerran, Carleton instructed Wallen to reduce the rations for the

---

[157] Ibid, Book Four, Chap. 5, "At Bosque Redondo." Letters to Gen. Lorenzo Thomas, 3/12/64, pp. 370-373.
[158] Santa Fe *Gazette*, 9/3/64, p. 2, col. 2.
[159] Santa Fe *New Mexican*, 10/31/64, p. 1, cols. 1-2.

Navajos. "I find it is their opinion that one pound of flour, or meal, or of meat, into soup, could be made to be enough, and is probably more nutriment per day than they have been accustomed to obtain . . . . I can barely see how they can be supported until we get provisions from the States, or their corn becomes ripe enough to pluck."[160]

The General wrote to General Thomas on March 12, 1864. "The War Department, General, has performed its whole duty in having brought these Navajo Indians into subjection and now, in my opinion, stands ready to transfer them to the Department of the Interior."[161]

The National Intelligencer, on February 26, 1864, printed an account of the controversy between Judge Knapp and General Carleton. The paper reported Attorney General Bates' reply to Judge Knapp. Bates and President Lincoln had discussed the matter, but the Attorney General wrote Knapp that he was unable to change the situation. He

---

[160] Ibid., pp. 375-376.
[161] Ibid., pp. 371-374.

referred to the General's insistence that he had jurisdiction in the district under martial law.

Apaches in Arizona, now formally declared a separate territory, continued strikes against military units. During May and June of 1864 Lieutenant Nelson H. Davis led a detachment of 111 men of the California Fifth Infantry and First Cavalry against plundering bands of Gila Apaches. The men marched from May 9 to June 3. Several *rancherias* and many wheat and corn fields were destroyed.[162] Two chiefs and fifty-one Indians were killed. Seventeen Indians were wounded, while women and children were captured. The stolen property of Anglo men who had been recently massacred was recovered. Despite the extermination, Apaches were still a danger in much of New Mexico and Arizona.[163]

---

[162] Rancherias were Indian villages.
[163] Masich, Andrew E., *The Civil War in Arizona*, Chap. 8, "California's Soldier-Correspondents to the San Francisco Daily Alta, California,", 1862-1865," p. 283.

Another Army expedition was conducted during August. It involved a thirty-day drive of the California Volunteers in search of hostile Apaches in central and eastern Arizona. There, ten Apaches were killed, and two captured. Twenty acres of corn, pumpkins, and beans were destroyed.[164] The Apache War was not over, only a few tribes surrendered.

Across the nation people strained for relief from the tight money market. Businesses were stressed by the labor shortage, and in New Mexico, the Army's Quartermaster's Department announced that corn was selling at the highest market price.[165]

In July, the Santa Fe *New Mexican* related that the farm of Lucien Maxwell of Mora County announced the erection of a steam grist mill capable of turning out 300 barrels of flour per day.[166]

---

[164] Colton, Ray C., *The Civil War in the Western Territories,* Chap. 7, "Indian Campaigns," pp. 135-136.
[165] *The New Mexico Press*, Albuquerque, 7/26/64, p. 1, col. 3. Originally taken from the *Topeka Tribune*.
[166] Santa Fe *New Mexican*, 8/12/64, p. 2, col. 1.

The California Column miners' activities were not reported. There was an official effort to keep silent about these valuable government mines. Mining was being conducted, even as early as 1863. Indian attacks held back mining for some months during this period. Seasoned miners included Private Peter W. Kinsinger who discovered silver ore at Pueblo Springs in Socorro County in 1863.[167]

In southern New Mexico, California Column officers, Colonel George W. Bowie and Captain Charles A. Smith, were linked with El Paso politician William W. Mills, the customs officer at the Mexican border. These men took legal possession of the Stephenson Mine in the Organ Mountains. Their claim was based on the mine's abandonment when the Confederates fled New Mexico. The local owners' departure with the Confederates risked appropriation of the mine by Union loyalists.[168]

---

[167] *NMHR*, LIII;1, 1978, Darlis A. Miller, "Carleton's California Column: A Chapter in New Mexico's Mining History," p. 10
[168] Ibid., p. 23.

The Organ Mountains in southern New Mexico were the site of another claim in 1864. In August, Captain William McCleave and Surgeon William H. McKee united with Bowie, Smith, W. W. Mills, and a local miner, Nepomuceno Carrasco, to mine three mines. One of these three, the Calzada, was being actively mined by fifteen men in November,1864.[169]

Clearly, the need for support and goods from the states by rail, and the improved transportation of the Territory's abundant ores to ready markets, were economic measures sorely needed.

---

[169] Ibid., pp. 23-24.

Chapter Seven: A Navajo Crisis

March 1864 – December 1864

Beginning in March 1864, Dr. Steck was in Washington for his confirmation as Indian Superintendent. He made urgent appeals to officials and Congressmen for the Navajo tribe's acute needs. A special appropriation would provide clothing, blankets, tools, and sundries for the coming winter. Finally, a March 31 letter from Secretary of War Stanton to Interior Secretary J. P. Usher prompted a recommendation of $100,000 to relieve the Navajo and "enable furtherance of the colonization plan."[170] Steck returned home to Santa Fe by May 21, 1864.[171]

Steck's entreaties met with sympathy and agreement in the halls of Washington, but most authorities were unwilling to speak out in time of war. Army officers had confirmed that the military establishments of New Mexico had cost "not less than $3,000,000 annually, independent of land warrant bounties."[172]

In June, the War Department sent a board of officers to discover the cost of supplies purchased for the captive Navajo. Evidence proved that in the four-month period of March through June purchases came to $510,000.[173] Steck pointed out that this didn't include supplies for the troops assigned to the Bosque, or the cost of transporting the Indians, as well as the expense of the buildings Carleton ordered to be erected. There was also the payment of sixty

---

[170] Keleher, William A., *Turmoil in New Mexico*, The Long Walk, Book Four, Chap. Seven, "Dr. Michael Steck," p. 415.
[171] Santa Fe *New Mexican*, 5/21/64, Page 2, col. 2, "Dr. Steck."
[172] Ibid., p. 414.
[173] Keleher, William A., *Turmoil in New Mexico,* Book Four, Chap. Seven, "Dr. Michael Steck," p. 417.

laborers employed by the military, and the cost of obtaining oxen teams.

In New Mexico, there was local opposition to Lincoln's election voiced by the Santa Fe Democrat newspaper, *The Gazette*. It was generally recognized that Carleton had taken control of *The Gazette* and its editorial policy.[174] Editor Collins' departure for Washington was in April and his hostility toward the Lincoln administration was a matter of record. General Carleton endorsed General McClellan's election.

In May *The Santa Fe New Mexican* became ardently opposed to General Carleton and his policies. They asked why Carleton supported McClellan's men with articles on the editorial page of the Democrat *Gazette*. The Republican newspaper later criticized the General in bitter and accusatory terms in a two-column diatribe.[175]

---

[174] Ibid., Chap. Eight, "Carleton on the Defensive," p. 441. Santa Fe *New Mexican*, 3/24/65.
[175] Santa Fe *New Mexican*, 5/12/65, "General Carleton's Analysis."

In Washington, on July 5, 1864, Senator William P. Fessenden was pressed into service to fill the place of Salmon P. Chase who had been encouraged to resign as Secretary of the Treasury. *The New York Journal of Commerce* reported on Fessenden's address to the associated banks of New York. The date was August 13. Fessenden stated that the previous fiscal year compared favorably with other years. His description of the country's financial status reassured the attending bankers. They recommended loaning $50,000,000 to the Treasury, provided it would be credited by them to the government and drawn upon as credits are drawn by private borrowers.

Afterward, *The Journal of Commerce* commented that "if this arrangement is carried out, the inflation has reached its limit, at least for some months. Speculators in stocks, securities of every sort in produce, may as well arrange for a 'crisis' and all dealers may govern themselves accordingly."[176]

Although the leading Republican newspaper of the Territory seldom published Dona Ana County news, the county's August 21, 1864 elections to the legislature appeared in its columns in early September. Steve Elkins of Mesilla and Pablo Melendres of Dona Ana were announced in both Territorial newspapers, as the county's representatives to the 1864-1865 legislature. Elkins was elected to the House, and Melendres to the Council.[177]

In Santa Fe, General Carleton drew modified fire from the press, the judiciary, and the Indian service concerning the Bosque Redondo. The press warned Carleton in tactfully worded editorials that his policies were not popular with the public.[178] Dr. Steck, an Indian agent since 1853, as superintendent, had questioned the General's dictation of Indian policy and noted its likely disastrous effects for the whole Navajo tribe. Carleton finally

---

[176] *New York Journal of Commerce*, 8/13/64.
[177] Santa Fe *New Mexican*, 9/2/64, p. 2, col. 3.
[178] Keleher, *Turmoil*, p. 399.

attempted to defend himself with a speech to the public and several articles published in the Santa Fe *Gazette*. [179]

When the Santa Fe *New Mexican* became completely disenchanted with the General, it published an article in October 1864 telling citizens of the status of Carleton's policies.

      Congress should pass a law to enlarge the Apache reservation to provide
      for the Navajos, but they were told the tribe numbered from five to seven
      thousand, that they would have to do much to sustain themselves this year
      at this location. They will now see that they have been deceived; that they
      number over 15,000 souls, that they have done comparatively nothing to
      sustain themselves, and that the poor wretches now . . . . . are carrying
      mesquite roots, on their backs, from eight to ten miles, and cedar or pine

---

[179] Ibid., p. 445.

wood from 15 to 20 miles to cook their food. What is to become of them in the winter?[180]

Responsible men reported that there was not enough water in the Pecos during the summer for irrigation in the fields. That was when only 3,000 Indians were planting. Ten or twenty thousand could not be sustained. The Navajos said only half their tribe was at the reservation. The authorities agreed. The newspaper suggested the tribe be returned home where 40¢ per day would cost the government $2,889,000. Such an allowance would not include salt, buildings, transportation, and clothing. Each Navajo needed at least one pound of beef and one pound of bread per day.

At one point in 1864, when beef and flour sold for twenty dollars on the hundred, the nearly starving civilian population blamed Carleton because he used government

---

[180] Santa Fe *New Mexican*, 10/28/64, "The Reservation Question," p. 1, cols. 1-3.

gold to outbid them in buying supplies for the army and the Indians.

The *New Mexican* told the Territory's citizens:

> ". . . . . . it is high time you look into this matter. The program [Carleton's] contemplated the location of 20,000 Navajos and Apaches in your midst, your grazing land which we have turned over the Indians not your own, but those of another territory. Your interests must suffer that the Arizonans may prosper. Those having mining interests there may be enriched by your loss. Yes, you are to be made the willing asses upon which they ride to wealth and power. Let their rations be stopped from failure of Congress to make an

appropriation, or from invasion and you have a [disaster.]"[181]

In October, a *New Mexican* reader reported General Carleton gave a young Navajo girl to a sutler.[182] The public recalled that Carleton, in an earlier assignment in 1851, sold his two black slaves to Governor Lane before leaving the territory to command a regiment of dragoons on the Utah border.[183] The "gift" of a child was not the act of a man committed to the abolishment of slavery, and the rift between Carleton's political allies and the Radical Republicans in Santa Fe grew larger.

Michael Steck submitted a report to the Commissioner of Indian Affairs on October 21 from Santa Fe. He reported that the Navajos were still at war and stealing sheep from the settlers. He recommended that the

---

[181] Ibid., col. 2.
[182] Ibid, 12/9/1864, p.2, col. 3.
[183] Hunt, Aurora, *Kirby Benedict: Frontier Federal Judge*, "To Recapture Tucson," p. 112. Also, Keleher, *Turmoil in New Mexico*, Book Four, Chap. One, "First the Apaches," p. 279.

tribe should be placed on a large reservation in their own country and be guided gradually to make their own living. More than half of the tribe was still at large. Only the poor were at the reservation. They were unable to mount a resistance. If the Navajos were returned to their own country and fed at once, the cost would be $200,000. If not, the next year the cost to feed the Navajos would be $2,000,000.[184]

Judge Knapp was encouraged to open court as presiding judge once more and did so in November 1864. Shortly after District Court opened, Frank Higgins, District Attorney, and Attorney Watts entered. Steve Elkins, the newest and youngest territorial attorney, stood to argue on Knapp's behalf, but the judge was forced to adjourn court before anyone else could speak.[185] They announced that

---

[184] Ibid., Book Four, The Long Walk, Chap. Seven, "Dr. Michael Steck," pp. 418-421.
[185] *New Mexico Historical Review*, 55:4 1980, "The Resignation of Judge Joseph A. Knapp," Darlis A. Miller & Norman L. Wilson, Jr., pp. 335-344.

Judge Knapp was not authorized to hold court and the assembly was closed.

By December 1864 matters at the Bosque had reached a climax. Congress refused to continue to support the reservation project. When the legislature opened on December 1, Steve was the newest member. He strove to be silent and allow himself to learn from the senior members, most residents of many years. He watched as they argued whether Secretary Arny should be allowed to go to St. Louis to have the Territorial Law Code printed in Spanish and English. He suppressed defending Arny who had been the primary writer and laborer in a committee of three. However, he was proud to vote with the majority to be rid of General Carleton for good in the Territory. Arny was finally approved for the trip to print the Code.

On December 7, Delegate Perea met President Lincoln. He disparaged Secretary Arny, Dr. Steck, and John Greiner. He suggested Charles Clever be appointed

Secretary, Felipe Delgado as Indian Superintendent, and James Collins as manager of the Federal Depository.

Three months later he proposed John Watts be given the Depository position.[186] Lincoln still chafed at Treasury Secretary Salmon Chase's embarrassing interference in his campaign of the late summer. Chase had continued his efforts to be named the Republican nominee for President. Lincoln finally arranged for Chase's removal from the Cabinet. When Chief Justice Roger Taney died in mid-October, Lincoln recognized Chase was the most qualified man for the Supreme Court position. He overrode his own personal resentments of the man's intrigues against him. Chase was told of the President's choice on December 6, 1864. He wrote at once to Lincoln conveying his heartfelt gratitude for the President's confidence and good will.[187]

---

[186] Murphy, Lawrence R., *Frontier Crusader: W. F. M. Arny*, Chap. 7, p. 129.
[187] Goodwin, Doris K., *Team of Rivals*, Chap. 25, "A Sacred Effort," pp. 679-680.

Chapter Eight: A Telling Census

October 1864 - April 1865

There was trouble between the Comanches and the Kiowas with the Navajos at the Bosque. The grama grass plains where the Comanches grazed their stock adjoined the Bosque Redondo. General Carleton had to feed the Navajo. He wasn't responsible for the Plains Indians. In 1864 twenty ounces of meat and twenty-two of flour was authorized to be given to adults monthly on Ration Day, and a proportionate amount for the children. Now only half-rations were available.

The Navajo were starving due to two years of crop devastation and Congress' refusal to extend appropriations.

General Carleton hinted that "If the Navajos had the spirit with reference to the Comanches which they ought to have toward their hereditary enemies, a war party of 500 of the former, could go out and get all the stock they wanted . . ."[188] Although common practice, it was contrary to policy, and Carleton was reckless in making such a suggestion.

In 1864 and 1865, hundreds of freight wagons headed west from Fort Larned on the Santa Fe Trail. Comanche and Kiowa Indian raids were made on nearby caravans and the fort itself. One hundred seventy-two post animals were stolen there in mid-summer 1864. Military escorts were scheduled for protection of caravans on certain days of the month.[189]

---

[188] Keleher, William A., *Turmoil in New Mexico,* Book Four, Chap. Five, "At Bosque Redondo," p. 379, 10/64.
[189] Dary, David, *The Santa Fe Trail,* Chap. Fourteen, "The Civil War,

In the same mid-summer, two bands of Plains tribes attacked trains and murdered travelers at Walnut Creek. They robbed the train of a well-known Albuquerque merchant and gathered at Pawnee Rock where they attacked another train, killing and scalping five men, and carrying off five small boys as captives.

General Carleton was determined to chastise the Plains Indians. On October 22, he put Kit Carson in command of an expedition against the Kiowas and Comanches. He urged speed and action.

The plainsmen were angry to have the Bosque Navajos stealing their cows from the Staked Plains. They complained to no avail and twice attacked the reservation.[190]

Like the Navajos, the 1,500 Utes and Jicarilla Apaches at the Cimarron reservation had to be fed. At the end of 1864, the army had withdrawn provisions to both

---

1861-1865," pp. 271-272.
[190] Ibid. Also, Records of Fort Sumner, New Mexico, 1862-1869, Records of the U. S. Continental Army Commanding, 1826-1920, RG 393, microfilm. Headquarters, letter from Gen. Carleton to Brig. General Crocker, Oct. 14, 1864.

reservations. Maxwell was a major contractor for the Bosque and Cimarron reservations, but the corn and wheat crops had been decimated by storms and worms, a problem shared by most farmers that year. He held many unpaid bills the government owed him.[191] The tribes at the Cimarron reservation were hungry. They were soon called on to assist the campaign against the Plains Indians. Carson and Maxwell asked the Utes and Apaches to act as scouts for the mission. The two men approached Kaniache, the Ute chief. They promised the chief provisions if the braves of the Cimarron agency would act as scouts and fight the Comanches and Kiowas. The tribes were traditional enemies. General James Blunt, with 335 troops from Fort Bascom and the area, would supply the main attacking force. The reservation would be fed in their absence and the Indian fighters would share the rations provided the

---

[191] Murphy, Lawrence R., *Lucien Bonaparte Maxwell*, Chap. 6, "The Cimarron Indian Agency," pp. 130-132.

soldiers.[192] The fight was retribution for their attacks on settlers' and merchant's wagons.

On the last day of October 1864, the troops gathered at Fort Bascom for the assault on the plainsmen. A deep snow fell in southern Colorado and covered Raton Mountain. It lay on the route they followed to Adobe Walls. Afterward, the temperature dropped to freezing so that range cattle and wild animals were soon destitute. Fleeing antelope herds were hindered by the fine crust which followed brief warming periods. Only bears and wolves benefited from the vulnerability of the shorter haired creatures.[193]

On November 10, Kaniache and his seventy-five Mohuache Utes and Apaches arrived at Fort Bascom near Las Vegas. Snow was on the ground. They traveled by night in double file. They were told not to light even a

---

[192] Oates, Harvey Lewis, *Dear Old Kit: The Historical Kit Carson*, Univ. of Oklahoma Press, Norman, 1968.
[193] Howard, Irving, *Memories of A Lifetime in the Pike's Peak Region*, G. P. Putnam's Sons, New York and London, The Knickerbocker Press, 1925.

cigarette. The troops faced a 200-mile trek to Adobe Fort. They were supplied with adequate provisions, rifles, and howitzers. The two-week journey required a change from wagons to pack mule transportation. About thirty miles west of their destination the Utes spotted the enemy. Carson rode closer to the Kiowa village of 150 lodges while his troops followed him. There were signs the Indians had abandoned their camp and traveled the four-mile distance to Adobe Fort.[194]

Carson ordered the troops to keep absolute silence. They advanced in light marching order. Just before dawn, he halted the men, called for a dismount, and commanded them to stand by the horses holding their reins. The Utes and Apaches wore buffalo robes for warmth. They hid in a chaparral thicket. When the bugle sounded, they threw off their robes and appeared in their war paint and feathers.

---

[194] Keleher, *Turmoil*; Book Four, "The Long Walk", Chap. Seven, "Dr. Michael Steck," p. 429. Also, Colton, Roy C., *The Civil War in the Western Territories, "Indian Campaigns"*, pp. 145-146.

They splashed across the shallow Canadian River for the enemy.

Suddenly, as if from nowhere, at least a thousand whooping warriors on fine horses surrounded the federal troops, firing their rifles.[195] The warriors charged and were repulsed by the cavalry, only to charge again. The Kiowas' reinforcements were nearby. Facing an overwhelming force of Kiowas, some Comanches, Arapahos, and Apaches, the howitzers were put in place. Their work dropped many Indians, but new reinforcements were continually made.

The Indians of the nearby Kiowa village saw their tipis being raided and burned. Enraged, they set fire to the dry prairie grass behind the soldiers, allowing them to use smoke to get within firing range. Carson countered with a backfire, his howitzers behind them allowing retreat. He found high ground and set fires in his rear to halt the Kiowa's attack. Carson consulted with the Utes and

---

[195] Ibid., p. 429.

overruled the army officers. He allowed the Utes to raid the Kiowa village before it was burned. They fought a full day. He ordered a return to Fort Bascom. When the Union saw the depth of their enemies' reinforcements, they recognized the wisdom to withdraw. At four p.m. the federals began a retreat to the wagon train in the rear.

The retreat saved many of his men, so outnumbered by the enemy. Carson estimated the Plainsmen lost 100 men, while two soldiers were killed, and twenty-one were wounded. One ambulance could not hold them. The injured were loaded on the gun and ammunition carts. The Kiowas followed them but thought it foolish to prolong the fight against a strong enemy. They turned back. The troops arrived at Fort Bascom on December 20, 1864.

The Utes arrived at Cimarron with the Kiowa's large stores of dried meat, berries, buffalo robes, powder, and cooking utensils. They also took a buggy and spring wagon belonging to a Kiowa chief. The tribe hailed them as heroes. As promised, the remainder of the tribe was fed while the warriors supported the troops. The provision crisis was over for the winter.[196] The Cimarron reservation tribes could survive until spring.[197]

The legislature was in session when news of the Adobe Walls attack reached them. A messenger rushed to the podium to deliver the battle's outcome. Governor Connelly read several accounts of the confrontation. Formal and informal reports contradicted each other. There was no consensus.

The Governor interpreted the reports. Carson and General Blunt were vastly outnumbered. They had stumbled onto the site of several Plains Indians' villages. The tribes were warned of their approach and had combined. The Union's howitzers were rendered useless when the Kiowas and their allied tribes started fires and

---

[196] Colton, Ray C., *The Civil War in the Western Territories*, "Indian Campaigns," p. 145. Seventy-five Ute and Jicarilla Apache Indian warriors were induced to accompany the troops.
[197] Hunt, Aurora, *The Army of the Pacific*, "On Duty in New Mexico," pp. 165.

created a smokescreen. They assembled to return before being further demolished. Thirty-five men were injured, and over one-hundred Indians were killed. The Union's safe return received a heartfelt welcome.

On December 23, the lawmakers read in the *New Mexican* that the bodies of "some fifteen Navajo Indians were observed a week or two since, exposed to the view of the traveler and the instincts of the wolf." The Indians' were frozen on the route to the Bosque where so many had died of starvation.

The newspaper reflected with irony that they might have been thinking of their destination, the Bosque Redondo. Their "sightless orbs may have dreamt of a paradise, and the Translator, had he been there, could have caught from their dying lips, it may be, the sweet expression, 'Content, content!' as in delirium they dreamed of the Pecos Reservation."[198] The reality was that Dr. Steck arranged for their burial.

The legislators fought over whether to support Carleton's policies. The General feared they would ask Congress for his dismissal. He arranged for monies to be distributed to affect the outcome. Samuel Ellison confirmed the bribery. He served in the legislature several times, was Supreme Court clerk, House Speaker, librarian, and held other positions of authority as well.[199] Carleton's effort was successful, and he remained in command, at least for a time.

Steve Elkins avoided notice as a new representative from the controversial third district. His fair hair, complexion, height, and youth set him apart from the older and darker men of his acquaintance. He needed to be accepted with respect. He had arrived with Reverend Reade and the Aguirres, and now had a well-regarded practice. He was presently visible as a Republican from a Democrat

---

[198] Santa Fe *New Mexican*, 12/23/64, "Starved to Death," p. 2, col. 4.
[199] *NMHR*, 1/1937, "Memoir of a Kentuckian in New Mexico 1848-1884," p. 9. Also, Santa Fe *New Mexican*, 1/26/66, p. 1, col. 1, "Carleton's Resolutions of Last Winter."

district. He remained mostly silent. He was soon recognized for his expertise in the application of Robert's Rules of Order.

During this session, General Carleton had several of his subordinates distribute inducements to leaders of the House and Council to vote in his favor. He had been forewarned of the plan to remove him. The result delayed the decision of the assembly to ask the President to withdraw the Commander.

Elkins' party allegiance was likely unquestioned when he was nominated as Dona Ana County's representative. The county, and Elkins with it, was assumed to be unanimously Democratic. Costly formalities of printed ballots were not used. Elkins abstained from issues of conflict and soon became known as a conciliator.[200]

In the late summer, Congress finally agreed to send the reservation Indians $100,000. Purchases could be made

---

[200] Mills, W. W., *Forty Years at El Paso*, "John Lemon," pp. 71-72. Steve Elkins was said to have obtained a retraction of a slander which settled a matter and avoided a duel between two prominent men.

to relieve the Navajo by having the Quartermaster's Office at Fort Leavenworth conduct the requisitions. The expense of freighting to the Bosque was a major concern for the quartermaster. The location was far from regular transportation trails. Dr. Steck's wife died in October. Steck's assistant would meet Colonel Leavenworth on the plain in Kansas to approve the critical shipment.

In November 1864, a month after Mrs. Steck's death, the doctor waited to meet his assistant at Fort Union. He had attended to his wife's care, and after a period of mourning, handled business involved with her death. Colonel Leavenworth was assigned to order the Navajos' supplies from the $100,000 allotment made by Congress.[201]

The Colonel made the purchases, traveling to Chicago alone. When he returned, he met Baker mid-way between Fort Leavenworth and Fort Union, New Mexico.

---

[201] *The Overland Monthly*, Vol. 10, Feb. 1873, No. 2, "An Indian Reservation" by George Gwyther, M.D., pp. 123-134, spec. p. 126.

Before Baker could check the supply crates, Colonel Leavenworth had returned to his fort.

Baker met Steck at Fort Union. It was nearly Christmas. After an inspection of the goods, they discussed the unsatisfactory outcome. The items, agricultural tools, cloths, blankets, and some clothing, were clearly flawed. They couldn't reject the goods and show up empty-handed. They determined to distribute the gifts but have the sutler at Fort Union establish the real value. They would be able to verify the amount of the fraud. The gifts had to be made since the tribe was told to expect Christmas gifts.

The afternoon before the distribution, several observers were invited to stand by. Dr. George Gwyther frequently commented on the sub-standard goods. Blankets were needed by all, but few were available. Gwyther suggested the blankets be weighed and the result recorded. The weight was less than half of the Army's standard blankets.[202] The Army paid $18.50 per pair for the Navajo.

The military purchase price was $5.50. Cloth was cut into squares of two-and a half yards and calico into three-yard pieces so that everyone was able to keep some item.

The day and evening of the occasion, the tribe appeared at the fire lit for them in front of the fort, not far from where their monthly flour and meat were distributed. Their haggard faces were expressionless, eyes solemn, shuffling unshod feet, few rags covering their bodies. Dr. Steck noted their numbers and pieced out the items so that he was able to give each person some tool or shred of cloth which might serve them in some fashion. As dark closed in, the last few souls faded into the waning light as only spectral shadows.

A census was taken the same week Steck and Baker were at the reservation. There were 8,354 Navajos at the Bosque, consisting of 1,782 families. They owned 3,038 horses, 143 mules, 6,962 sheep, 2,858 goats, and 630

---

[202] *The Overland Monthly*, Feb. 1873, Vol. 10, "An Indian Reservation," pp. 123-124.

looms. Also residing on the reservation were 405 Mescalero Apaches and 34 Apaches of other tribal branches. Over a thousand Navajos died of malnutrition and disease in the previous year.[203]

The Bosque's commander for only two months, General Marcellus Crocker, would soon be recalled to command at another fort in the east.[204] He had strenuously resisted the assignment at the reservation, to no avail. Until the census, Crocker was deceived about the true status of the Navajo, their health services, provisions, and structures arranged to provide for them.

The General's Adjutant, Captain Robert Lusby, died on February 20, 1865. He was commemorated in a service given him by the Brotherhood of Masons shortly afterward.[205]

---

[203] Keleher, Wm. A, *Turmoil in New Mexico*, December 31, 1864, Book Four, Chap. Five, "At Bosque Redondo," Navajo Census, December 1864, p. 380. Also, fn.105., p. 502. Also, OR Series I, Vol. XLVIII, pp. 522-569.

[204] Headquarters records of Fort Sumner, NM, 1862-1869 (Microfilm) Record Group 393, Genl. Orders 2, Extract, p. 19, Special Order No. 477 series of 1864 – Gen. Crocker at Fort Sumner, is ordered to report to the commanding General of the Cumberland and [relinquish the command of this fort – Fort Sumner.] Date: Feb. 20, 1865.

[205] Santa Fe *Gazette*, 3/11/65, "Death of Capt. Robert Lusby," p. 2,

General Crocker began at once to tighten security on the methods used to provide food and essentials to the Navajo. Transportation of supplies from Fort Union was unsatisfactory. Crocker had not been made aware of the problem. He was made commander in late September 1864 and arrived from Missouri only shortly before then.[206] Concern for the shortage of grain was not reflected in headquarters' records until a letter received from Quartermaster McFerran on December 18, 1864, revealed it.[207]

The sutler's evaluation of goods delivered to the Navajo at Christmas did not satisfy General Carleton. General Crocker had his officers do their own assessment of the merchandise. The sutler's report requested by Superintendent Steck listed the total value of the flawed merchandise as $30,000. There was no doubt Leavenworth,

---

col.4.
[206] Ibid., Headquarters file. Letter of A.AG. General Benjamin C. Cutler, 9/24/64 from Office of General DeForrest.
[207] Ibid., Letter to General Crocker from J. C. McFerran, QM, 12/18/64.

in collusion with Carney & Stevens, contractors, stole at least $60,000 in the transaction.[208]

The year had been tumultuous with the Apaches continued attacks in the southern region. Political infighting occurred among the Republicans. Democrat Carleton fought off his critics on all sides, and the Navajos suffered near extermination in a pest-ridden forty-square mile prison. They were without adequate shelter, hospital, food, or supplies. Carleton refused to bend in his insistence that the Navajo could not find a better location than the one on the Pecos.

The Cimarron reservation did not provide land for the Utes and Apaches to farm, but the grant owner was continuously aware of the reservation's needs. Thanks to Kit Carson and Lucien Maxwell, the Ute and Jicarilla

---

[208] Gwyther, Dr. George, *The Overland Monthly,* Feb. 1873, Vol. 10, "An Indian Reservation," pp. 123-134. Also, Paul A. Lester, Doctorate Dissertation, "Michael Steck and New Mexico Indian Affairs, 1852-1865," Univ. of Oklahoma, Norman, OK, 1986, p. 214.

Apaches at Cimarron held the Kiowas' stores. These were provided for them during the harsh winter months.

The earliest issues of Santa Fe's January newspapers indicated the sources of each editor's news. Notice of the Kiowa and Comanche Indian battle appeared in the Santa Fe *Gazette* as the Army's full and official report made on December 27, 1864.

The leading story in the early January issues of the *New Mexican* was a complaint of discharged California soldiers. Five men represented the Californians who expressed the enmity between General Carleton and the citizens of the southern district. The soldiers testified to the unjust treatment of citizens and their own distaste for their part in enforcing Carleton's rule.[209]

It was only the beginning of a letter writing campaign against General Carleton's military policies and actions of nearly three years. The departing soldiers

---

[209] Santa Fe *New Mexican*, 1/6/65, "California Volunteers vs General James H. Carleton," p. 1, col. 1.

expressed gratitude for the acts of kindness tendered them by the citizens of New Mexico.

Covering all other matters of recent note, *The New Mexican* published its summary of the Governor's Message to the Assembly. The newspaper's report cited the "solemn Treaty of Fort Defiance." It reminded citizens that the government had never permitted a savage enemy to locate on public lands. The editors maintained the lands of the Pecos belonged to the United States and the Indians were wards of the state. The editors attacked the Governor for his stance on the reservation as "forty miles on the Pecos exchanged for 400 miles of pastoral and mineral land formerly in possession of the Indians."

Carleton's refusal to withdraw the passport policy impeding Knapp's trips to court in Santa Fe, his usurpation of civil authority, his Army contract favoritism, his use of gold to subvert the marketplace, and many other improprieties under the aegis of martial law drew Knapp's insightful criticism. The final insult was John Watts' delivery of Knapp's resignation papers to him at the President's door.

Knapp's wife was ill. He intended to leave New Mexico for his former home in Illinois that spring. He began a series of eight open letters to Carleton which were published between January 13 and May 6 on the front page of the *New Mexican*. On April 14 he charged Carleton with pursuing a "black flag" policy in dealing with Indians. He wrote that the military was responsible for the death of Mangus Colorado and portrayed it in minute detail.[210] His letters also pointed out that a springtime expedition of extermination was continued. The revelations were climaxed by the convening of the Dona Ana County Grand Jury on June 10, 1864.

The apparent response from Washington was the notification that a Senate investigating committee would

---

[210] Santa Fe *New Mexican*, 4/14/65, p. 1, col. 1. Also, Keleher, William A., *Turmoil in New Mexico*, Book Four, Chap. One, "First the Apaches," p. 294.

arrive in July. The committee would explore the Indian problem and focus on the Bosque Redondo.

At Santa Fe on February 15, 1865, Carleton ordered General Crocker to send the Navajo chiefs to him. The chiefs were Herrera Grande, Guando Blanco, Delegadito Chequito, Burbon, El Chino, El Luhador, El Largo, and Ganado Mucho.[211] When they arrived, Carleton spoke with them through an interpreter. Governor Connelly and former Congressional Delegate Jose Manuel Gallegos were present. The chiefs were instructed to go to the old country and tell Manuelito and the Navajos remaining there to come into the Bosque Redondo. This was their last warning. If they would come now, they could keep their stock. If not, five weeks after this notice, the people, backed by the Utes, would fight them and they would be destroyed. The chiefs were to return at once after they contacted their tribesmen.

---

[211] Report of Capt. Francis McCabe, 1st NM Vol. Cavalry submitted to Carleton 1/7/65. OR Series I, Vol. XLVIII, pp. 522-529. Also, Keleher, Wm. A., *Turmoil in New* Mexico, Book Four, The Long Walk, p. 381.

Chief Herrera Grande and his lieutenants traveled nearly 400 miles to reach Manuelito. He answered that his god and his mother lived in the west, and he would not leave them. It was his tradition never to cross the three rivers, the Rio Grande, Rio San Juan, and Rio Colorado. He could not leave the Chusca Mountains. He would suffer all the consequences of war or famine. His life was all he had to lose. He had never robbed or wronged the Americans or Mexicans, but had lived on his own resources. If he were killed, innocent blood would be shed.[212]

In late March Chief Herrera Grande returned to Santa Fe to report the news of Manuelito's decision concerning surrender. Carleton did not like the answer. He sent a message to Major Julius Shaw, Commander at Fort Wingate. It was March 23. "Try hard to get Manuelito. It will be a mercy to others whom he controls to capture or

---

[212] Ibid., Book Four, The Long Walk, Chap. Five, "At the Bosque Redondo," p. 382.

kill him at once. I prefer he be captured." He added that, if he attempts again to escape that he should be shot down.[213]

When the legislature adjourned, attention returned to the Bosque reservation. Trouble between Apaches and Navajos broke out over the Apache claims to their produce. The fields of the Apaches were shared with the Navajo against the Apaches' wishes. Carleton's treatment of the Apache agent, Lorenzo Labadi, enraged the Apaches. Carleton's claims of Labadi's stock grazing on government property were baseless. The Apaches who were strong enough began to escape the Bosque.[214] They returned to their own country to scratch for their existence, hunting, and fishing in the Sacramento Mountains.

On January 26, 1865, the letter of a reader of *The Santa Fe New Mexican* written from Peralta said that the winter was the coldest of his experience.[215] He had heard that Carleton's Indians at the Bosque did not appreciate the

---
[213] Ibid.
[214] Ibid., Also, p. 385 and Chap. Seven, "Dr. Michael Steck," p. 427.
[215] Santa Fe *New Mexican*, 1/26/65, p. 2, col. 2.

change of weather, noting that the freezing temperatures kept the Indians from raiding his herds. However, he reported that on the 13th of January 100 head of cattle were stolen from a herd belonging to people of Los Padres and Casa Colorado.

Sleet and snow were especially troublesome and uncommon for the area. Due to the scarcity of hay at Fort Sumner, it was necessary to cut the ration to twelve pounds daily for each public animal. However, the issue of breadstuffs to the Indians was increased to one pound daily on February 5.

Among the Navajos, over a thousand had died, mostly of syphilis, diphtheria, smallpox, pneumonia, and malnutrition. To these maladies, malaria was added in the new year, caused by standing water and mosquitos.

On February 18, Assistant Quartermaster Will Rynerson received a draft for $10,000.[216] Rynerson

---

[216] Records of Fort Sumner, Endorsements, signed by Major Wm. McCleave on April 23, 1865. See also pp. 12-13, 22, and 32 of endorsements.

complained the funds were insufficient to build a decent hospital building and a makeshift one was erected. Rynerson could not find laborers suitable to carry out the more complex work. The amount was inadequate to hire laborers and order supplies.[217] Weeks later, Rynerson was ordered to select a site where a slaughterhouse and corrals could be built for the cattle to be killed and issued to the Indians.

In Washington, Congressman Perea of New Mexico had an appointment with President Lincoln. It concerned the widespread criticism of General Carleton and the President's dismissal of Judge Knapp of the 3rd District Court. Indian Superintendent Steck continued to beg for help for the Navajos. Too much money was required for their care and too little went to the troops.

Perea had been Congressman since 1861 and was elected as a Republican. He saw Dr. Steck as an adversary

---

[217] Ibid., Book Four, The Long Walk, Chap. Seven, "Dr. Michael Steck", p. 427.

of the President's program to strengthen the mining operations. He advised the President to replace Secretary Arny with Charles Clever, Steck with Felipe Delgado, and John Greiner of the Federal Depository with James Collins, all Democrat replacements. These changes would pacify General Carleton, a Democrat who was heavily under fire from the New Mexico legislature.

The President made only one change, Michael Steck, the most respected and noticeable of the group. Steck had visited Congressional offices in the spring for a Navajo relief sum to be applied on their behalf. President Lincoln agreed to replace Michael Steck. Former Judge John Watts, and Lincoln's colleague in Illinois in their early legal practice, were friends. By 1865, Watts had been a New Mexico Judge and Congressman who supported Delgado as well.

Although the New Mexican constituency was Democrat, and Republicans were barely accepted as a genuine party, the people did not appear to feel threatened by Lincoln.

As the spring wore on, it became clear that there was widespread devastation suffered from crop losses due to weather, corn worms, grasshoppers, and locusts. The springtime flood waters on the Rio Grande had washed out the flood plain serving wheat and corn fields in Bernalillo County. People fled to the hills. A hundred-mile distance down the Rio Grande and westward from Albuquerque to Fort Wingate, grasshoppers and corn worms devoured every leaf, branch, and twig. South of Albuquerque, several communities were submerged.

Where the Rio Puerco and Rio Grande met, flood conditions drove people from their homes at Las Mesa and Sabinal. At Las Cruces and Mesilla, the Rio Grande changed its course and flowed on the west of Mesilla. The previous year, the loss was only to the corn crop, but this year there was a total crop failure. There were no fruits, no pumpkins, no wheat or grain, and no beans, squash, or tomatoes.[218]

At Mesilla, so many Confederate townsmen had abandoned the town for the south that there were few people left to attend to the community's ditches. A major rebuilding of homes and businesses would have to be undertaken. Other communities were faced with the same crisis. The Pueblo people would be called on for aid in supplying emergency provisions.[219] They were respected for their thriftiness and their carefully conserved grain storages as well as their peaceful and independent habits. They were prepared for the emergency.

Unannounced to the public, the New Mexico District could not provide enough food to sustain the soldiers in New Mexico and Arizona. Volunteer enlistments began to expire in late 1864 and offensive operations ended.

---

[218] Ibid., p. 383. Also, Santa Fe *Gazette*, 6/17/65.
[219] Ibid.

The California men sought to return home, but discovered they were forced to remain in Arizona. One bitter soldier wrote the *Alta* newspaper in San Francisco. He reported that two thousand men were suddenly thrown on their own resources with only eighty dollars for rations and transportation back to California. The Quartermaster would not sell to citizens. There were coils of red tape everywhere. They were forced to re-enlist.[220]

On March 16, as the legislature adjourned, California Volunteers were notified they would be released from service. Their promise to be paid to return home was not fulfilled. The weather further complicated their return without money or supplies. Ten men signed the testimony of the notice written at Las Cruces for New Mexico's newspapers on January 13.[221] They had heard from other Column veterans and friends in California that efforts were

---

[220] Masich, Andrew, *The Civil War in Arizona*, Chap. 8, "Arizona Dispatches," p. 306.
[221] Santa Fe *New Mexican*, 1/27/65, p. 2. Also, Masich, Andrew, *The Civil War in Arizona,* "A Soldier's Letter from Arizona Territory," dated 8/29/64, p. 305.

being made to have the California legislature provide rations and transportation.

In Arizona, near Fort Whipple, a tragedy occurred. George Vicroy, a member of the investor's group who traveled with the new territory's officials, had acted on the government's offer to support a full-scale development of new mines. In early 1865, when the Navajo saw signs of a reduction of troops, they realized they could shut down the model mine. It was built only a few miles from Fort Whipple. They killed the main employees and burned all the buildings. The Navajo braves met no resistance. The company's costly equipment was destroyed. Carleton had written his promises to Vicroy for the troops' protection. A suit against the government was begun to cover the losses.

Steve Elkins was still engaged in opening his law office in Santa Fe. He had a visitor one afternoon who offered her husband's services in making his move.

Mary Aguirre also came to ask him a question about General Carleton. How could they make the Army pay for the loss of their mules? According to Colonel Frank Chaves, Epifanio's mules were lost crossing the Rio Grande in taking the Arizona officials to Camp Whipple.[222] They had tried many times to recoup their loss but appeals to the General were in vain. They had borne the cost of the military escort that accompanied them from Fort Leavenworth when they left Missouri. The soldiers were fed from the wagon train's provisions. At least they should be compensated for the lost mules!

Steve advised Mary to have Epifanio write to General Mason, now in charge of the District of Arizona at Tubac.[223] The debt would likely be attributed to his department. The debt was on the Governor Goodwin party and belonged to Arizona. Steve likely considered the

---
[222] Moynihan, Ruth B., Susan Armitage, and Christine Fischer Dichamp, *So Much to Be Done*, Part III, Chap. 19, "It Was All A Wonder to Me," Mary Bernard Aguirre, pp. 145-154.
[223] Masich, Andrew E., *The Civil War in Arizona*, Chap. 10, "Arizona Dispatches, 1865," fns. 21-22, p. 327.

Arizonans had better resources which apparently came from California.

The cost of war in mid-1865 was estimated to be $ 2.76 billion dollars. The country's debt before the war was $64 million. As a result, speculation was high concerning the gold market. In the spring of 1865, *The New Mexican* carried an article from the *Missouri Democrat*. The paper's editor reasoned that the amount of gold thus diverted from the U. S. without touching New York averaged over one and a half million each month.

The enormous sum was considered part of the country's exports and against it would be counted heavy imports of foreign goods, paying gold duties into the Treasury. The gold balance was therefore, still against the U. S. in transactions with Europe.[224] This was occurring despite the arrival of "small sums" by steamer to New York and Boston. The "small sums" shipped from San Francisco

---

[224] Santa Fe *New Mexican*, 4/28/65, "The Price of Gold," p. 1, col. 1.

amounted to nearly four million each month. Recently, at least one other mint was added at Denver. A third may have been in operation in Oregon.

Gold's value declined in the early months of 1865. The experts agreed that gold would not advance until the war ended. However, the flow of gold from Europe to America had resumed.[225] Current testimony seemed to indicate that the immediate cause of the arrival of gold from abroad was a demand for United States bonds by capitalists of England and Germany. Since December 1862, the principal part of the treasure shipped from California abroad had been sent directly to England by English steamers from Aspinwall to Southampton. Previously, it was sent to New York and then to England. It was hoped that at the end of war California gold would be sent directly to New York as it had been formerly.

---

[225] Ibid.

Hugh McCulloch took the Treasury office in March 1865. When Secretary Chase left office, he had considered the country's enormous debt and recommended a radical new tax on income and a system of national banks. The legal tender notes were anathema to him. On April 28, the flow of gold from Europe to America resumed. At home, exports exceeded imports.

At some time in this period, a tax on the cost of war was assessed New Mexico, apparently with the concession of Delegate Perea. The President was desperately in need of additional income. How quickly this was leaked to the public is not known. However, it would come out before the next election of a congressman. Delegate Perea's allowance of it would be fatal to his career.

When President Lincoln was assassinated on April 14 the war had scarcely ended. The first sign the Territory learned of the assassination was May 5 when the newspapers announced it. New Mexico celebrated war's end and mourned the President's loss in one gulp. The account of Lincoln's assassination was taken directly from the *Denver News*.[226] Five days later the military performed a 100-gun salute at Fort Marcy in Santa Fe.

Businesses were closed, and officials met in the Hall of the House of Representatives to acknowledge the solemn occasion. Ceremonies were held at each of New Mexico's forts.

In Santa Fe, a public meeting was called for the following Monday, to be held in front of the Governor's Palace. The Governor and Chief Justice spoke, and the Fort Marcy cannon was fired every half hour. All civil and military officials attended. It was the largest citizen assemblage ever seen in the Territory. Across the territory, draperies were hung in public plazas, officers' quarters, porches of other civil officers, and before homes and businesses. They remained hanging throughout the month.[227]

---

[226] Ibid., 5/5/65, p. 1, cols. 1-2, from the *Denver News*, "Assassination of President Lincoln."
[227] LaFarge, Oliver, *Santa Fe*, "Weekly of the Wild Frontier," pp. 31-

At the Bosque Redondo, the Navajo were oblivious to the mourning of the Americans. The meat ration had been reduced to eight ounces daily for each Indian. Protesting their exile, many of the tribe refused to work in the fields. The rest searched for ways to escape, preferring death in the open to a humiliating defeat and confinement.[228]

34.
[228] Keleher, William A., *Turmoil in New Mexico*, Book Four, Chap. Seven, "Dr. Michael Steck," p. 427 and Chap. Five, "At Bosque Redondo," p. 385. Also, Santa Fe *New Mexican*, 4/28/65, "Contentment at the Bosque," p. 2, col. 1.

Chapter Nine: Politics and Indian Investigations

May 1865 – December 1865

Andrew Johnson took the Presidential Oath of Office three hours after Lincoln's assassination. He soon granted amnesty to Confederates who took the oath of allegiance. He recognized the loyal governments of Arkansas, Louisiana, Tennessee, and Virginia when Congress was in recess.

President Lincoln's nomination of Felipe Delgado as superintendent of the Territory's Indian Affairs was not known to Dr. Steck until April. [229] He was formally notified of his removal on May 10. He was told his replacement was "for the good of the service."[230] The newspapers did not publish the resignation for several months. Other arrangements were being made for the doctor.

When Steck first learned of his replacement he was in Gila Apache country. He returned to Santa Fe and called on a friend who wanted to rent his house. He arranged for the Jose Jaramillo family to take his home for fifteen months.[231]

Steck met with his three agents to receive their accounts. The last was delivered on April 21. He then left at once for Washington to close his own Department's

---

[229] Murphy, Lawrence R., *Frontier Crusader – W.F.M. Arny*, Chap. 7, "Secretary of the New Mexico Territory," p.130.
[230] Keleher, Wm. A., *Turmoil in New Mexico,* Chap. Seven, "Dr. Michael Steck," p. 434.
[231] Dailey, Martha Lacroix, "Michael Steck: A Prototype of Nineteenth Individualism," PHD Dissertation, Univ. of New Mexico, 1989. Chap. VI, p. 268.

accounts. He planned to find out who maneuvered his dismissal.

There was an urgency to settle the protests of many New Mexicans regarding property claims which awarded the government these assets. The landowners were accused of treason, stated as "libel" in the court's reports. Most demanding, were those of Texans whose valuable properties were in the vicinity of El Paso, only forty miles from Mesilla.

When General Carleton arrived in 1862 with his 2,500 troops, there were not enough provisions to feed them. They had no shelter. The only available property to satisfy their basic requirements was the flour mill at El Paso. It belonged to Simeon Hart, a Confederate contractor. The flour mill supplied the Rebel army over a large portion of northern Texas and southern New Mexico.

The mill was abandoned during the Confederate escape. Carleton appropriated it under the Confiscation Act of 1862. The Confederates were forced to relinquish Fort Bliss when they were driven back from Santa Fe without provisions earlier that year. They fled to forts in central Texas.

At the end of war, the issue of property ownership was the primary concern of businessmen who needed incomes and could not use their land to resume stores and sell grain, or beef, etc. The issue was not only one of Texans, but of local people who were in loyal Union communities. People in the 2nd district of New Mexico suffered property losses as well as Texans and Mesillans. The matter had to be addressed by the U. S. Court in Mesilla where Judge Houghton was assigned. Theodore Wheaton was District Attorney there, and U. S. Marshal Abraham Cutler had jurisdiction. As soon as the war ended, business owners like Simeon Hart went to Washington to plead their cases for a pardon. Such action promised the fastest results. A court in northern Virginia registered the pleas as soon as Virginia declared itself a part of the Union and signed its loyalty papers.

New Mexico responded at once by setting up court cases to accommodate the angry property owners. President Johnson arranged to have the hearings which would allow protesters' recourse to repossess their lands. He appointed new officers of the court in the 2nd and 3rd districts. Steve was made District Attorney for the 2nd District, replacing Theodore Wheaton. Wheaton, Cutler, and Judge Houghton were put on trial. The confiscation's legality itself was in question.

In Washington, just before the adjournment of Congress in April, the Pennsylvania Representative, C. F. Buckalew, was called into the Indian Commission room by Senator Doolittle to see former Judge and Congressman Watts. Watts told him that he had secured for Steck "a much better situation as Superintendent with a great mining company in New Mexico." He further urged Buckalew's cooperation in the selection of a new Superintendent.[232]

While in the capital, Steck learned from J. McCarty, a Washington attorney, that John Watts told him of his [Watts] part in the dismissal. Watts reported to McCarty that he and his friends were "going to give Steck a position in the mining company" which would "suit him better." [233]

The eastern public knew the New Mexican Quartermaster's Department was being examined for irregularities. Now the public knew that the reservation Indians were being starved. The problem of inadequate supplies had not been resolved although many months had passed between the New Mexico quartermaster department's articles and the census.

Senator Doolittle was Chairman of the Senate Committee on Indian Affairs. Judge Knapp alerted him the year before to General Carleton's Indian wars and their

---

[232] Ibid., p. 278.
[233] Ibid., p. 269.

negative effect on the area's settlers. It was decided in Washington to take reports from Indian departments nationwide to see what practices were being followed and how to improve conditions.

When the committee of three men arrived in July, a massacre had recently been committed by volunteer troops led by Colonel John Chivington. It happened on a Cheyenne and Arapahoe village at Sand Creek, Colorado. Once the situation at the Bosque was addressed, the one in Colorado had to be studied as well.

General Carleton appeared in Santa Fe for the hearing at the Capital. He announced that martial law was abolished. He seemed to host the speakers who were both former reservation managers and community leaders at Santa Fe. The officers at Fort Sumner who managed supply issues and distributions also spoke. The community leaders were those who had knowledge of, or visited, the reservation. No conclusions were drawn.

Senator Doolittle announced that the Interior Department would send a special agent to the next legislature. He would tour the Bosque Reservation and pronounce whether its operation and facilities were deemed satisfactory to fulfill the Navajos' needs. After several days the committee finished its work and set out for Colorado.

In late July, Steve's advertisement for his attorney office appeared in the Santa Fe *New Mexican*. He gave the names of those who endorsed him. He named Robert Campbell of St. Louis, a noted government contractor and prominent banker, also a popular hotel owner; Joab Bernard, of Westport, Missouri, a large merchandizer, and supplier; his nephew and partner, W. B. Bernard, a judge in Kansas City. A. A. Warfield of Westport was a known figure in the Territory. The prestige of these men was easily recognizable to everyone. Elkins' first cases were conducted with other well-known attorneys in Santa Fe. They were mostly garnishments and attachments. The

Santa Fe New Mexican shortly followed with a few brief remarks liberal in their praise of the new attorney.

On July 28 Judge Houghton was commissioned by President Johnson as 3rd District Judge at Mesilla.

In August, the first of a series of letters written by former Judge Knapp appeared in the *Santa Fe New Mexican*. It condemned Judge Watts' use of political power for his own purposes.

At the end of August, it was known widely that Dona Ana County was going in heavily for J. F. Chaves. The Republicans began publishing their party's name as "The Administration Party of New Mexico" when a convention nominated candidates for county offices at Santa Fe. Steve was a speaker for the event. At the end of September, John Greiner replaced James Collins as Receiver of the Land Office and Depository.

The Gazette began to call itself the Union Party in late August. When challenged by Republicans, they charged Frank Chaves with being the pro-peonage candidate. He stood up for the practice of retribution, defended by many New Mexicans based on the slavery of Indians who had committed raids on settlers' homes and stock. Citizens often humored the Indians' Christian defenders, missionaries, usually ineffective in their influence with the tribes. The Republicans added to their name, "The Union Administrative Party". These terms were primarily used in local political races. *The Gazette* hammered *The New Mexican,* calling Chaves the head of the pro-peon party.

Chaves had a penchant for putting his own slant on issues to defend his acts. Chaves prepared for the upcoming Congressional race against Attorney General Charles Clever. He hired Herman Heath, a man known for his tendency to adopt irregular means to gain ends which suited his own purposes. Heath was known to have sought an executive appointment with the Confederacy during the war. He was also reputed to have stolen horses at war's end while an Army Quartermaster assigned in Nebraska.

Heath and Chaves developed a strategy for getting favor with the largest portion of the native Mexicans in Santa Fe. Rio Arriba County held the largest number of voters who spurned acceptance of the Chief Justice. Chaves and Heath would take advantage of the rising tide and join Slough's detractors. The county's normally Democrat voters became friends of Chaves, hoping Slough would be withdrawn.

By September the Administration Party announced their majority by 1,054 votes in the local election. The outcome was expected. Democrat Perea who led his party's ticket was complicit in allowing the Territory's payment of a tax to cover the war debt. No other territory was assessed a war tax. He supported General Carleton's retention as well. His record in office made no important gains for the Territory.

Perhaps calculated to aid Perea's election, "Uncle Dick" Wooten, a faithful Democrat, completed his toll road across Raton Pass by the end of August. Wooten was considered a citizen of Colorado. He lived in Trinidad, on the Colorado side of Raton Mountain. The work was done by the Army and reported to Captain B. C. Cutler at Santa Fe, New Mexico's Assistant Adjutant General, just before the New Mexico election.[234]

The toll road benefited Wootten and his partners. The stage carrying citizens to and from the states followed the Cimarron to Taos route. Traffic would now be heavy across Raton Mountain. The land acquired by Wootten was, in part, received from Lucien Maxwell in early 1865. Wootten's deed, granted by Maxwell and his wife, stated that the Maxwells would "travel without charge" over the toll road.[235]

---

[234] Santa Fe Weekly *Gazette*, 9/16/65, "Road Repairing on Raton Mountain," Fort Union, NM, 8/28/65, by Patrick Kealy, Capt. 1st Infantry, NM Volunteers, Commanding Road Party.
[235] Pearson, Jim Berry, "The Maxwell Land Grant," Chapter Eight, "Developing the Grant's Resources," pp. 162-163.

September was nearly upon them when Chaves showed up to campaign. Although the Union Democrats campaigned enthusiastically for the incumbent, Francisco Perea, it was clear his tenure in Congress was at an end. His record of accomplishments was dismal. Perea had failed to accomplish any of the advances made by George Chilcott, his Colorado counterpart. New Mexico had no land office while Colorado boasted a new one near the New Mexico border. Perea was led by John Watts', involving him in covering for Watts' favors to Lincoln.

These decisions undermined Perea's ability to support the best interests of the Territory, especially regarding the territorial tax. When the results were tallied, Chaves won by a majority of 2,599 votes. The full accounting was made by September 15.[236] The *New Mexican* commented, "Colonel Perea carried two counties out of ten; how humiliating after all the blowing about his

---

[236] Santa Fe *New Mexican*, 9/15/65, "Election Returns," p. 2, col. 1.

popularity and 'overpowering influence.'" Chaves received nearly two-thirds of all the votes cast in the current Congressional election.

Meanwhile, former Secretary Arny began a series of articles he developed while touring the Territory. He wrote of advances in agricultural, pastoral, and mineral experiments, and new mining claims. He also informed citizens of the status of the Pacific Railway.

An article of *The New Mexican* published in late October indicated that the army had fixed the price of grain in the local marketplace at Mesilla. A further investigation revealed that two merchants selling in Mesilla were in league with Carleton to sell supplies from the Bosque Redondo to merchants Higgins and Griggs for the Army's and merchants' profits. The secret pact came out when Assistant Quartermaster Rynerson, and a reservation subordinate of his, pointed to Lieutenant Hofedank as the guilty party. Hofedank committed suicide when unable to shake his colleagues' charges.

In Washington, by October 6, a report came out that the District Court of Virginia was chiefly occupied with confiscation cases, and pardon seekers had rallied in force. Events in New Mexico proved that there were many men of the El Paso area who were included in this group.

By November 11, *The Champion* newspaper of Pueblo, Colorado carried news of the Atchison, Topeka & Santa Fe Railroad. Willis Gaylord of the railroad was appointed its chief engineer. He was scheduled to make a draft of all funds necessary to complete the survey of the road for the 150 miles southwest of Topeka. The survey would continue beyond Council Grove. The two considered routes would be subject to studies on the feasibility of each. The work was expected to take a year to be completed.

General Carleton remained at the helm of the *Santa Fe Gazette* in November. At the *New Mexican*, the editors charged Carleton with assessing contractors for their share toward the support of his newspaper and the Congressional election campaign. Contracts had also been made conditional on their support of him.

The race between J. F. Chaves and his first cousin, Jose Perea, was dominated by the strong dislike for General Carleton's arrogant dismissal of the advice of others. After Carleton's assumption of *The Gazette*'s editorship, there was no question of Perea's ultimate defeat. The Territory's war tax was the final straw. The Republicans crowed that after so much ballyhoo about the overwhelming popularity of Perea, he had sunk into oblivion with scarcely a whimper.

Thomas Tucker was added as co-editor on the *New Mexican*'s staff. Thereafter the pages written in Spanish were increased.

When Governor Connelly addressed the 1865-1866 legislative assembly on December 1. *The New Mexican* declined to print the speech due to its length. Instead, the newspaper listed the new officers of the House and Council. These men were elected in September and were unanimously Republicans. They further published the assembly's resolutions regarding the character and integrity of Judge Benedict and Secretary Arny. Connelly likely used some of former Secretary Arny's news accounts to deliver positive information to the assembly. He congratulated the New Mexico Mining Company for its profits, calling it the most productive gold mine in the country.

The decision to publish the resolutions was a response to charges from *The Gazette*. The Democrat paper was irreverently critical of Judge Benedict who they had for months charged with writing many of *The New Mexican*'s articles and profited thereby. On the other hand, *The New Mexican* gave a generous and tactful account of Benedict's long New Mexico career. It was so typical of

Steve's established respectful nature that no one questioned who wrote it. The remarks honored both the Territory, and the Chief Justice, keeping the man's dignity intact.

The tribute of support was made because the two men were being replaced in the new Johnson administration. When Arny heard of his replacement, he wrote Secretary of State Seward. He reminded him of the fact that his appointment was assigned for "four years and dated February 18, 1863." Unless it was revoked, his term would end February 18, 1867. He also reminded the Secretary of various aspects of his service to his country as well as to the Territory. No more was said, and he temporarily remained in office.

The Governor received a request for volunteer troops submitted to the Secretary of War the year before. The volunteers remained to protect citizens and travelers from Indian raids. They were later told additional forces could be provided from the States. However, there was no haste to do so.

The Governor's call for an enabling act would begin the process of preparing a written constitution for a citizens' election. It was a step in the direction of applying for statehood. At least three other territories were undergoing the same process. The act received the assembly's full support. Convention delegates would meet on the fifth Monday of April in Santa Fe to write the Constitution. The fourth Monday of June the Constitution would be submitted to a popular vote. They stipulated that the restrictive Free Negro Act must be repealed as well as an earlier act that legalized the system of involuntary servitude. Colorado and Nebraska were among those attempting to enact statehood measures. Their enthusiasm was contagious.[237]

---

[237] Records of the New Mexico Legislatures, State Dept. Territorial Papers, NM, 1851-1872, Roll 3, 1/6/65-3/15/71.

The Governor introduced Julius Graves, the Interior Department's Special Agent, on January 1. Graves reported his visit to the Bosque Redondo in the week before his appearance at the legislature.

Graves represented the Indian Department as well as the Department of the Interior.[238] He had spent a month or more investigating the Bosque Redondo for his Department.

Graves presented questionnaires for the lawmakers. Their primary concern centered on the selection of the Bosque as the Navajo's permanent home. The agent gave Governor Connelly and the assembly blank ballots. He asked them two questions about the Navajo: Should they be held as prisoners at the Bosque? If not, what should be done with them? Graves recommended the Bosque as a permanent home for the Navajo. Most of the legislators refused to answer Graves who supported Carleton's

---

[238] Keleher, William A., *Turmoil in New Mexico: 1846 – 1868*, Chap. Four, The Long Walk, "Post War Indian Policy," pp. 364-367.

policies without exception or qualification. Graves believed, according to his own figures, that the tribe was reduced by half since 1853 when there were 13,500 Navajos. He attributed the decrease to incessant warfare.

Volunteer expeditions, or whites' campaigns against the Navajos to retrieve their cattle, resulted in the capture of slaves. The Indians were then sold, which kept up a state of hostility against the whites. Graves suggested Congress should put a stop to the practice of retaliatory campaigns. He declared that slavery was the universally recognized mode of securing labor in the Territory. He reported 400 slaves in Santa Fe alone.

Agent Graves declared that two kinds of slavery existed in New Mexico, practical enslavement of captive Indians and service for debt. The depth of New Mexico's entrenched prejudice, and continued hypocrisy, could be illustrated in the case of the Superintendent of Indian Affairs, Felipe Delgado, who held six slaves. Graves announced that the policy of General Carleton had an excellent effect.

Graves later submitted his pro-Carleton report to the Secretary of the Interior. The assembly continued its business after Agent Graves' departure.[239] They then passed a memorial condemning Carleton and asking for his removal. This time there was no interference or hesitation. The regular acts of pardon, incorporations, charters, commissions, adoptions, and such, continued to the end of the session. Ultimately, General Carleton would be removed when the legislature petitioned the Secretary of War and President for his resignation.

After Graves' remarks about the favored form of slavery in Santa Fe, pinpointing Felipe Delgado, Lincoln's Indian Superintendent appointee, as an example of local hypocrisy, the man soon fell into disgrace.

---

[239] Keleher, Wm. A. *Turmoil in New Mexico*, The Long Walk, Chap. Four, "Post War Policy," pp. 364-368.

In Washington, Congress heard a report from the Committee on Reconstruction in January. Argument commenced with a speech from the Treasury Secretary to activate a contraction of the currency. There would be an early resumption of specie payments. It was stated that the business interests of the country would admit, and pledge themselves to cooperative action to that end, as soon as possible. The resolution passed by a vote of one-hundred-eleven to six.

The confiscation cases involving New Mexico and Texas were of the greatest interest to New Mexicans. The *New Mexican* began reporting on them on December 8. Steve had been named District Attorney for the 2nd District at Bernalillo, replacing Theodore Wheaton.[240]

The distinction of the confiscated properties in Texas from those in New Mexico did not arise until a Texas resident noted it in a news article from Franklin,

---

[240] Santa Fe *New Mexican* 12/8/1865, "The Maid and Her Milkpail", p. 2, col. 1.

Texas. Judge Houghton had allowed the Fort Bliss property to be claimed by Albert French of New Mexico. It occurred in an auction conducted by Marshal Abraham Cutler in mid-December. French was a member of Carleton's California Column and resided in the Mesilla vicinity.

The Santa Fe New Mexican reported that Fort Bliss, Franklin, and El Paso were outside New Mexico's authority. Judge Houghton was handling the case. John Watts appeared for the U. S., Steve and Charles Clever, Attorney General, for the defense of accused and disloyal citizens. Judge Houghton ordered Marshal Abraham Cutler to attach the properties. He ruled in favor of the U. S. and the right to claim Confederate properties across the border. Cutler initiated a Texas property auction.

The confiscation cases involved several successful mines in the southern New Mexico district and Texas. Elkins was trained in mining law by one of his mentors, Joab Bernard of Westport, or Kansas City, Missouri. A geologist, Bernard had mined in Michigan's copper fields. His profits enabled his investments in Missouri, and later New Mexico. He was associated with the Aguirres, and the New Mexico Mining Company while primarily a Westport merchandizer.

The New Mexican's editors argued that such cases should be heard before a commissioner appointed by the court, or a jury, rather than denying to the charged even the right of cross examination. They cited several decisions of the New Mexico Supreme Court pertinent to those on the national stage.

The auction was entirely illegal since the New Mexico Supreme Court pronounced that the Territory had no jurisdiction outside its boundaries. Steve, as District Attorney, took charge of the hearings which followed. He decided that Judge Houghton was influenced by District Attorney Wheaton and should not be held responsible since he was a trusted citizen. He was generally well-informed as an attorney, but untrained formally. He was appointed due to the shortage of legal counsel in New Mexico. He had assembled his own law books and attended to his own education in legal cases since the 1840s. He had been misled by Theodore Wheaton.

When the cases were retried in 2nd and 3rd District Court, John Watts represented the U. S. Steve Elkins and Charles Clever, Attorney General, argued for the property owners who had been charged with treason. Watts cited maritime law, not applicable to the type of cases in question. Local citizens rejoiced in the restitution of peoples' properties and the undesirable implication that these people were not loyal to their country. Cases heard in court over confiscation matters would continue for more than two years.

Steve sent the results of the trials to U. S. District Court in northern Virginia where many property owners awaited the decisions of the court there to reclaim their properties.

On February 16, it was announced that Governor Connelly would not be reappointed. Bobby Mitchell would be Governor with George Este, a former Union officer, serving as Territorial Secretary. Mitchell was a former Nebraska General, experienced with Indian warfare. On March 14, 1866, John Slough, former hero of the Battle of Glorieta, was named Chief Justice.

At home in Santa Fe, Sam Jones, Steve's former Rebel sympathizing friend, who represented his Pinos Altos Mining Company, prepared to leave for the east. *The New Mexican's* account reported that Jones would return to Missouri to procure the necessary capital and machinery to successfully develop the valuable mines owned by his company. His partners were mostly successful Mesilla merchandizers.

It was at nearly the same time that Steve received a call from his family to come home. His mother was dying. He began to pack at once, realizing briefly that he would miss the Constitution's writing and the opportunity to vote. He sought out John and Michael before he looked for a senior executive like John Slough. He must forward a request for a leave of absence. Slough could not be found.

The required leave of absence was certainly acceptable in his case. He would need John Greiner to forward it on to Washington for him.

Under the circumstances, the Missouri trip would require at least eight days. Steve had a busy agenda on his arrival in Kansas City and Westport. His mother's burial would be delayed for his arrival. Parting with his mother would transition to adopting a life partner with Sallie. He would soon need to change his schedule accordingly. He certainly realized how much he needed a partner for his legal office. A women's college was said to have been located near the University of Missouri. Sallie was likely trained by Steve to help with his correspondence and keep his files. He would have double support in finding a law partner.

Once home in Westport, he must have quickly become aware of how familiar people avoided him. Joining the Union made him an outsider. Having served as a spy for the enemy, he was a castaway. What could he expect? Fortunately, he found it was published that he was made District Attorney for the court at Bernalillo. His treatment was not as a pariah, although not as a hero either.

While in Missouri Steve learned his four-month stay there was not sanctioned by the courts. An article in the Santa Fe papers shortly followed his own announcement he would be absent for several months. His district attorney appointment was withdrawn for failure to request a leave of absence in a timely manner. His urgent request was not that unusual. Others like it had been granted for such personal reasons.

There were no notable cases on the docket in the 2nd district. Someone had undoubtedly intervened against him. Theo Greiner was appointed in his place. He was training Theo and could remain as his assistant. He would offer his assistance to other attorneys for a reduced fee. His income would not be seriously affected.

Steve was certainly thrilled at his reunion with Sallie, his brothers, and father, Philip. How long the family remained skeptical would be difficult to say. Nevertheless, within a year their presence would be visible in the Santa Fe area.

It was through Sallie that Steve met again with Tom Catron, a former classmate of his at the University of Missouri. They both studied law. Tom was evidently a neighbor of Sallie and her family. When Steve and Sallie prepared for their wedding, Tom appeared. He had been a

Confederate officer in the war. Former Confederates were not granted attorneys' licenses at war's end. He had been helping his father on the farm.

The two young men renewed their friendship and Steve offered Tom some help making a new career in New Mexico. They would not reveal their prior connection. They would travel to New Mexico separately as if unknown to each other. Tom could learn Spanish and begin in Mesilla where a former Confederate officer would be welcome. He would soon apply for a license and shortly run for office.

Someone felt threatened by Steve's legal presence in the Territory. He was aware he had at least one enemy since his firing from the Fort Fillmore position.

The unexpected reunion with a college friend was providential for Steve. Letters indicate Steve, Sallie, and Tom, had a circle of friends in common. As a result, he was a perfect candidate for Steve's law partnership.

An agreement was made between the friends to travel together in the same wagon train to Santa Fe but appear unknown to each other. As soon as possible he would run for office and begin to merge their legal association. A further *New Mexican* article states Steve's and Sallie's arrival was in a private coach. They may have taken the coach from their last stop on the trail, but their belongings arrived in the wagon train.

Steve would read in mid-August that Interior California had sent $3,000,000 in gold to San Francisco in one month's delivery. Gold production was likely at its peak since war's end.

Chapter Ten: Michael Steck

November 1865 – December 1866

It was November 1865 when Michael arrived in Santa Fe from his visit with the New Mexico Mining Company's Philadelphia investors. The introduction had helped solidify his authority over the mines.

His initial conversations with John Greiner gave him confidence all would be done to affect the company's success. Adding Steve's knowledge of legal affairs would cover updating important documents. He arranged to see his freighting partner, P. R. Tully. They could manage business affairs once he established his lodgings at the mine. He left at once for Dolores and the Placer Mines.

Turning south toward the Tuerto mountain divide, about twenty miles beyond the town of Tuerto, there was a gradual descent to the village of Dolores. Over the years perhaps a dozen homes had grown around the mining site. Grama grass on the camp's perimeter was yellow and worn from trampling. There were no trees amidst the buildings although a few birches and cottonwoods outlined the town's boundary. Beyond the few trees to the west was a rich forest of fragrant pines. The ground along the Old Placers location was torn as if by an army digging trenches along the surface for miles.

The road beside Galisteo Creek was made of a red and brown sandstone. Scattered about the creek banks were large masses of petrified wood, branches, and tree trunks. Across the creek lay two springs. The one was composed of syenite, the other, fresh-water limestone. Above these, on a slight elevation, were the remnants of an ancient pueblo, only portions of its walls remaining. The former enclosure was now two-hundred feet square and defined by its stone foundation. [241]

Michael had spent many hours with John considering the various aspects of the mining operation. He began to plan for a business which could yield a profit for many people. He was no longer limited by the constraints of Carleton and the military.

An inventory of the mining equipment was the first concern. He examined the windlass and the main shafts. He checked the buildings to determine their usefulness and looked for the company's tools. He found none.

There was no income. Where would they begin? The market for wood held the greatest potential. He adapted the steam engine on the site to serve as power for a

---

[241] Meline, James F., *Two Thousand Miles on Horseback*, Letter XIX, "Camp in the Valley of the Tuerto Mountains, July 31, 1866. Also, "Camp in the Valley," August 1, 1866," pp. 128-134.

sawmill and produce dimension lumber for the underserved Santa Fe market.[242] The timber would also serve as beams for roof supports in the tunnels, replacing the rotten ones. The shafts and tunnels must be cleaned, the buildings and roads repaired. He set his priorities. Most expensive would be straightening the tunnels. The work was vital. It would take a great deal of time to start up operations and get the money necessary to begin. It would be many months of grinding work to be able to leave the mine site for any time at all. He looked forward to the arrival of his half-brother, Frank, who would help him.

The machinery arrived in late January and a sawmill was erected.[243] Lumber was sawed for building the stamp mill and repairing the dilapidated buildings. It was late May when they began restoring the mines. They cleared away

---

[242] *NMHR*, XLVI: 1 1971, Townley, John, "The New Mexico Mining Company," p.67.
[243] Dailey, Martha LaCroix, *Michael Steck, A Prototype of Nineteenth Century Individualism*, PHD Dissertation, Univ. of New Mexico, 1989, p. 275.

rotten timbers, rock, and dirt from the shaft floors as deep as fifteen to twenty-five feet.

Michael heard from John and neighbors about the Johnson appointees. John was replaced by James Collins, the *Gazette's* editor, and Democrat leader. The new Governor, Bobby Mitchell, was involved in the southern district's mining. When he arrived in New Mexico he joined a tour of the southern mines immediately. It was generally understood that the Governor was more concerned with investing than with governing. He understood from Arny that Governor Mitchell knew the new Chief Justice, John Slough, who was on the same tour. John and Michael regretted being separated, but John had expected to be replaced.

Meanwhile, Michael and John Greiner hired an experienced engineer to help temporarily solve the water problem.

Michael regretted to report to the company president in Washington that Watts owed the company over $4,000. He had left Santa Fe without telling him, or anyone in the company, where he was. Watts often made trips to the Montoya Grant near Fort Bascom. At the time, his son, who lived in the city, also could not report his whereabouts. Watts' expenses had fallen back on Michael. What could the company do to retrieve the money?[244]

He was convinced that a five-stamp mill would not pay expenses. He recommended the building of a railroad to bring ores to the mill, and once again a reservoir to collect and retain water so that it would later channel the water through pipes to the mill. His expenses were always greater than earnings. They were still a growing company.

Many weeks were taken up with assessment and preparations for a trip to Santa Fe to further purchase

---

[244] Steck to President Kidwell in Washington, D.C., 6/15/66. Steck Papers of the NMMC, Univ. of NM, Center for Southwest Research, Coll: MSS134, Box 2, Folder 4.

blacksmith and carpenter tools. His half-brother, Frank had arrived.

Until the mill could be fully restored the miners put their major efforts to the job of blocking out new deposits of free-milling ores.[245] The ten additional stamps he ordered in St. Louis were on the way. Their arrival time depended on the weather. The company store needed to be stocked. He would put up a mill to grind wheat and corn for the local people as well as the company's employees. Some sales could be made to outsiders.

After the trip to Santa Fe, Michael sat down to write Fred Jones, the company treasurer, and the board. He was paid $14,000 of the $20,000 promised him and the money was spent by the time he arrived at the mines.[246] He

---

[245] Ibid. Free-milling ores are gold and silver which can be crushed and amalgamated.
[246] Michael Steck Papers, NMSU, Center for Southwest Research, University of New Mexico, dated June 13, 1866, letter to Fred Jones from Superintendent Steck.

reminded the board that the cost of setting up the equipment was $2,000.[247]

The five-stamp mill was operative in mid-April. A visitor brought him a newspaper in late April. It told how federal officers who left the Territory without filing a timely leave of absence were being withdrawn from their appointments. Michael was concerned how Steve might take the set-back, but he pursued his own course fervently. He would spend the rest of the year in milling rock as fast as it could be delivered.[248] He directed the miners to block out the new deposits, but the mill still needed restoration. He continually wrote the company for money to expand the water sources. The directors considered the prospect too expensive.

---

[247] Dailey, Martha Lacroix, *Michael Steck, A Prototype of Nineteenth Century Individualism*, PHD Dissertation, Univ. of New Mexico, 1989, pp. 274-277.
[248] *NMHR,* XLVI:1 1971, Townley, John, "New Mexico Mining Company," p. 67, Also, Santa Fe *New Mexican,* April 6, 1866, p. 2, and May 25, 1866, p. 2.

Michael had met a young woman during his negotiations. He had been visiting with his uncle and some of his friends in the Muncy Valley. He had a lively conversation with a lovely single lady, and he asked if they might correspond. He continued his letters to Lizzie. He longed to make them more exuberant and colorful. He committed himself to at least one letter each week. Daily life at the mine offered little to enliven his written conversation.

He told Lizzie nothing of his difficulties with the company. Money had not been sent. At the time of contract, he promised to buy up the gold found in the vicinity by other companies. The company agreed to $10,000 in cash and $10,000 in credit for this purpose.[249] He was using his own resources for essentials and asked for cash payments. He told the officers more stock must be sold, twenty-thousand shares insufficient. He needed his

---

[249] Dailey, Martha Lacroix, *Michael Steck: A Prototype of Nineteenth Century Individualism*, PHD Dissertation, p. 272.

up-front money refunded. He suggested the stockholders increase the stock's value by enactment. Two-thousand shares of increased stock should be sold immediately.

Each night he found the correspondence difficult, being engaged in such common and demanding tasks. He wrote and rewrote, collecting the best of his expressions for his final draft.

Lizzie was an accomplished painter. He would emphasize the beauty and healthful aspects of the Territory if he could entice her to join him.[250]

Each morning he awakened to a tedious routine with little sign of the opportunity to explore the shafts. It was several weeks later, when the men had cleared most of the tunnel and shaft debris, an experienced engineer accompanied him to search for an exposed vein. Luck finally blessed them, and quartz began to be visible. They tackled the job of straightening the tunnels and found three

---

[250] Ibid., pp. 278-283.

openings where the vein was exposed. The findings promised ore deposits which would yield paying rates. The ores were gold and quartz.[251]

Collins' new position was announced in June as Receiver at the Depositary.[252] Steve was teaching his son and mentoring him through several cases.[253] Theo could now claim some income and John could return home to other pursuits.

Michael and John were sorry to be separated. They had been companions for a long time. Their goal for the company was to support their retirement. There were no provisions for retirement without substantial investments in large businesses for men in their official positions. They talked of what could be done to improve the company before John's departure. John advised Michael to have the company purchase the cabin he had occupied for a time. It

---

[251] Ibid., p. 277.
[252] Santa Fe *New Mexican*, 6/8/66, p. 2, col. 2.
[253] Santa Fe *New Mexican*, 6/10/66, case advertisements.

could be used to advantage in various circumstances. Michael agreed.

Michael ran the stamp mill on one battery, but soon found that he didn't have enough water to run more than five consecutive days. The reservoir needed to be drained and enlarged to twenty by sixty feet. He supervised the digging of a drain 150 feet long running into the reservoir. The work increased the volume of water enabling three batteries to operate.

Income still did not cover expenses. The mill itself required wood, engineers, and laborers. He wrote the company officers. He made more recommendations to cover the time the miners took in walking to the operations. They needed several homes at the site to make the work more accessible. Small sheds needed to be built to cover each shaft and protect the men from bad weather. A railroad would be vital to bring ores to the mill. Another reservoir was needed to collect and hold water. It could later channel water through pipes to the mill while it was running.

Although the mining site at Dolores was isolated, Michael followed the Ute reservation's problem and learned more of the Bosque Redondo at the same time. In mid-summer the previous year, while the Doolittle Committee met, General Carleton was desperate to feed the Indians at the Bosque and corn worms infested their harvest. He learned that Carleton wrote to Washington that the failure of the corn crop at the Bosque Redondo was a visitation of god. The failure of the crops across the entire Territory forced him to cut down their rations . . ."[254]

Steck knew of these developments only in a second-hand manner. He had been negotiating his position as New Mexico Mining Company superintendent. The Navajo prisoners remained starving, heartbroken, and suffering

---

[254] Keleher, William A., *Turmoil in New Mexico: 1846-1868,* Chap. Five, "The Long Walk," p. 384.

diseases without a hospital. Great numbers had left the reservation in the late summer and fall of 1865.

Crop yields were nearly non-existent at war's end. People in Dona Ana County reported that scant food was available to supply the poorer members of the surrounding communities through the winter.

Although the Military Department of New Mexico had been abolished on July 27, 1865, many former soldiers remained through the year, usually mining. Unofficially, General Carleton remained in Santa Fe and at Fort Union, still wielding authority and managing the mining operations at Pinos Altos. It was clear that mining ventures would be the preferred businesses in 1866. At least two mines had filed charters in 1865. Since 1840 the Placer mines at Dolores produced an excellent grade of gold.

At first, in 1853, Greiner established the company as a partnership with several other men. The group had to make allies of most of the Territory's officers and legislators. After incorporation in 1858, five thousand $100-par shares were distributed among members of the legislature.[255]

Former Governor Abraham Rencher, Governor Henry Connelly, and Miguel A. Otero, freighting company owner formerly elected to Congress, were several of the prominent partners. The bill to incorporate was established in 1858 by the Territorial legislature. Congress confirmed the incorporation on March 1, 1861. Its land area was established as 69,458.33 acres.[256] Michael and John soon consulted Steve concerning the company's right to keep others from surface mining, a practice of many years.

Steve had returned by July. The three men, John, Michael, and Steve sorted through the company's history. There was no indication they had a right to operate on the surface. All documentation evidenced only the company's sub-surface rights. They decided to proceed until

---

[255] *New Mexico Historical Review*, LVI:1 1971, John Townley, "The New Mexico Mining Company," p. 63.
[256] Ibid., p. 64.

challenged, mining on the surface only when necessary. Their stockpiles would need security for protection.

The territory's model mining company, in which so many powerful local interests were concerned, must perform at an unprecedented level, within an extremely limited budget. Michael's reputation and management skills were at stake as never before with his duties as Indian Superintendent.

Before the war, the Dolores mines led New Mexico's economy and provided a source of income for perhaps thirty or more people. Under John's leadership, the company invested $20,000 in milling equipment. At the end of the war, they owned an additional ten square miles of land. The ore came from both surface and tunneled mines. During the war operations were suspended.

After the war, John Greiner led the company and John Watts served as its attorney. Watts, Greiner, and Steck, with John's associates in Ohio, served as company directors. However, Michael did not trust Watts who at one time owed him a monetary sum that had been long overdue.[257] He was forced to hire a collector to retrieve his money.[258]

At first, in 1853, John Greiner established the company as a partnership with several other men. The group had to make allies of most of the Territory's officers and legislators. Congress confirmed incorporation on March 1, 1861, and the land area was established as 69,458 acres.[259] Michael's contract with the company had clauses which stipulated his salary was $2000 annually with several incentives. Before dividing the net profits to the shareholders, he would receive one-tenth of the returns. The company's money could be used to buy gold, clean it, and sell it for a profit. The mining company would progressively increase his pay. The company's officers did not allow Michael to add Steve to his employees. They

---

[257] Ibid., p. 269
[258] Dailey, Martha Lacroix, "Michael Steck: A Prototype of Nineteenth Century Individualism," PHD Thesis, 1989, Chap. VII, p. 269
[259]

feared the power of John Watts' associates and protected him. Michael took on Steve as his private attorney.

Michael learned some time since Governor Connelly arranged in late December 1863 for General Carleton to be given 100 shares of the company's stock. Although Michael did not approve it, Watts insisted that the General be awarded these shares.[260]

Their stock had to be promoted. It was decided to use a favorable report by Professors E. T. Cox and R. E. Owen provided in December 1864 on the mining potential of the company. It would serve as an advertising tool. It was considered attractive to new shareholders.

The three men, John, Michael, and Steve, sorted through the company's history. There was no indication they had a right to operate on the surface. All documentation evidenced only the company's sub-surface rights. They decided to proceed until challenged, mining on

---

[260] Lester, Paul A., "Michael Steck and New Mexico Indian Affairs, 1852-1865," Dissertation, p. 193, fn. 47 and p. 194, fn. 49 and p. 230.

the surface only when necessary. Their stockpiles would need security for protection.

Michael's contract had clauses which stipulated his salary was $2,000 annually with several incentives. Before dividing the net profits to the shareholders, he would receive one-tenth of the returns. The company's money could be used to buy gold, clean it, and sell it for a profit. Twenty thousand was committed to start-up expenses. He asked for the remaining $6,000 owed him from the original contract agreement, but they did not comply.

Chapter Eleven: The Utes Revolt

July 1866 – October 1867

During the summer, events on the Ute reservation threatened the Territory's Indian Agency and its new superintendent, A. B. Norton. Superintendent Delgado was fired when it became known that he owned peons.

When Steve arrived in July, he had already learned the news of his replacement before leaving Missouri. He visited Michael at the mine soon after he returned home. He reassured Michael that he would manage. He would offer his partnership in upcoming cases until he could find more work.

Steve's activities in Missouri are not a matter of record. He was a mere territorial visitor in Kansas City. Later events would indicate his attendance at his mother's funeral and the arrangements which were made leading to his wedding to Sallie. It was through Sallie that he was reunited with Tom Catron. The families may have been neighbors. Tom was also a graduate of the University of Missouri in the same year as Steve. Letters of the period suggest the two young men had a circle of friends in common. Steve's need for a legal partner was certainly on his mind. He asked Tom what he had done to seek employment as an attorney. Missouri law did not permit a former Confederate Army officer to be admitted to the Bar Association. The rule would likely ban him for at least several years. Steve offered to help him get started in New Mexico, but it would be only between them.

Steve and Tom would conceal their prior relationship as students. They traveled in the same caravan.

When they arrived in New Mexico Tom would establish Mesilla as his new home. As a former Confederate officer, he would be readily accepted in the southern district. Once he learned Spanish, he could take cases to court, become familiar to citizens, and run for office. He would gradually become Steve's partner.

In late July, Steve slowly unpacked his and Sallie's belongings, including wedding gifts. He settled Sallie in their Santa Fe home and introduced her to several families who lived nearby. Michael and his brother were introduced and invited to dinner. Steve was ready to return to work at the mining office, although only part-time.

At Dolores, Michael had the men run the mill continuously, removing the stockpile, while channeling water. If the company resisted further expenses, the only solution would be to start an auxiliary water company. Michael would initially fund the water company. If necessary, Steve could handle a petition for a

Congressional land grant to cover the sixty ditch miles to the Pecos River.

They examined an earlier attempt to gain right-of-way for additional water. They set up their prospects for raising money. By October Michael had enlarged the stopes and reached the water level in the main shaft at 140 feet.[261]

When the gold was produced, cleaned, and refined, it would be sent to San Francisco. Interest in gold, and the San Francisco mint specifically, had not waned. Gold production was likely at its peak since war's end.

Exploration drifts were being driven into newly opened shafts of the lode. They would wait to order new equipment until they blocked out the vein's ore reserves and could estimate potential profits. On July 21, 1866, the Governor was inaugurated.[262] Shortly afterward, the newspaper reported that Governor Mitchell and Colonel A. B. Davis left on the previous Monday for the Pinos Altos

---

[261] Santa Fe *Weekly New Mexican*, 10/6/66, p. 2. Stopes were blocks of ore, marked by stakes, situated above a drift, and ready for extraction.
[262] Ibid., 7/21/66, p. 2, cols. 1-2.

mining district.[263] They would tour the area and introduce themselves to several mining superintendents who welcomed new investors.

On August 25, it was announced that a three-company post would be established at Pinos Altos and Colonel A. B. Davis had gone to select the site.[264] Steve read in mid-August that Interior California had sent $3,000,000 in gold to San Francisco." [265] This was a sign the country's debts were being reduced.

At Cimarron, there was a shortage of both grain and appropriations in the Sangre de Cristo area and Superintendent Norton halted Lucien Maxwell's normal issuance of provisions to the Ute and Apache Indians on the reservation. They were being threatened to move to the Ute reservation to join the one over the border in Colorado.

The news was devastating to the tribe. One Ute brave set out alone for a nearby ranch and asked for food.

---
[263] Ibid., 8/11/66, p. 2, col. 2.
[264] Santa Fe *Daily New Mexican*, 8/18/1866, p. 2, col. 2.
[265] Ibid., 8/18/66, p. 1, col.2.

He was offered a partially butchered cow and quarreled with the rancher resulting in his death. The reservation tribes threatened blood for blood. The dead brave was the son-in-law of Chief Kaniache.[266]

Kaniache argued with the reservation's agent and was told he must leave and could not return. Many of the Chief's people followed him into Colorado near the other Ute reservation at the territorial border. The tribe took corn and provisions from farms and ranches on the route they traveled. Settlements along the route were aroused. The ranchers called on troops to defend them and shots were fired before Maxwell was alerted to the incident. He called on military friends to intervene and withdraw the troops.

Secretary Arny was asked to mediate in a resolution of the crisis.[267] Certain that depredations would continue unless food was provided to the tribes, Arny authorized

---

[266] Ibid., 9/8/66, 10/6/66, and 10/20/66, each on the newspaper's page 2.
[267] Ibid. Also, Murphy, Lawrence R., *Lucien Bonaparte Maxwell*, chap. 6, "The Cimarron Indian Agency," pp. 132-139.

Maxwell to issue beef and flour at once.[268] The Secretary promised Maxwell that he would be paid if he had to go to Washington himself for it. Arny told the Utes that the Mexican accused of killing the Chief's son-in-law would be tried according to American law.

Kaniache agreed to serve as hostage until the trial would be held. It would take place three months later. A judge at Santa Fe awarded four hundred dollars to the dead man's heirs.[269] The money was used to buy the 1,300 Cimarron Indians enough sheep to feed themselves through the winter. Kaniache agreed and was released on October 1, 1866. Peace was finally restored in a rare act by an Indian chief to accept American legal recourse.

It was reported that Maxwell was visibly shaken by the circumstances. He leased the reservation for twenty years and feared the government would not reliably feed the Indians. They depended on game, continually

---

[268] Murphy, Lawrence R., *W.F.M. Arny, Frontier Crusader*, Chap. 8, "Agent at Abiquiu," pp. 136-137. Also, Santa Fe *New Mexican,* Ibid.
[269] Ibid. Also, Santa Fe *New Mexican,* 8/26/66, 10/6/66 and 10/20/66.

diminishing, to supplement their diet. He could not be sure when he would be paid for the tribes' provisions. He and his family might be forever caught in the crossfire.

Meanwhile, the Congressional race between Chaves and Charles Clever, the latter the Democrat's candidate, began. Chaves knew that Secretary Arny was leaving at the end of February. He had requested that Herman Heath, a former Nebraska officer, be appointed to follow Arny. Heath arrived in Santa Fe in August. Chaves was not there to greet him. The campaign would not begin until late September. Chaves' boast that he would win the contest by over 4,000 votes would not be forgotten.

That summer, Lucien offered the government his forty by sixty-mile tract of land for only $250,000. He conveyed the message to Indian Superintendent A. B. Norton. Maxwell's farm was known to be the largest in the Territory. He cultivated 5,000 acres and had at one time employed 500 hands. It was thought his farm property covered ten square miles. His animals included a thousand horses, ten thousand cattle, and 40,000 sheep.[270] Agent Norton advised Washington of the offer in his 1866 report to the Interior Department.[271] His flour mill was worth over $50,000, a sawmill, storehouse, barns, corrals, and dwellings collectively added a substantial amount to the value of the raw land. However, Washington was not interested.[272]

The government could not likely determine the value, lacking a survey on the land. The boundaries would raise controversy and set precedent for the settlement of other grant claims.

At the same time, in Colorado, the Sangre de Cristo, also a former Beaubien holding, was for sale. In 1860, all Mexican grant owners were invited to a Court of Land

---

[270] Meline, James F., *Two Thousand Miles on Horseback*, "Letter XXIII, Santa Fe, New Mexico, August 4, 1866.
[271] Ibid., Chap. 6, "The Cimarron Indian Agency," p. 136. Also, Santa Fe *Weekly Gazette*, 12/1/1866.
[272] *New Mexico Historical Review*, 55:1, 1980, L. R. Murphy, "Master of the Cimarron," p. 20. Also, Murphy, L. R., *Philmont: A History of New Mexico's Cimarron Country,* "Crisis at Maxwell's," Chap. VI, p. 82.

Claims in Washington to state and give evidence of claims. The Beaubien-Miranda had sent a claims agent to represent it.

By September 1866, Maxwell, as a federal contractor, supplied over a hundred tons each of beef, wheat, and a ton of salt, to the Cimarron and Bosque Redondo reservations for a year. He received $33,462.88 for his services.[273] However, the military was slow in paying its contractors. Maxwell had a generous nature, but there was a limit to how far he could extend himself. He could not supply the agency when inadequate funds and little food were available.

In Santa Fe, the race for Congress between Chaves and Charles Clever commanded the public's attention in September and October.

When the results came in from each county Heath posted them in his office. There were ten counties, and the

---

[273] Murphy, Lawrence R., *Lucien Bonaparte Maxwell, Napoleon of the Southwest,* Chap. 6, "The Cimarron Indian Agency," p. 140.

results took a week to arrive. In Santa Fe County the two men were tied. Mitchell took the certificate of election from Heath's desk and signed it. It showed Clever had the lead with only several votes. Chaves entered the Secretary's office and had Heath submit a challenge. There had been a challenge to Rynerson's claim of election in Dona Ana County. A new voting district was named within the week of the election. Sam Jones, the Democrat, claimed the victory.

    Chaves and Herman Heath had set the strategy to win over the Rio Arriba County voters by joining the legislators and attorneys against Slough. It brought Chaves back into the political circle of insiders among his colleagues. The Rio Arriba citizens sensed he had their best interests at heart. The judge had been too harsh. They had counted on rejoicing when Slough returned to Colorado. Chaves and Heath would be forced to recount the ballots in each county before the end of 1866 and the results of the

Presidential election. When the 1867 new year would begin in Congress, Chaves' appeal for a final examination of the polls would result in his favor. The Republican candidate was General Ulysses Grant of the victorious Union.

Meanwhile, on Baldy Mountain and Maxwell's property, a Ute Indian discovered a peculiar earth formation and gave his find to William Moore, Fort Union's sutler. Moore recognized the mineral as copper. He chose several prospectors to follow the Ute to the source of the material. It was near the summit of Raton Mountain. Lucien, William Moore, and William Kroenig, all prosperous local men, made a claim together on the copper site.[274] The prospectors they sent had their own placer claims and were seasoned miners who camped on Willow Creek. During the search they panned the nearby creek and found gold flakes. It was nearly winter, and they needed to

---

[274] Pearson, Jim Berry, *The Maxwell Land Grant*, Chap. One, "Lucien Maxwell, Big Land Owner," p. 16.

wait for spring to dig into the earth. It was difficult to keep the find a secret. Word got out at Fort Union.

The next spring, would-be miners, claimants from Fort Union, arrived on the grant. Further exploration turned up more gold.[275] While a little gold still lay on the ground, Matt Lynch and his prospecting party searched, traveling upstream for several miles, retracing their steps back and forth many times. They carried their shovels and pans. In June, they put away the shovels for picks and blasting powder. They began clearing the surface of a small depression partly filled with decomposed vein matter. Very little sign of gold was there.

They climbed the hill further. On a ridge between Ute Creek and the Ponil River they uncovered three veins of rotten quartz. Each was nearly three feet wide and six feet apart. Gold was visible in each one. Threads could be seen, as thick as knitting needles, some threads much

---

[275] Ibid., p. 21.

smaller. In many places, small pieces of gold-bearing rock were hung by fibers of pure gold.

They rushed to tell Lucien of their find. He began to develop the site at once. He sent to Chicago to purchase a fifteen-stamp mill to process the ore. A sample was sent to the U. S. Branch Mint in Denver.

In late August or early September, Mitchell and Slough came to Cimarron and proposed leasing the whole mining district. When Lucien refused, they tried another ploy. They knew Lucien's daughter, Virginia, was his greatest pride and joy. They suggested another town should be built and called "Virginia City." William Moore had already established Elizabethtown, naming it for his daughter. He had sold lots to businesses as well as individuals. Many soldiers from nearby Fort Union came to enjoy the new conveniences.

Lucien soon realized he had missed a major opportunity on his own grant property. Furthermore, when he looked at the maps with these two Territorial executives, he understood that no one knew the boundaries of his grant, much less himself. He began to claim the entire Moreno Valley as his property. No boundaries had been established. He would declare them. He had been elected Mora County Probate Judge and had Charles Holly, a resident and formerly an official of Colorado, handle the busy office.

Meanwhile, in the southern Pinos Altos area where the authorities sought investments, Will Rynerson owned or co-owned at least nine mines. These mines were no longer a secret. The Amberg was his favored mine and was registered on October 15, 1866. It was organized by civil and military officers in the territory who visited the mine in late July. The investors included Governor Mitchell, Judge Slough, Colonel Enos, and General Carleton.[276] The mine's name, "Amberg", indicated that Santa Fe merchant Jacob Amberg was likely the original financier.

---

[276] *NMHR*, "Carleton's California Column, A Chapter in New Mexico's Mining History," Darlis Miller, LII:1 1978, p. 13.

The new Territorial officials also visited another nearby mine, one of three copper mines and four gold claims of the Bay State Pinos Altos Mining Company. Its officers were petitioning for a charter in the upcoming 1866-67 legislature. Steck understood that Albert French, a former California Column officer, and other owners, discreetly deeded two hundred shares of the company to Carleton for the sum of one dollar.[277] It was October when Carleton was formally transferred from New Mexico, although he periodically returned.

The Gazette reported that Carleton was "the only officer in this district equal to the situation." *The New Mexican* took the opportunity to remark that the "community at large would rejoice at his removal."[278] The newspaper further stated, ". . . instead of placing troops where they were needed for the protection of the settlements, he has stationed them where it would be most

---

[277] Ibid., p. 12.
[278] Santa Fe *New Mexican*, 10/27/66, "Carleton Removed," p. 2, col. 1.

lucrative to speculators and favorites."[279] Its editors added that to imply Carleton was superior to other officers displayed "the most abject nauseating toadyism [and] is a great injustice to others."

Mitchell was soon off on another money-raising project. The Virginia City project was too far from Cimarron and had no special attraction. Lucien Maxwell built the initial business locations, but few people were interested. They debated the alternatives. He and John Watts would be able to get investors in New Mexico mines of their interest with a trip to Washington. They became confident they could get Watts recognized as a Territorial Congressman at the Special Session of Congress. They planned an immediate trip, missing the legislature so that they would not return to the Territory until March. They intended to win the seat for Watts who had been a Congressman in 1861 on Lincoln's appointment. Mitchell

---

[279] Ibid.

gave Arny only a few days' notice of his departure. A week later, they were notified by assemblymen in Santa Fe to come home, there were serious consequences if Mitchell did not appear. The two optimists telegraphed home that they would return in March.

The Democrats of the Assembly argued that Secretary Arny no longer held the position he claimed. Secretary Arny and Steve agreed to challenge Mitchell whose contempt for rules and his own authority must be met with their own challenge. Arny replaced several Democrats Mitchell ordered him to appoint, with Republicans. Before the stand-off began, Tom Catron was made District Attorney of District Three, appointed by Mitchell. His office was not challenged. Steve was named by Arny as Attorney General, replacing Charles Clever.

When the arguments rose to a climax, Democrats asked for Catron's support. He told them he never stated he was a Democrat. The moment brought shocked silence to the assembly. An outcry followed. Steve's appointment by Arny again raised questions of the Secretary's continued authority. Arny stanched his critics once more, telling them he was making a trip to Washington when the session ended. The entire assembly was aware Arny's trips to the Capitol always ended favorably for him. The news silenced the grumblers.

At the same time, a vital judicial matter was being settled by Judge Slough, Judge Houghton, and Judge Sidney Hubbell. The Territorial Supreme Court, in its February 1867 third district session, considered the plea of Thomas Heredia of Dona Ana County. He was forced to make a contract to pay a debt. He had escaped from his master and been held against his will. The case came before the court in Dona Ana County regarding his appeal for habeas corpus relief. In Santa Fe, the judges ruled unanimously that New Mexico's peonage law was unconstitutional. Judge Slough wrote the opinion on

February 2. He stated that servitude bore a strong resemblance to Southern slave codes. Heredia was set free. He had been held on a charge of debt. The opinion did not sit well with Congressman Chaves who defended the practice in Washington. Slough challenged the Territory's "power elite" who held Indian peons from raids on settlers' stock.

The Judge appointed two highly respected individuals to enforce the law: Samuel Ellison and F. D. Thompson. Their success was small, and Governor Mitchell declared all of New Mexico at variance with federal statutes.

Chaves, in his new campaign for Congress, welcomed the opportunity to be rid of Secretary Arny. He was an abolitionist who would never have bowed to Chaves' opinions and decisions. Chaves had searched for a secretary who would serve him complacently, not questioning his acts and orders. He found Herman Heath who had been an officer in Nebraska. Mitchell may well have suggested Heath. Heath reputedly was suspected of having sold Army horses from the Army's paddocks' shelter for his own gain.

During the early part of Judge Slough's tenure as Chief Justice he did little to make friends. He was thought a tyrant by most New Mexicans because of his overwhelming concern for courtroom discipline. He often dismissed juries, unpaid, and punished clerks for minor errors. He did not discuss the law's interpretations or accept the opinions of other attorneys. In short, he was a malcontent in the opinion of many. He tried to do at least one thoughtful deed when he applied to the assembly for a memorial to be built in honor of the Civil War soldiers who died in New Mexico's battles.

Slough had at least two conflicts with Steve on important matters before the law. One concerned whether it was legal to vote when an attorney was in a different county than where his official duties forced him to be present. If he had a case elsewhere, Judge Slough thought not. Elkins voted outside the county in question and was correct. Judge Slough never spoke of it or made a modest nod that he was in error.

Steve had an important case involving whether the Llano Estacado was Indian country. Slough insisted there was no official Indian country in New Mexico. He was in error in this case as well. Steve offered to show him the decision which cited the Llano as Indian country, but he would not go to the law books to seek the answer with Steve.

Slough's inclination to punish court officers for infractions became visible when he presided over a case in San Miguel County. The Baca family was extremely influential in that county, and they were Republicans. Their young son was assigned to serve as a court clerk there on one of Slough's appearances. Although the youth was familiar with the rules, he allowed two jurors to be excused for a brief period where they were able to speak to each other. When Slough learned of the offense, he sentenced young Baca to a short jail term. Las Vegas citizens were incensed. The young man was seeking entry to an eastern college of some distinction. His reputation was compromised.

In December, after the Civil War Memorial ceremony, Slough approached Mitchell at the public gathering. The two men were speakers. After the event, he attempted to speak with Mitchell who was walking with friends. Mitchell rebuffed him. Slough was so irate that he went to the street and shouted alone in the plaza that he was no friend of Mitchell. He said that Mitchell had asked him to come to New Mexico, but he wished he had never done so. Slough also attempted to mail a letter of resignation, but at the last minute withdrew the letter at the post office.

Slough unquestionably knew that a strong flavor of antipathy against him was in the atmosphere. However, he seemed unable to cast the spell away. When the legislature gathered on December 1, he was in his office working on papers. No one came to bring him to the assembly for an address, the traditional welcome. Somewhat later, he sought to find Secretary Arny, thinking the man had incited the rebuff. He came up behind Arny, in plain sight of all, and grabbed his shoulder forcefully to have Arny look at him directly. Arny announced that he would not be goaded into a fight. He placed his hands in his pockets. Later, Arny complained of being accosted on the street by Slough. He went to the Justice of the Peace Court to register his charge.

At court two days later, Slough insulted the Judge and left the court in a temper. A later formal retraction did not improve his standing. Secretary Heath reported the events in a complaint letter to the Assistant Attorney General of the United States,

Secretary Heath continued his attack through action in the legislature's Council. He wrote a series of eleven resolutions against Slough. He presented them to the most respected member of the Council and asked him to introduce them to the assembly. Don Jesus Maria Pacheco studied them but did not want the responsibility. He turned them over to Will Rynerson, the newly certified Councilman. The certificate had not gone through the proper channels.

In Dona Ana County, Will Rynerson had supported Chaves' campaign, turning away from Carleton's mentorship. At the same time, in the summer, he brought a crushing mill from California to the mines. Other miners could rent from him to use it. A popular move, he drew nearly all Democrats out of the convention to nominate a Republican candidate, Chaves. Now he was awaiting a reward from the Republicans and Secretary Heath needed a favor. Someone must read the list of Slough's improprieties in the Council's Judiciary Committee report to the assembly. The document denounced the Chief Justice for a list of his acts of professional misconduct.

The first Councilman Heath approached read the petition and refused, suggesting he speak to someone who was not already a Senator. Heath arranged for Rynerson to be certified the senator from Dona Ana. Although contested by Sam Jones, the other candidate, Heath overruled. Heath's act was irregular, but not protested by the assembly. Heath duly signed a certificate verifying the majority votes for Rynerson were genuine.

Heath had no authority to carry out these acts. The Senate's authority to immediately make Rynerson a member of the Judiciary Committee, then to be chosen to read the incendiary document, were also illegal acts. Nevertheless, no-one objected.

On the night of Saturday December 15, Judge Slough looked for Rynerson at the Fonda Bar. He saw him at the billiard table. He sat down some ten feet away, next to Sam Tappan. Rynerson laid his long arms against the pool table's frame to spot his shot. The Judge made several derogatory remarks about the big man. Rynerson, and the men nearest him, did not hear the insults for the roar around them. When the Judge left soon afterward, the remarks were conveyed to the manager of the bar. After Slough left, manager Tom MacDonald passed the remarks to Rynerson, who left, seeking Slough but not finding him.

Slough had some sense of his vulnerability. He sought someone who could give him a pistol. John Watts' son passed him at the Plaza. An Army officer and official courier, he carried arms. Slough stopped him and asked for a pistol. He apologized. He had only a small derringer. Slough thanked him and put the object in his pocket.

The next day Rynerson went to the Exchange Hotel for Sunday dinner. He was dressed in his usual black suit, with it a cloak draped like a cape over his shoulder. A bell was sounded for the meal. When Slough appeared from the doorway of another representative's room, Rynerson confronted the Judge. He said that he heard the Judge was looking for him and had called him a "son-of-a-bitch and a thief." A challenge was made. Several exchanges occurred.

"Take it back or I'll shoot you," Rynerson told him.

"Shoot and be damned!" Slough stormed back.

The shot rang out as Slough reached for the derringer from his vest pocket. It dropped as he was hit in the hip and fell to the floor. He was taken to be examined by doctors who were called. The next morning, December 17, Judge Slough was dead.

A great number of Democrats protested in the street for several nights after Slough's death. There must be closure to the affair before the eastern public caught wind of it, the Republicans insisted. They pressured Steve to assume the case as soon as a substitute judge could be found. Judge Hubbell was seriously injured by a fall in

October and had just taken retirement. The absence of an appropriate judge must come from Washington to be decided.

The confrontation and its fatal result, even the public outcry, continued to the courts. The problem delayed hearings on pretrial motions in January. Steve was chosen to defend Rynerson by the Washington Republicans. Former Judge Benedict would assist him. Will Rynerson's guilt was considered in February in Santa Fe County. Steve requested change of venue the same month. He argued there was too much local bitterness in Santa Fe. In March the case appeared in San Miguel County Court. The case arose at the same time General Grant was campaigning for President. The Republicans in Washington wanted the matter closed as quickly as possible.

Local citizens in Santa Fe placed blame on Secretary Heath who illegally certified Rynerson for office. The Democrats wanted to lynch Heath, but cooler heads prevailed. Judge Houghton managed the pre-trial motions and the bail determination. Rynerson was held in the Fort Marcy jail.

When Judge Brocchus was finally appointed and arrived, it was because he had served as a judge in New Mexico two years before. Steve argued to move the case from Santa Fe where the general sentiment was prejudiced against Rynerson. Change of venue was granted to San Miguel County where Judge Slough had offended the ruling political family by briefly jailing their son. The star student had accidentally allowed two jurors a deliberation break simultaneously. Rynerson's charge was murder. The San Miguel jury which Slough had offended the previous year acquitted Rynerson of murder in the fourth degree on March 22, 1868.

News of another gold strike at Lucien Maxwell's place in Mora County soon became the latest topic of extreme interest. Many civilian workers at Fort Union left their jobs to join the gold rush to Maxwell's property. Maxwell invited some of his friends to make claims. The wealthiest men of the area funded many projects. Among them was an attempt to bring needed water to the many placer operations in the Baldy Mountain area where the mines were located.

There were new developments in nearby Colorado. Ex-Governor Gilpin was trying to sell the adjoining Sangre de Cristo grant. He had an important agent in Europe, Charles Lambard, a director of the Union Pacific Railroad. The price was $1,500,000. The grant was only half of the Sangre de Cristo. William Blackmore perceived that the Sangre de Cristo must be divided in half to appeal to European investors. The half nearest the expected western transcontinental site on the Colorado line was where the transcontinental was expected to be located continued to be called the Sangre de Cristo. The other half was called the Costilla Estate. It adjoined the Maxwell property.

Watts would soon join the group who followed the money. Steck likely considered the promises of John Watts to be like desert mirages. He had not yet accomplished the acquisition of the Rio Grande bottom land. If it didn't materialize, the loss would deflate the company's resources. Watts would certainly be after his next big chance with the good fortune his friend, Lucien Maxwell had found. Instead, Watts was temporarily named Chief Justice in 1868 to replace John Slough. He had been both a judge of the New Mexico Supreme Court and a Congressman from the Territory. He alone had the experience to manage the position. The U. S. Judiciary would seek another candidate in the next few months of 1868.

Many Union soldiers leaving the service rushed to make claims in the Pinos Altos area. Hundreds of men were camped in the locale in 1866.[280] In the spring sixty

---

287 NMHR, LIII: I 1978, Darlis Miller, "Carleton's California Column: A Chapter in New Mexico's Mining History," p. 12.

California Volunteers planned to muster out of service. It was announced that they had organized to mine in the Territory under the direction of experienced civil and mining engineers.[281] Before leaving the Army, the soldiers would have the advantage in making claims. The government would support them.

There was now a personal income tax to be paid on the daily cost of war.[282] Before the war the national debt was sixty-five million. There was a great deal of argument over the true cost. The damage in economic terms alone, was catastrophic. A national banking system was recently put in place to regulate loans, interest on savings bonds, and trade. California's currency was based on gold and the East's currency based on scrip. California and the rest of the nation would have to compromise between gold, silver, and scrip, or paper notes, as legal tender.

---

[281] Ibid., 4/6/66, p. 2, col. 2.
[282] *Barrons*, 4/9/2011, "The Cost of Civil War," John Steele Barron

On October 29 Michael wrote a check to Steve for $500, a typical amount to retain an attorney as counsel for a mining company. It was recorded in the company's account book, its ledger. Joab Bernard, Steve's mentor and a major investor of the company, appeared at Dolores and asked Steve to replace Carleton as collector for the Pinos Altos miners. He would be expected to change the destination of the gold from San Francisco to the Denver Mint.

The Denver mint was established by an act of Congress in 1862. Clark, Gruber & Company was one of three companies manufacturing gold pieces at the time. They produced the most coins of the three. Jerome Chaffee was president of Clark, Gruber & Company. Congress appropriated $75,000 to meet expenses of a new mint in 1863. A committee was appointed by the Treasury to establish a location for the mint. Clark, Gruber & Co. offered property for the project and the institution was erected in September 1863.

Jerome Chaffee was a renowned and successful mining company owner. He was also president of Denver's largest bank in 1866. In 1867 he was running for Congress in Colorado. Many New Mexicans preferred to bank at the 1st National Bank of Denver than at the Santa Fe Depository. It was a familiar and trusted location for New Mexican citizens.

Michael and P. R. Tully, his freighter, conferred about the mines seeking charters in the legislature. An appeal to the new mines might give them access to other sites than those at Pinos Altos. Gold could be cleaned and treated profitably. The company could certainly use some profits.

At the New Mexico Mining Company in December, a two-year ore reserve was blocked out. Capital was raised to free Michael to purchase new stamps. He was anxious to return to Missouri and Pennsylvania. He did not conceal his loneliness and Lizzie's responses were sympathetic. He intended to propose.

Steck reached Hughesville and Lizzie two days before Christmas. It was a time of great joy for Michael and cause for much celebration.

As miners and fortune hunters poured into the Cimarron area, the reservation Indians became more restless and agitated. In the spring of 1867, a conference of Utes was called for the Colorado Ute reservation near the New Mexico border. Chief Kaniache attended. He signed an agreement for his tribe to settle on the southern Colorado reservation. When the New Mexico tribe learned of it they withdrew his rank as chief and shunned him. He began to follow Lucien Maxwell whenever it was possible. He dressed in American clothes, finding bins for used clothing. He often wore a Union officer's uniform, his favorite.

Lucien tried to calm the reservation Indians, but they had problems with their agents who came and went too often. In August 1867, when William A. Bell of the Union Pacific Railroad's survey crew met Maxwell, he assumed the owner was also their agent. Maxwell was in his shirt sleeves and sitting on the front step of his house. Surrounding him were many of the reservation Indians, squaws, papooses, and warriors. Bell related to others, "They all seemed on the most familiar terms with him – talking and laughing while the children played around."[283]

---

[283] Murphy, Lawrence R., *Lucien Bonaparte Maxwell,* Chap. 6, "The Cimarron Agency," pp. 129-130.

Chapter Twelve: An Election Scandal

January 1867 – March 1868

In mid-March and at home in Santa Fe, Steve and Sallie welcomed their first child. They named her Lizzie. Steve was unable to be with Sallie for the birth's occasion. He was countering the offers of the negligent Governor, Bobby Mitchell.

At nearly the same time in Pennsylvania, Michael Steck and Elizabeth Wood were married on February 13, 1867. Limited time and means dictated the length of their honeymoon. They visited Philadelphia and New York City.

They toured Washington until it was time to leave for the Southwest. They took a train at Independence and hired a wagon. Michael wanted Lizzie to see the West in its most glorious array. He determined to return to New Mexico by way of the prairie in May. Her awe at the prairie's sweeping grandeur, its tall grasses, and colorful wildflowers, convinced him he made the right choice in bringing her there on the way home.[284]

In Santa Fe, Michael's house was prepared for them. He would stay at the Placer Mines, but in warm weather Lizzie would stay at the camp with him. She planned to bring her canvas and oils with her to record her surroundings.

Meanwhile, Governor Mitchell and John Watts had arrived in New Mexico in the second week of March. The legislature had closed at the end of February. The Governor at once began a denunciation of Secretary Arny and Steve

---

[284] Dailey, Martha Lacroix, *Michael Steck: A Prototype of Nineteenth Century Individualism,* PHD Thesis, Univ. of New Mexico, 1989, "The Mining Years," p. 282.

as the instigators of a plot to unseat Mitchell's chosen appointees. There being no forum for a confrontation, the dispute was carried out in a series of letters published in *The New Mexican.*

As the Acting-Governor, Arny began in January to award printing contracts and sign official commissions. His aggressiveness and assumption of authority prompted angry protests from the Democrats. They insisted he was already relieved as territorial secretary eight months before. Arny countered that his tenure would not expire until the new appointee arrived. The Republican majority defended him and voted into law a group of Arny-favored measures.

The Governor did not want to create a sensation over his Congressional visit because he and John Watts received a formal rebuke for their unsolicited appearance in Congress. Instead, they visited Congressman Chaves, attempting to excuse their absence. They had learned Steve was named Attorney General in place of Charles Clever, Mitchell's intended recipient of the office.

Aware of Steve as Chaves' opposition, they asked Chaves the best way to remove Steve as Attorney General. The Congressman suggested they have President Johnson rename him for a district office. When Mitchell's letter to Steve arrived to suggest that he accept an alternative office, he stated it would be Attorney General for the 2nd District of New Mexico.

Steve countered the Governor's error. He pointed out that Mitchell named a nonexistent office, combining a federal and a territorial office as one and the same.

Enraged by public exposure of his error, Mitchell declared he would veto every Republican measure raised in the present assembly's session. Steve responded that he had no cause to thank Mitchell for his offer, that the Congress had cleared him as District Attorney the year before. He would accept the appointment as District Attorney since there was now an opening for the position at that very time.

Shortly after, Secretary Arny's term of office was confirmed by Congress the same month. This disposed of the minority Democrats charges against him of a false claim of extension of office.

Mitchell's ignorance, or carelessness in writing Steve, made him more intractable and aggressive than ever. His ignorance was now clear to all citizens and his pride offended. On his arrival, Mitchell issued certificates of office to the Democrats he initially named, renaming Clever, and still including Tom Catron. It was entirely irregular, and his administration would be continually scrutinized for similar acts throughout his term.

Steve was named District Attorney for the 1st District at Santa Fe. It put him in direct line to be named U. S. Attorney after a normal period of a year or more of successful performance in the office.

The Taos County delegation assembled themselves and wrote a formal protest. They refused to acknowledge the executive power of the Territory. They had not joined the Legislative Council in hearing Governor Arny's address. His new appointees were scrutinized.

The *Gazette*, representing the dissenting Democrats, named William Breeden, Arny's chosen assessor, claiming the officer was not a citizen of the Territory and was chosen by Congressman Chaves.[285]

Secretary Arny's term of office finally ended in February 1867. Frank Chaves was now reinstated as Delegate through the Republican majority Congress. The votes of each county were reexamined, and Chaves' recount gave him a victory. Chaves chose Herman H. Heath, who, as Secretary pro-tem, participated in the recount. He was a former Nebraska officer, and now Arny's successor. His character was questioned by some

---

[285] Poldervaart, Arie, *Black-Robed Justice*, Chap. 8, "The Outlaw Dusters," pp. 78-82.

because of the loss of army horses at war's end.[286] He was expected to be a willing subordinate, serving Chaves without question.

Congressman Chaves' early March address to Congress on the Navajo was still the talk of Santa Fe. He had challenged Congress to honor the nation's several treaties with the Navajo, a bold affront to Congress. It was thought that only a man as imperious as Chaves would call for Congress to free the natives to go home. The *New Mexican* carried the speech in early April.[287]

The Santa Fe *Gazette* took the opportunity to call Chaves "the head of the peonage party" in New Mexico. Another item from *The New Mexican* concerned Steve's reappointment.

The *Daily New Mexican* wrote of Steve, "*S. B. Elkins, Esq., having been appointed and confirmed U. S.*

---

[286] Roberts, Gary L., *Death Comes to the Chief Justice*, Chap. 1, "The Republican Ascendency in New Mexico," p. 31.
[287] Santa Fe *New Mexican,* 3/2/67, p. 1, col. 1. Also, Roberts, Gary L., *Death Comes to the Chief Justice*, Chap. 2, "The Zealot and the Politicos," p. 38.

District Attorney for the First District of New Mexico, has taken the oath of office and is now duly qualified to attend to 'any and all' business connected with his responsible position. Mr. Elkins has won for himself an exalted place in the esteem and affection of the people of New Mexico, by his genial courtesy, perseverance, and energetic fidelity to all trust hitherto reposed in him. A future is before him of brilliant promise."[288]

As for Steve's war service, he always declared himself a non-combatant, but carried the designation of Captain, U. S. Army.

Governor Mitchell was known among his familiar circle as "Bobby." He was a former Civil War general in Nebraska's Indian Territory. A Democrat, the President likely thought his knowledge of Indians would be beneficial to the issues in New Mexico. He would also

---

[288] *Santa Fe New Mexican*, 3/30/67, p. 2, col. 1.

relate well to Judge Slough, a hero of New Mexico's Battle of Glorieta, the Territory's major battle of the Civil War.

Mitchell was undistinguished in appearance, of average height and weight. He wore his dark hair in the style of the times, just below his ears. His beard and moustache were full and his expression normally serious, assessing those he encountered with a penetrating stare.

The Governor's first few months in the Territory had introduced him to many mining ventures as he traveled New Mexico, learning its business practices, and familiarizing himself with its entrepreneurs.

At Santa Fe, only a week after his wedding trip, a letter was waiting for Michael at the Santa Fe Post Office. Fred Jones was on his way to visit the mine and would arrive momentarily. The company expected some reliable sign the mines were productive. Dr. Kidwell wrote the company was sending Jones to Dolores for a report on the company's status. Jones was an attorney, company treasurer, and active company director.

One set of directors, those in Washington, appeared to have reservations about Michael's statement of the company's advances. The directors in Philadelphia were satisfied. The Washington office was receiving the gold produced. Michael was quite put off about Dr. Kidwell's concerns, suggesting that he was not trusted.

At Cimarron, Lucien agreed to be a partner in the new Virginia City project with efforts to gain government buildings for the town. He began collecting rent wherever he could and started a series of business ventures which included Governor Mitchell and Chief Justice Slough."[289] Two leading Colorado capitalists were also added, Charles P. Holly and Henry Hooper. The Fort Union men, investors as well as claimants, resented the officials' interference. Immediately after the Territorial officials' visit, Lucien

---

[289] Ibid., p. 155.

claimed the land grant comprised the entire Moreno Valley, nearly two-million acres.

Meanwhile, when Michael was away in the winter with Lizzie, the New Mexico Mining Company demanded John Watts' payment of $6,000. Watts resigned. His prestige was such that the board feared certain damage to the company in releasing him. They refused his resignation. The increased land holdings of his present work were employed as a negotiation tool. His normal fee would be counted as partial payment of his debt. The title would include land from Fort Craig to fifty miles below Fort McRae. If the property was acquired, it would amount to 50,000 acres of Rio Grande bottom land.

When Jones arrived in Santa Fe on May 15, Michael was waiting for him at the Exchange Hotel. He showed him the Placer Mines article he provided for the newspapers as soon as he arrived. It told of newly ordered stamps and the 800 tons of $75-$100 ore waiting to be processed. The next morning, they toured a portion of the 70,000-acre Ortiz property belonging to the company. Michael explained the property's value. Steve had just sent the title to the property to the company President, Dr. Kidwell in Washington.

Michael took Fred to the stockpile and primary mine shaft. He then pointed out the recently graded track site for the tramway. It would be a mile and a half long. Several engineers had been consulted on its construction. He had just enough time to prepare the site. A test run of his stockpile was expected. Fred wanted to take back a gold sample. Michael had expectations of his own for the company. When Fred returned, he would expect him to relay the need of funding for the tramway and tunnel.

The two men spent several days studying the company books with John Risque, the accountant. Michael was not following regular business procedure for his books, and they did not agree with the company's accounting.[290]

They would need to develop a method which could be practiced and understood by both locations. Fred suggested a second set of books. Jones was due to leave after one week. He was quite satisfied that everything was in order. He carried with him a gold nugget which he showed to Amos Steck when he arrived in Denver.[291]

Amos Steck was a former mayor of Denver and Michael's cousin. Fred was delayed in Denver, his choice of route, by an Indian war on the road east. Bad weather held him up even more, and he did not arrive in Washington until June 3rd. He relayed to Steck that he should advance his plans and expect to keep the mill running continuously. They believed that the fifteen-stamp mill could produce $2,000 in gold by November 1.[292]

In June Michael and Steve met to discuss a means to draw water from the Pecos River. Such a plan was

---

[290] Univ. of NM, Center for Southwest Research, Steck Papers, Coll. MSS 134, Box 2, Folder 4, Letter of Steck to Jones, 6/22/67
[291] Ibid., Jones to Steck, letters, Coll. MSS 134, Box 2, Folder, 4, 6/3/67.
[292] Ibid.

addressed by an engineering firm in 1865 before Michael became superintendent. They referred to the papers in the file. The plan would involve paying the landowners on the route for the right to cross their property. They believed at least one route was affordable. They would file for a company charter in the upcoming legislature to prepare for the spring season.

Michael considered the Washington directors' demands, the reluctance to answer his own needs definitively, and his continued uncertainty that he would be paid what the company owed him. He wrote Jones on June 22 that he planned to leave the company since a satisfactory settlement and other matters had not been addressed.[293]

Meanwhile, the public heard much more of Pinos Altos prospects and news of the mine find on the Beaubien-Miranda land grant. *The Gazette* began to call the Beaubien-Miranda the Maxwell Grant. The new officials,

---

[293] Michael Steck Papers, Univ. of New Mexico, Center for Southwest Research, Letter of Steck to Jones, 6/22/67, MSS 134, Box 2, Folder 4.

Governor Mitchell and John Slough, were still interested in the property and visited him in early November. Elizabethtown was named for William Moore's daughter. Moore was Fort Union's sutler. Fort Union soldiers often bought from stores there, used the barber shop, and other facilities.

The second Mora County town was protected against an uprising or an Indian raid. The officials had told Lucien that the entire gold region would be secure by undertaking the project. Mitchell would send out volunteer troops if an uprising broke out.

Lucien began to realize that the officials, and everyone else, did not know the grant's boundaries. He was free to state them himself. He would claim the whole Moreno Valley. The size would be two million acres, he speculated. He would apply for a post office and any other government office to support the town so that it would surpass Elizabethtown.

At Cimarron, the 1866 copper find on Baldy Mountain turned up gold at a deeper level. Mining began near the town, with placer mines in the Territory's northeastern quadrant in mid-year 1867. The most pressing need of these mines was the development of an adequate water supply. The Michigan Company from Fort Union, under the leadership of Pete Kinsinger, Tom Lowthian, and Colonel Edward J. Bergmann, a former Union commander, may have been the first to employ the use of hydraulics.[294] Water was sprayed on the mountain from powerful hoses. The Michigan Company group led the valley miners to form a lawful, orderly location and working of their claims. They first met on May 13, 1867.[295]

It was late June 1867 when Michael heard that Will Rynerson had gone to California for a quartz mill. When he came home, he sold a one-fifth interest to Carleton for $3,000.[296] Shortly afterward, there was a nominating

---

[294] Murphy, Lawrence R., *Lucien Bonaparte Maxwell*, Chap. VII, "Developing the Moreno Valley," p. 87.
[295] Ibid.

meeting held for the Congressional election. When Rynerson heard Clever's name called, he stood to nominate Chaves. He was told to sit down. He refused. The meeting continued without recognizing him. He interrupted and announced that he was going into the street to nominate Chaves. Those who agreed with him could join him. It was noteworthy because it signified Rynerson's break with Carleton. Nearly everyone in the room followed the big man.

In early July Michael's friends asked him to run for the legislature. He told them he hadn't time to run for office. Business was too demanding. They insisted that he was the best-informed person on Indian affairs and business matters. They argued that the company officers would be in favor of his participation. He would not have to campaign; he was too well known. The mine would be idle in the

---

[296] *New Mexico Historical Review*, LIII:1 1978, Miller, Darlis A., "Carleton's California Column, A Chapter in New Mexico's Mining History," p. 13.

winter months during the session. He was forced to concede.

On July 23, Fred wrote Michael that the company would fund the railroad.[297] He asked for specific instructions concerning what materials must be sent. They agreed to purchase John Greiner's house. He told Steck that shares were being sold, 507 taken at the present date. He begged him to stay with the company and enjoy the fruits of his labors. New Mexico's ex-Governor Rencher stood in a meeting and said that he wanted evidence that the fifteen-stamp mill could produce something substantial. All shareholders in the room agreed with him.[298]

By August 14 Michael wrote Jones that he had too much investment to abandon the company at present.[299]

In August it was revealed that the trip Watts and Mitchell made to Washington in December was intended to

---

[297] Univ. of New Mexico, Center for Southwest Research, Steck Papers, MSS 134, Box 2, Folder 4..
[298] Ibid., Letter of 8/17/67, Jones to Steck.
[299] Ibid.

give Congress Watts's credentials which would enable him to take a seat as Delegate to the December Special Session. There was a change of time for the meeting of Congress, and Watts offered to serve as Delegate and represent the Territory. There had not been an election and Governor Mitchell presumed to appoint Watts. When the news came out, New Mexicans were made aware of Watts' propensity for power and his inclination for secrecy to secure the highest office in the Territory.[300] Governor Mitchell was a willing party to the act. Both men paid dearly in the public's loss of respect.

In July 1867 a group of miners came from the west side of Baldy Mountain and entered "what is claimed to be Mr. Maxwell's grant."[301] They prospected near Lucien's sawmill in the Cimarron Canyon. Finding a promising location, they began to dig for water nearby. Maxwell came along and ordered them off his land.

---

[300] Santa Fe *New Mexican*, 8/31/67, p. 2, col. 2, "Mitchell's Delegate."
[301] Ibid., pp. 153-154.

When William Bell visited the Maxwell ranch, they walked some of the property together. Bell noted that Lucien seemed to welcome the miners who first came to make claims at Cimarron. Lucien explained the genesis of the land grants from Mexico. His father-in-law owned the Beaubien-Miranda Grant and the neighboring property in the present Colorado, the Sangre de Cristo Grant. Charles, or Carlos, Beaubien received these properties as gifts from the governor of the northern-most province of Mexico before the Mexican War. The new owners were to encourage settlement. The Beaubien-Miranda was awarded first and the Sangre de Cristo somewhat later.

Beaubien had been considered the most likely person to make the proper contacts for settlement. The Sangre de Cristo was awarded to Beaubien's son. There was later an Indian rebellion over the property and the son was killed. Beaubien wanted nothing to do with the Sangre de Cristo afterward. However, actual title still resided in his name until his death when a contract with Colorado's ex-Governor Gilpin resulted in Gilpin's ownership of title.[302]

Currently, United States taxes threatened Gilpin and he took measures to sell the grant. These included dividing the grant into halves for a more practical sale.

In early July Michael's friends asked him to run for the legislature. He told them he hadn't time to run for office. Business was too demanding. They insisted he was the best informed person on Indian affairs and business matters. They argued that the company officers would be in favor of his participation. He would not have to campaign; he was too well known. The mine would be idle in the winter months during the session. He was forced to concede.

On July 23, Fred wrote Michael that the company would fund the railroad.[303] He asked for specific instructions concerning what materials must be sent. They

---

[302] Brayer, Herbert O., *The Spanish-Mexican Land Grants*, Vol. I, Introduction, p. 26 and "The Costilla Estate," pp. 66-67.
[303]

agreed to purchase John Greiner's house. He told Michael that shares were being sold, 507 taken at the present date. He begged him to stay with the company and enjoy the fruits of his labors. New Mexico's ex-Governor Rencher stood in a meeting and said that he wanted evidence that the fifteen-stamp mill could produce something substantial. All shareholders in the room agreed with him.[304]

In August the new mill was operating and by month's end the regular clean-up of the mill totaled $1800.[305] On August 17, Fred wrote that the Territory's Ex-Governor Rencher stood up in a large meeting of shareholders and said that "unless something in the shape of returns is received from the fifteen-stamp mill, [they] should feel like abandoning further efforts.[306] The mass of the stockholders agreed with him.

---

[304] Univ. of New Mexico, Center for Southwest Research, Steck Papers, MSS 134, Box 2. Folder 4.
[305] NMHR, XLVI:1 1971, Townley, John, "New Mexico Mining Company," p. 68.

By August 14, Michael wrote Jones that he had too much investment to abandon the company at present.

Michael considered the circumstances critical. He would go to Washington and speak to the shareholders' meeting in late September. He would provide the evidence they wanted. However, he needed assurance that the company was fully confident of his integrity and performance. He would leave by September 17. His return at once would be necessary to meet his obligations in New Mexico, one for the mines, the other for the legislative session on December 1. When September 2 and election day arrived, he traveled to Santa Fe to vote. He planned to leave for Washington several days later.

The last two days were spent at the mine. He looked forward to time at home with Lizzie who was now expecting their baby.

Michael learned the details of the Congressional election after his return home. Governor Mitchell created two new precincts in Dona Ana County. Herman Heath, the hand-picked choice of Congressman Chaves, arrived in Santa Fe in July. He illegally declared Will Rynerson the winner in Dona Ana and certified him for the council seat. It was entirely irregular, but the Republican dominated Council accepted him. They further assigned him to the judicial committee. Sam Jones, the Democrat candidate, tried to contest the election's totals and Heath's award of the certificate to Rynerson.

Although Santa Fe County appeared tied between Chaves and Clever, Clever had won overall. Chaves claimed before the election that he would win by over 4000 votes. Such a statement proved absurd. Chaves arrived in the Territory to campaign a little over a month before election day. He was taken by surprise by a near tie. Chaves entered Heath's office where numerous people stood by, reading the vote count from a chalk board. Secretary Heath was overwhelmed by the presence of

Governor Mitchell who took the certificate of election, named Clever the winner, and signed it immediately. Chaves, arriving late, barely saved the day. He signaled Heath to challenge the election.

Heath and Chaves planned their strategy to win the seat by the change of year when President Grant and the Republicans would control Congress. They intended to run a canvass of the counties suspected of irregularities. The case would be submitted to Congress for review and final decision. Clever would hold the seat until Congress determined otherwise.

On September 13, at the Placer Mine, Tully sent Michael fifty-three ounces of gold dust. It was then received by Michael's half-brother, Frank, who carried out such procedures when Michael was absent. Because Tully did not have a "written order" he was unable to send one hundred and fifty ounces. The order accounted for the transfer of currency. He promised to send the balance "by the first safe chance."

Tully gave their status: they were "even with our contracts winding up our business in Tucson and I will settle in Las Cruces and do nothing but merchandize. If that gets too lean, quit, and go to New York or San Francisco." He said, "We should be able to earn $100,000 capital in cash and if we can't make anything with this, we are not any account. When we get all fixed up, I want to see you and if we can fix so as we three can make anything we may make a C & go at .7; it takes three men to do any large business in this country. Be patient old friend. I shall not wish to keep you out of what is yours. Your friend, P. R. Tully."[307]

Several letters arrived from Charles Krause, prospective Superintendent, and John Risque while Michael was in Washington. All was well and many

---

[307] Ibid., Tully to Steck, "Transfer of Gold Dust," 9/17/67, Box 2, Folder 5.

visitors had been at the mine. Michael was told that Charles Clever was one who stated what many others said, there are too many men in the company. Its main office should be in Santa Fe and the company officers should be local men. He advised Michael to get his money in cash from the company at once.[308]

The election was over when Secretary Heath called a public meeting on railroads for October 5.[309] It would be held in the Palace. Advance notice alerted officials to begin the research and organization on September 21. General Palmer told citizens that correspondence should be developed with approaching railroads to provide the best information about the Territory. Their location might be chosen as the route to California. New Mexico officials had heard from the Union Pacific Railroad whose engineers

---

[308] Letter of Charles Krause to Michael Steck, 10/26/67, Michael Steck Papers, University of New Mexico, Center for Southwest Research, MSS 134, Box 2, Folder 4.
[309] Santa Fe *New Mexican*, 10/5/67, pp. 1-2.

were presently in the area creating two surveys for a route to the Pacific.

The current meeting produced a committee designed to assemble a mass of data on the soils, location of coal and other minerals, timber, water, mountain passes, sources of local traffic for a railroad, and many other relevant facts helpful to the selection of New Mexico as an ideal railroad site.

The research and reports were required within a week. General William J. Palmer, chief engineer for the Union Pacific Railroad, western division, was expected to address the people of Santa Fe on October 12.

According to schedule, the meeting was held at the Palace on October 12 and General Palmer laid out the problem.[310] The cost to complete the connection between the Central Pacific rail line in California and the Union Pacific in Wyoming would be less than the cost to construct

---

[310] Ibid., 10/12/67, pp. 1-2.

the Union Pacific line now at Kansas with the Pacific Ocean in southern California. The cheaper line would cross Colorado and Denver, then Wyoming to Utah. He encouraged people to use every political means at their disposal to persuade Congressmen to choose the southern route. He told the assembly that the loss of business in crossing the nation by a northern route was inestimable.

Back home in Santa Fe, Michael found letters from his staff sent to Washington and returned to Santa Fe. While he was gone his freighting partner wrote him, "Elkins will give you $1060.03 in gold dust at 22.37 per ounce as per your agreement. You will look over the statement. Inside it contains a true statement of our business and when Mr. Elkins pays you the $1,060.03 # in gold dust we will be even to this date as far as I know anything about our [accounts]. I have done in this not what is fair, and I will do no more, and if you will recollect it is more than our agreement. I will be up soon to see you . . . ."[311]

As his friends predicted, when the legislative election took place his own position as Santa Fe County representative was won handily.

In Santa Fe, it was whispered in the Palace halls that a jurisdictional coup was arranged when Judge Hubbell resigned just before the election. Chaves believed that if one more federal judge were removed from New Mexico the Republicans could have a firm hold on the judiciary. Judge Slough had made himself unpopular among the native New Mexicans with his courtroom reforms and emphasis on discipline. The native New Mexicans would appreciate any moves Chaves would make to be rid of the temperamental and argumentative Judge Slough.

It was thought that Chaves and Secretary Heath planned to embarrass Slough and cause his resignation. The Judge was offended on the first day the legislature met. Traditionally, the Chief Justice swore in the members in the

---

[311] Ibid., Letter of Tully to Steck dated 11/17/67.

opening session. When he was overlooked and Secretary Heath chosen, Slough blamed Secretary Arny. Later that day he accosted Arny on the street. Arny refused to respond to Slough's rough grasp on his shoulder. The Judge raised his hand to strike Arny but withdrew it when Arny stated he would not be drawn into a fight. He put his hands in his pockets. Arny chided the Judge for his intemperate outburst and further sought redress in Justice of the Peace court.

When Judge Slough appeared in court, he insulted the court officer. A later formal retraction did not improve his standing. Secretary Heath reported the events in a complaint letter to the assistant Attorney General of the United States.

The secretary continued his attack through action in the legislature's Council. He wrote a series of eleven resolutions against Judge Slough. He presented them to the most respected member of the Council and asked him to introduce the resolutions to the assembly. Don Jesus Maria

Pacheco studied them but did not want the responsibility. He turned them over to Will Rynerson. The new Council member investigated them for several days. He recognized he owed his seat to the Secretary. He agreed, and on December 7 was assigned to the council's judiciary committee. The next morning, he introduced the resolutions relating Judge Slough's blasphemies, alleged drunkenness, political partisanship, dismissal of juries without pay, and other signs of irrational behavior.

On the night of Saturday December 15, Judge Slough looked for Rynerson at the Fonda Bar. He saw him at the billiard table. He sat down some ten feet away, next to Sam Tappan. Rynerson laid his long arms against the pool table's frame to spot his shot. The Judge made several derogatory remarks about the big man. Rynerson and the men nearest him did not hear the insults. When the Judge left shortly afterward, the remarks were conveyed to the manager of the bar. After Slough left, manager Tom

MacDonald passed the remarks to Rynerson who left, seeking Slough, but not finding him.

The next day Rynerson went to the Exchange Hotel for Sunday dinner. He was dressed in his usual black suit, with it a coat draped like a cape over his shoulder. A bell was sounded for the meal. When Slough appeared from the doorway of another representative's room, Rynerson confronted him. He said that he heard the Judge was looking for him and had called him a "son-of-a-bitch and a thief." A challenge was made. Several exchanges occurred.

"Take it back or I'll shoot you," Rynerson told him.

"Shoot and be damned!" Slough stormed back.

The shot rang out as Slough reached for the derringer from his vest pocket. It dropped as he was hit in the hip and fell to the floor. He was taken to a table to be examined by doctors who were called. The next morning, December 17, Judge Slough was dead. A great number of

Democrats rallied in the street for several nights after Slough's death.

The confrontation and its fatal result, even the public outcry, continued to the courts. The absence of the Supreme Court judges delayed hearings on pretrial motions in January. Will Rynerson's guilt was considered in February in San Miguel County. Steve was chosen to defend Rynerson despite his role as District Attorney. The case arose at the same time General Grant prepared to run for President. The Republicans in Washington wanted the matter closed as quickly as possible. Local citizens in Santa Fe placed blame on Secretary Heath who illegally certified Rynerson for office. The Democrats wanted to lynch Heath, but cooler heads prevailed. The San Miguel jury which Slough had offended the previous year, acquitted Rynerson on March 22, 1868.[312]

---

[312] Roberts, Gary L., *Death Comes to the Chief Justice*, Chap. 5, "Justice – of a Sort," p. 109.

The Legislative session was deeply scarred by the scandal. Little was accomplished. It was March before positive work could be done on major issues such as the railroad committees' reports sent to the Union Pacific and other interested parties whose surveyors were in the area.

News of a large gold strike at Lucien Maxwell's place in Mora County soon reached Michael. Many civilian workers at Fort Union left their jobs to join the gold rush to Maxwell's property. Maxwell invited some of his friends to make claims. The wealthiest men of the area funded many projects. Among them was an attempt to bring needed water to the many placer operations in the Baldy Mountain area where the mines were located.

There were new developments in Colorado. Ex-Governor Gilpin was trying to sell the adjoining Sangre de Cristo grant. He had an important agent in Europe, Charles Lambard, a director of the Union Pacific Railroad. The price was $1,500,000.[313]

Watts would soon join the group who followed the money. Steck considered the promises of John Watts to be like desert mirages. He had not yet accomplished the acquisition of the Rio Grande bottom land. If it didn't materialize, the loss would deflate the company's resources. Watts would certainly be after his next big chance with the good fortune his friend, Lucien Maxwell, had found. Instead, he was made temporary Chief Justice until a more suitable judge could be found.

---

[313] Brayer, Herbert Oliver, *The Spanish-Mexican Land Grants*, Vol. One, "The Costilla Estate, 1843 – 1870, p. 75.

Chapter Thirteen: Empty Promises
April 1868 – January 1869

Steve returned to his Santa Fe attorney duties immediately following the San Miguel trial. His friend, Tom Catron, was appointed District Attorney for the 3rd District by Governor Mitchell, and shortly afterward confirmed by the Legislative Council. Throughout January and February, the newspapers carried accounts of the several trials involving the death of the Chief Justice. In February, the Pecos and Placer Mining and Ditch Company was incorporated in the legislature.[314]

During the legislative session the question of Governor Mitchell's conduct concerning his office was considered by a committee. A vote was taken to make a

---

[314] Santa Fe *New Mexican*, 2/11/68, p. 2. Republished with names of original incorporators, 2/18/68.

formal complaint to Congress. The complaint made several charges and appealed to Washington to take measures to relieve Territorial officials of the Governor's obstruction of the operation of government. He was deemed unworthy of his position by a vote of seventeen to five in the House of Representatives and eight to three in the Council. A copy of the report was sent to the Secretary of State and the Chairman of the Committee on the Territories. As a result, Herman Heath, Territorial Secretary, assumed the duties of the Governor.[315]

The President discharged all federal officers, but Grant did not exonerate Steve, who was kept, from the fight over the Assessor's case of William Breeden, until mid-year. Steve's name appeared as prosecutor in the peonage trial held in early August. Steve served his District Attorney's duties as usual.

---

[315] Santa Fe *New Mexican*, 5/5/68, p. 1, col. 3, "Troubles in New Mexico," from the Leavenworth Times.

Throughout January and February the newspapers carried accounts of the several trials involving the death of the Chief Justice. In February, the Pecos and Placer Mining and Ditch Company was incorporated in the legislature.

At Cimarron three seasoned miners searched diligently for a lode strike, following a hunch from gold flakes seen in Ute Creek the previous May. Rich deposits became visible in melting snow by November 1867, but extensive development was not feasible until spring. Although they tried to keep the secret, the news was leaked over the winter.

In the early spring they prospected upstream, and on the hills above. They found a thirty-foot depression full of rotten quartz that shimmered with gold near the convergence of Ute and South Ponil Creeks. There, three well-defined veins three feet wide and a foot apart were located.[316] They rushed to tell Lucien Maxwell at once.

---

[316] Murphy, Lawrence R., *Philmont*, Chap. VII, "Bonanza on Baldy Mountain," pp. 93-94.

Lucien set about developing the property right away. He hired E. H. Bergman, a retired army officer to superintend the mine's installation and operation. A sample of the ore was sent to O. D. Munson, assayer at the U. S. Branch Mint at Denver. They must wait several months for a report of the single ton's value. They called the mine the Aztec.

The men at Maxwell's placer mines cried for water to separate the dirt from the minerals. The investors conferred with a former officer under General Carleton. He suggested the construction of an elaborate ditch system to transport water from the Red River at Taos. Michael and Steve followed Lucien Maxwell's "Big Ditch" work at Cimarron. Many would-be miners had filed claims in the past year. The strain on water resources on the Maxwell property was far greater than their own. There had been over a thousand claims made in the Moreno Valley. Maxwell hired Captain Nicholas Davis, a former Carleton officer, to plan the water system.

Maxwell incorporated the Moreno Valley Mining and Water Company in January.[317] Several of his friends, wealthy citizens of Mora and San Miguel Counties, joined him. It was said that Maxwell contributed most of the $115,000 from his own money to build a complex ditch and overhead trough system for water from the Red River at Taos. The Pecos River ditch would be far less costly but was still a major undertaking.

Lucien hired E. H. Bergman, a recently retired army officer, to purchase and superintend the mill's installations and operation of the Aztec's needed equipment. The mill opened in October 1868. Its 435-pound stamps could soon be heard over a five-mile radius as they pounded onto an iron base thirty-three times a minute. There were forty-eight men employed in the mine and mill. The mill and a twelve-horsepower engine occupied a frame building at the base of Aztec Ridge. A new settlement formed around the

---

[317] Murphy, Lawrence R., *Lucien Bonaparte Maxwell*, Chap. VII, "The Greatest Gold Producer on the Globe," p. 158, fn. 19, p. 245. (*Mining and Scientific Press,* San Francisco)

operation. It was dubbed "Baldy Town." A shaft was sunk in the mountain and tunnels were dug into the rich ore bodies.

A weekly clean-up produced more than $8000 worth of gold with a daily yield of $1,000. Lucien had the gold molded into what looked like guinea hen sized eggs.[318]

In March it was announced that Steck and Elkins' ditch company received a large amount of public land along the proposed ditch line through a bill passed in the Senate earlier in the year.[319] They began to raise money for ditch construction at once. The company's profit would profit the ditch company as well. The mill could not operate continuously without supplemental water. They hired a Californian, former Colonel McMullen, to manage the ditch connection between the mill and the Pecos River nearly sixty miles away.

---

[318] Ibid., pp. 94-95.
[319] Santa Fe *New Mexican*, 3/31/68, "New Mexico Progressing," p. 2, col. 1.

In late March railroad construction became the focus of work at the New Mexico Mining Company. It began in April. The stockpile and fifteen stamp-mill were ready for production.

The cost of transportation from the stopes to the mill site was the primary expense of the operation. The mules used in the past to transport the ore were too slow for current equipment and could not haul enough rock to allow the mill to work at full capacity. They would supplement the railroad.

The narrow-gauge railroad, at one and a-half miles, ran down a rough slope. The loaded cars were controlled by gravity and brakes controlled the speed. Its descent was at fifteen miles per hour. The track was built of hardwood with a metal strip nailed to the top. Two cars carried the ore. Michael set production at one hundred tons per day, five times the normal scale. The mill operated at peak capacity from August to December.

In late April, Major Magruder was in Santa Fe and exhibited two large gold nuggets from the Placer Mines. He reported that operations of the mines under Steck were more than satisfactory "in the extreme." In sixteen days, the company netted more than $2400 using new equipment and machinery. Expectations for an improved system would provide greater results in a shorter time.[320] For March, April, and May there was a net profit of almost $5,000. Michael was putting up a new mill with a capacity for twenty stamps. He predicted there would be no big profits for two years, but "great future wealth."[321]

On the first of March Steck wrote to Fred Jones that his contract indicated his resignation notice must be given to the company three months in advance. He wrote, "I will not be in the employment of the company longer than the 17th of August."[322] The figures for his total income,

---

[320] Ibid., 5/12/68, "Nuggets," p. 2, col. 1.
[321] Dailey, Martha Lacroix, *Michael Steck: A Prototype of Nineteenth Century Individualism*," Chap. VII, "The Mining Years," p. 287.
[322] Ibid.

dividends, and bonuses collected in his three years as superintendent, allowed him to become financially independent. Lizzie had just delivered their first child, a baby daughter.[323] He would remain in Santa Fe until the next year. He wanted to return to Muncy and make the home for his family he had longed for so many years.

The company delayed its reply for several months. In June David Guildersleeve wrote him that "they had sunk nearly a quarter of a million dollars in the [sic] enterprize." Guildersleeve reminded him that he was one of the largest stockholders in the company and a replacement had to be found. They wanted him to train the man for six weeks before leaving. He had as much to gain as anyone. After two weeks of negotiation, Steck agreed. At the end of the year, he owned one thousand shares of stock.

Between the end of 1867 and mid-May 1868 the outcome of the Delegate race recount of the previous year

---

[323] Ibid., p. 284

was unknown. J. Francisco Chaves attended the hearing on his contest with Charles Clever held in Washington sometime after May 27, 1868.[324] By May 19 Clever gave his concession to Chaves.[325]

In mid-May, the *Gazette* began its attacks on Chaves as the leader of the Republican peon party.[326] It raised the sensitive issue once again when a July trial was about to commence. The men to be tried were from Taos, Santa Fe, and Rio Arriba Counties. These were taxpayers who held peons. The *New Mexican* claimed that the object of these articles in the *Gazette* was to influence "foreign" readers. It was the *Gazette* and the Democrat Union Party who had always fought for the pro-slavery side in New Mexico. The *New Mexican* threatened its critics with publishing the names of people in the Democrat Union Party who held slaves.

---

[324] Santa Fe *New Mexican*, 4/14/68, p. 2, col. 3.
[325] Ibid., 5/19/68, "Clever on the Apologetic," p. 2, col. 1.
[326] Santa Fe *New Mexican*, 8/11/68, "Peonage in New Mexico," p. 2.

On June 9 General Sherman and Colonel Tappan of the Peace Commission were at the Bosque Redondo.[327] They asked the Navajos where they wanted to live. They all wanted to go home to the Canyon de Chelly country. They were awarded a three-million-acre reservation and given an escort to cross the 400 miles once more. There were certain benefits allowed, schooling, a small amount for each person to provide clothing, ten dollars annually if they would engage in farming, seeds, a few buildings to be built, separate schools for each thirty children, and $150,000 immediately to purchase sheep, goats, and cattle. At the time there were around 7500 Navajos who began the trek west.

The gathering of income tax information by Deputy Assessor W. W. Griffin yielded the revelation of many Indian peons in Santa Fe and its nearby counties. The people holding these peons were called to court on August

---

[327] Dunn, J. P., *Massacres of the Mountains*, Chap. XIV, "Cañon de Chelly and Bosque Redondo," p. 471.

11, 1868. Steve, as U. S. Attorney, and William Griffin, deputy assessor, planned to expose the continuing practice of peonage by means of the new tax canvass.

The *New Mexican* attempted to explain the trial which took place in early August by defining "Navajoe Captives."[328] The editors explained that during the war between the Navajos and the whites, Indian hostiles were captured. They passed into families of New Mexican citizens. They were often regarded as peons, but due to laws passed after the war abolishing peonage, the people became free and at liberty to go where they pleased. The article claimed the former captives now lived among civilized people and preferred their new status.

The two or three hundred people from Taos and Rio Arriba Counties were summoned to U. S. District Court. No indictments were presented, and Judge Houghton released the entire assembly. The primary reason was that

---

[328] Ibid.

no Navajo Indians appeared in court. Their names were not complete since none had the common first and last names used in formal documents. They were not able to read or write. No one was present to testify that they had not been paid for their labor. Many Navajos had gone home to Canyon de Chelly to join their countrymen who were freed from the Bosque Redondo reservation.

At Elizabethtown and Cimarron, the town's streets were crowded. Shortly after Maxwell invited a group of civilian workers at Fort Union to make gold claims on his grant, he recognized that many strangers would surround his home. They would interrupt the normal flow of his home life. One major concern was his eldest daughter, Virginia. His favorite child was seventeen.

The Menards in Illinois advised Lucien to send Virginia to a Catholic school in St. Louis to complete her education. He may have enrolled her himself. Arrangements were made with the nuns to let her board at the cloister. He planned to have her come home to Cimarron after one more year in school. Most New Mexican native fathers would receive offers from prominent single men in the Territory for a marriage contract. He was not inclined to let her go easily. In the meantime, he provided her with a liberal allowance for her personal use.[329]

In 1868 income tax was assessed in New Mexico based on the previous year's income. All people who made over a thousand dollars were published in the *New Mexican* with the amount of income they paid beside their names. Around eighty-five people were listed in alphabetical order. Most were merchandizers. Only six men earned over $4000. Lucien Maxwell was one of them.[330] Steve's income was the highest of the attorneys.

---

[329] Prince Papers, Historical Notes and Events, Maxwell Land Grant, Box 14020, Folder 8, *The Raton Reporter*, 7/18/72, Vol. XXXIV – Number 14, Reported by Melvin W. Mills, former attorney for Lucien Maxwell.
[330] Santa Fe *New Mexican*, 7/21/68, p.2, col. 3. Maxwell's reported income: $4,886.16 for 1867.

Maxwell owned several stores, but his primary income between September 1866 and August 1867 came from selling Indian supplies. The thirteen hundred Utes and Apaches received more than a hundred tons of beef and wheat and nearly a ton of salt from him. The total cost to the government was $33,462.88. When the accounts were submitted to the commissary officer, he noted that there were no additional charges for herding, renting warehouses, or butchering. Maxwell delivered the cattle on the hoof when they were needed, and the Indians did the slaughtering.

In mid-summer 1864, Maxwell had built a grist mill capable of turning out three hundred barrels of wheat a day, producing forty-four barrels of flour. The grist mill was built by an expert from the northeast. By 1869 miller Isaiah Rinehart estimated annual profits from the mill were $26,440.

After Matt Lynch and Tim Foley, seventeen companies staked claims along Willow Creek in the mining district. Prospectors covered nearby gullies on the western slopes of Baldy Mountain. One company at Cimarron anticipated the water shortage at the mines in early June. That company began construction of a ten-mile ditch. They planned to collect water from high mountain streams and carry it via wooden flumes and ditches to the mining operations on Baldy's slopes. Second and third companies started other water transport projects.

Lucien incorporated the Moreno Water & Mining Company in January 1868. Construction began on May 12.[331] He provided most of the initial $115,000 to start up the company. Other investors included William Kroenig, John Dold, Morris Bloomfield, V. S. Shelby, stage line owner, and Nicholas Davis, engineer. Davis was chosen to head up the project to find a way to channel a ditch line, or

---

[331] Murphy, Lawrence R., *Philmont*, Chap. VII, "Bonanza on Baldy Mountain," p. 92.

something similar, to bring water from the Red River at Taos to the Cimarron district.[332]

Lumber continued to be in demand for the immense ditch and flume project in the planning stage since May 1868. The ambitious water project at Cimarron was under way by mid-summer. Some predicted it would be complete by September. Four hundred men worked on the ditch, but wood for the huge wooden flumes to carry the water slowed the progress down.[333] All ditch projects needed lumber. The first sawmill used steam to power its saws and soon turned out 3,000 feet of lumber daily. William Kroenig and Lucien followed, erecting other sawmills to serve the district.

In 1868, many uninvited men came to Cimarron to make claims. Lucien had to hire an agent to provide them with leases. This year the leases cost two dollars per month per claim of two hundred feet. The newspaper had reported

---

[332] Murphy, Lawrence R., *Lucien Bonaparte Maxwell*, Chap. 7, "The Greatest Gold Producer on the Globe," p. 158.
[333] Ibid.

the earlier more liberal and cheaper claims. The new claimants felt betrayed. However, all around him Lucien encountered men who approached him for development capital. From time to time, he invested in promising prospects.

At nearly the same time as water concerns were addressed, road improvements were planned at costs estimated from $3,000 to $4,000 dollars. The Fort Union men, the Michigan Company, had organized the first eight claims at Grouse Gulch. The men who resigned from the Quartermaster's Department at the fort would expect soon to be forced to find other work. The Army was quickly retiring its civilians and the forts were closing.

Elizabethtown grew out of the need for a hotel, a blacksmith shop, stores, a barber shop, and other conveniences. Fort Union's sutler did much to organize the town's surveying and blocking of lots. The town honored him by naming it for his daughter, Elizabeth.

On June 9 General Sherman and Colonel Tappan of the Peace Commission were at the Bosque Redondo.[334] They asked the Navajos where they wanted to live. They all wanted to go home to the Canyon de Chelly country. They were awarded a three-million-acre reservation and given an escort to cross the 400 miles once more. There were certain benefits allowed, schooling, a small amount for each person to provide clothing, ten dollars annually if they would engage in farming, seeds, a few buildings to be built, separate schools for each thirty children, and $150,000 immediately to purchase sheep, goats, and cattle. At the time there were around 7500 Navajos who began the trek west.

In mid-year the Santa Fe *New Mexican* announced Grant and Colfax as the Republican nominees for President and Vice-President, calling the national convention of the previous week in Chicago the National Union Republican

---

[334] Dunn, J. P., *Massacres of the Mountains*, Chap. XIV,

party.[335] The National Democratic Convention met at Tammany Hall on July 4 and named their candidates, Horatio Seymour, and Francis P. Blair.

Finding work for the men of Fort Union was not a priority of either federal or territorial officials. Most of the fort's employees returned to their original homes in the east.

Employment for the men leaving the army was only one aspect of the area's problems. A more complex issue arose when Lucien realized he did not know the precise boundaries of the land grant. He had participated in the 1860 Court of Private Land Claims which gave grant owners the opportunity to get confirmation of their grants. The court was created by an act of Congress. His grant was confirmed, but none were required to have surveys performed. Instead, a Surveyor General had been assigned to New Mexico in 1853 to confirm the boundaries.

---

[335] Santa Fe *New Mexican*, 6/30/68, p.2, col. 2.

The Surveyor General's directions were so elaborate and burdensome that none were resolved. Lucien turned to his old political friend, John Watts.[336] Watts was a grant owner himself and was working on extending the boundaries of the New Mexico Mining Company. Watts accepted the new challenge to help Lucien have the land grant surveyed. At the same time, he had been appointed New Mexico's Chief Justice in August 1868. He would complete the term of John Slough and await the new appointee.

Michael watched and listened for developments on the Beaubien-Miranda Grant. He noted that the Santa Fe *Gazette* began to call the Mora County grant the "Maxwell Grant." Michael was interested to learn how the most knowledgeable experts would attempt to solve Maxwell's water and land boundary problems.

---

[336] Remley, David, *Bell Ranch*, Chap. 2, "John S. Watts," pp.33-52.

The Denver Branch Mint report on the 1867 Aztec's gold sample came back in September 1868. It yielded $19,455.37 a ton in gold and $189.08 in silver.[337] Lucien was surprised and gratified. A great deal of publicity followed. Baldy Town was built when the report came in. A fifteen-stamp mill arrived from Denver. The stamp mill and a twelve-horsepower steam engine were placed in a frame building. There were 435-pound stamps which pounded into an iron base thirty-three times a minute to pulverize the rock.

The Placer mines reported that their main vein was two and a half to six feet wide, and the depth was 172 feet perpendicularly. The tunnel or inclined shaft was 335 feet long. Another shaft 400-feet from the first was sunk 100-feet deep. The railway was in running order from the mine to the mill.[338] The tramway's cost was $20,000 and

---

[337] Murphy, Lawrence R, *Lucien Bonaparte Maxwell*, Chap. VII, "The Greatest Gold Producer on the Globe," p.60.
[338] *New Mexico Historical Review,* XLVI: 1 1971, Townley, John, "New Mexico Mining Company," p. 69.

constantly delivering to the mill. Michael left the company, remaining in Santa Fe while his home in Pennsylvania was being built.

His child, Rachel Wood Steck, provided a new joy for his life.[339] He was anxious to move on and resume his place in a society he understood better than the one in New Mexico. The Territory needed a railroad desperately to compete for business with Denver merchants whose freight charges were less than half their own.

Michael had to sink a substantial part of his savings to do what the company would not. However, he was satisfied that he had done his part and could enjoy a leisurely retirement. At the same time, John was able to declare that he had inherited $130,000 and would also retire.[340] They had fulfilled their promises to each other and

---

[339] Dailey, Martha Lacroix, PHD Dissertation, UNM, 1989, *Michael Steck: A Prototype of 19th Century Individualism*, Chap. VII, "The Mining Years," 284.
[340] Santa Fe *Daily New Mexican*, 9/1/68, p. 2, col. 3.

made the old Ortiz Mine work its magic after all. Michael wished he could share the thrill of success with John.

At Cimarron, sometimes Maxwell maintained control of a promising placer mine. He would share in both development costs and income. Near the Aztec Mine was the Montezuma, discovered by "Big Jack." It was southeast of the Aztec. Lucien owned most of the claim. It netted $1,000 a day by mid-November.[341]

Maxwell's ditch operation shut down in November. Nine more miles remained to be built. The longest above ground section involved 2800 feet of flume which was, at peak height, seventy-nine feet overhead. Work would be suspended for the winter.[342]

In December, an agreement was formed between the Union Pacific Railroad and the stockholders of the Denver Pacific Railroad. The Union Pacific would take over the land from Denver north to Cheyenne, Wyoming

---
[341] Murphy, Lawrence R., *Philmont*, Chap. VII, "Bonanza on Baldy Mountain," p. 95.
[342] Ibid., p. 92.

and build the northern link of the Kansas Pacific with the Union Pacific to the west coast. The railroad would assume the road's ownership when it was completed to Cheyenne. The financing was carried by European banking houses.

Chapter Fourteen: Selling Two Grants for A Railroad

January 1869 – December 1869

After President Grant's election in November 1868, the March 1869 Public Credit Act committed the nation to the payment of the public debt in gold.

The New Year, like most, arrived with mixed blessings. A new administration began in Washington. In

New Mexico, Governor Mitchell left the Territory once more without leave.

H. H. Heath became the Acting-Governor. Three new counties were established in the legislature, Colfax and Grant, a bow to the U. S. President and Vice-President. The third, a bow to President Lincoln. Tom Catron was confirmed as Attorney General. J. F. Chaves announced in February that he had won his seat in Congress and was reinstated. President Grant removed all federal court appointees from office, largely due to the bickering and retrials of the Breeden political case. Steve remained, but was continually fearful of dismissal.

A reaction was set off by the administration's support of Congressman Chaves and Herman Heath's reappointment. The public and other officials were revolted by the outbreak of violence resulting from the plot to drive the Chief Justice from New Mexico. Added to it was Chaves' appeal to the native Mexicans for their support.

The *Weekly Gazette* twice brought to light Heath's letter to the Confederacy in 1861 asking for an appointment,[343] without any valid response from the Administration Party's press, the *New Mexican*. They only defended Heath. In contrast, such newspapers as the Secretary's former residence in Iowa, stated that the man was an unconscionable coward and a shyster.[344]

In Colorado, the agreement made between Charles Lambard and Morton Coates Fisher, the latter representing the co-owners of the Sangre de Cristo, made it possible for Lambard to promote the grant's sale in England. The agreement was changed on January 5, 1869, to allow Fisher to be the sole agent for the grant in England since he had already been paid to work there. Lambard would confine his efforts to the European continent. He consented and sent a copy to William Blackmore, his sub-agent, who had

---

[343] Roberts, Gary L., *Death Comes to the Chief Justice*, Chap. 5, Justice – of a Sort," p. 116, fn. 47. Heath letter to the Confederacy printed in the Santa Fe *Gazette*, 7/18/68, 10/10/68, and 1/16/69.
[344] Brayer, Herbert O., *The Spanish-Mexican Land Grants,* Vol. I, "The Costilla Estate," p. 77.

not yet succeeded in obtaining any interested parties. Both agreed to the change.

Blackmore knew European investors and was aware few would buy a million-acre estate in the distant American West. However, quite a few might invest in a highly capitalized land company interested in immediate and substantial dividends where emigration and stock raising were the object.[345] Blackmore recommended the grant be divided in half and each part offered separately. He suggested the names "Trinchera" for the northern half, and "Costilla" for the southern. Two separate land companies were formed.

Blackmore produced a booklet on the Trinchera Estate to promote the Sangre de Cristo's sale. He drew up a special prospectus for the investors who would receive company stock.[346] He presented the estate as large, comparable to many English counties. A subscription form

---

[345] Ibid., p. 76.
[346] Ibid., p. 78 and fn. 40.

was attached to each copy of the prospectus. The purchase would be suitable only for a syndicated enterprise. The cooperation of English capitalists and emigrants would be necessary. Reports of such experts as Professor Hayden were provided.[347]

Once Governor Pile was agreed to the plan to be rid of Heath, the Republican forces were marshalled against him. In July 1868 and January 1869, the Santa Fe *Gazette* made public Secretary Heath's letter to the Confederacy in the opening days of war in which he asked for an appointment to office in the Confederacy.[348]

When Heath realized he would not be appointed governor, he and Congressman Chaves sought John Pratt's position, the able Democrat U. S. Marshal. Chaves had tried to blame Pratt for his lost seat in Congress. Pratt and his deputies oversaw the polls on election day. Pratt was popular with the Republicans, and they turned against

---

[347] Ibid., Introduction, p. 23.
[348] The Santa Fe *Weekly Gazette*, 7/18/68, 10/10/68, and 1/16/69.

Chaves. Pratt was also in charge of the census, a role he was prepared to assume.

Steve feared a replacement for his own position might suddenly appear in print. His name remained on the directory column of officials in *The Santa Fe New Mexican*, but his status as U. S. Attorney was uncertain. He began collecting endorsements from local officials to be sent to Senator Trumbull, Chairman of the Senate Judiciary Committee.

He watched with concern as the new appointee's names trickled into the newspaper's reports. He was employed by Lucien Maxwell and his advisors as attorney for their presentations to prospective grant buyers. He helped prepare the reports on the output of the mines. He was consulted on the planned survey of the vast property, but the new Surveyor General had not been named. Bill Griffin was an engineer and had applied, but his experience in Santa Fe was in banking. Someone else was chosen.

Governor Pile had not yet arrived from a trip he made to Missouri shortly after his first visit to Santa Fe. It was known that Heath, in seeking Pile's position, had made haste to befriend the Governor. It was not known what they had discussed, nor that Pile wrote a letter to the President endorsing Heath.

Governor William A. Pile was appointed by President Grant in early June. He arrived on June 15 and was immediately drawn into the controversy concerning Territorial Secretary Heath. When he returned to Santa Fe from his business trip, Steve spoke to him of his letter approving Heath to the President. Steve explained the unanimous support to rid the Territory of the man's undesirable presence. The Governor agreed to retract his approval.

Steve Elkins replaced General Carleton in the Arizona mining companies' management and their gold to be transported to the mint at Denver.

Steve and other members of the Santa Fe Bar organized a group to call together Democrats and Republicans. They would send a unified plea to the Justice Department. They asked officials to ban Heath from any office in the Territory. A telegram from over one hundred officials and citizens was sent to Senator Trumbull. It stated that Heath was entirely objectionable and asked for his withdrawal.

Governor Pile was at first friendly with Heath who clearly sought his approval. Shortly afterward, Pile met Heath's wife who hinted that a pay-off for the position may have been made to encourage the withdrawal of Edward Perkins from competition for the office.[349] John Pratt made an emergency trip to Washington to straighten out any further misunderstanding.

Attention was focused on the Federal Depository when it was learned that the Treasury Department in

---

[349] Roberts, Gary L., *Death Comes to the Chief Justice*, Chap. 5, "Justice – of a Sort," p. 120.

Washington was withdrawing all fractional currency. The printing award was stopped, and all current paper changed. Greenbacks were a different style from the ones currently in circulation. Treasury Department employees would be furloughed until May 15. A new paper mill was being used in a different city. Whisky and other revenue stamps were being turned over to the Commissioner of Internal Revenue. All the plates, dies, and other materials of the old money would be destroyed.[350]

Four days later, the *New Mexican* announced that a large deposit of greenbacks had been delivered by Colonel Bridgeman, Paymaster, U. S. A. Four hundred thousand dollars came in greenbacks and $300,000 credited to the Chief Paymaster, Colonel W. B. Rochester. One hundred thousand would be credited to the United States Treasury.[351]

On June 8, a robbery of the Federal Depository occurred on the eve of the new Receiver's arrival. The

---

[350] Santa Fe *New Mexican*, 5/4/69, p. 1, col. 4.
[351] Ibid., from Washington, dated 4/69, p. 1, col. 4.

robbery was committed on Saturday night. Colonel James L. Collins was found murdered in his office that morning. He had been shot in the heart with a pistol lying beside him. Scattered across the floor were various sealed packages of fractional currency and sundry piles of the same in small quantities. The money vault and iron safe had been broken open and all bills of large denominations taken away. The amount removed was believed to be not less than $100,000. Acting Governor Heath offered a reward. A committee of federal officers were inventorying all the public bonds remaining. They would be turned over to Captain Little.[352] He took charge on Sunday.

On June 15 the Santa Fe *New Mexican* announced in a brief item that $65,000 of the Depository's money had been found in the brewery north of town.[353]

The new Grant administration officers began to arrive in March and April. The Surveyor

---

[352] Ibid., 6/8/69, p. 2, col. 2.
[353] Ibid., 6/15/69, p. 1, col. 2.

General arrived on May 17. A letter from Lucien Maxwell to Surveyor General Spencer was carried by George Chilcott the same day. In it, Lucien applied to the Office of the Interior Department in Washington for the survey. It stated that work had begun and outlined some of its details. A check for $5,000 was included, the usual fee for the application. Charles Holly wrote the letter on May 16. It was sent to Santa Fe for personal delivery.[354]

When Joseph H. Wilson received the letter and check on June 28 in Washington, he became suspicious at once that the property described in vague terms was for a greater amount than that stated in the Treaty of Guadalupe Hidalgo ending the Mexican War. The treaty specified the ownership of a grant was limited to eleven square leagues per individual or twenty-two leagues to a partnership. He ordered Surveyor General Spencer to postpone the survey

---

[354] Murphy, Lawrence R., *Lucien Bonaparte Maxwell*, Chap. 8, "The Sale of the Maxwell Grant," pp. 173-179.

until the extent and locus of the grant was clearly presented to his department.

It was late June when Lucien Maxwell shared the news of his grant's survey. He telegraphed the Denver newspapers that survey arrangements were made on June 16. W. W. Griffin, accompanied by John Lambert, the survey's draftsman, and fifteen assistants, would be occupied with the survey for three months. They took wagons, pack animals, and provisions for the operation. Steve Elkins' brother, John, joined them as Griffin's apprentice.

The plan to sell the grant had been in motion for some time. Maxwell and his wife, Luz, granted Chaffee, Chilcott, and Holly an option to purchase their grant, containing about "two million acres of land" or to persuade others to purchase it. The option was granted on May 26, 1869. Ten days before, the transatlantic railroad was announced as complete.

At Cimarron, Maxwell excluded his 1,000-acre home ranch, cultivated land, and improvements. The Colorado capitalists paid Maxwell $5,000 for the option privilege. The price for the grant would be $600,000 to be paid to Maxwell and his wife and delivered immediately upon the grant's sale.[355]

A second option was made on January 28, 1870, which enabled the purchasers to complete the sale excepting the Cimarron home ranch of one thousand acres. The English syndicate purchasing the grant was scheduled to take up the altered option on April 30, 1870.

Surveyor General Spencer received Wilson's letter to postpone the survey in the third week of July. In late July Maxwell and his promoters carefully analyzed how they would respond to Wilson's order and refute its contents.

Unofficial reports have appeared that Griffin, a former officer of the Federal Depository, was contracted

---

[355] Pearson, Jim Berry, *The Sale of the Maxwell Land Grant*, Chap. Three, "Maxwell Sells the Grant," p. 49.

for the survey in Colorado based on the promise to take charge of the First National Bank of Santa Fe when the sale was made. Lucien's willingness to be the sole shareholder and give shares to the other directors suggests such an arrangement could have been offered. If so, Surveyor General Spencer was likely complicit.

The Maxwell team's argument against Wilson's position began by contesting the size limits he named. ". . . . regardless of what size limits might have been prescribed by Mexican statute, by its confirming act of January 21, 1860, Congress has in effect established a new grant which recognizes no limit" . . . and no federal agency has the authority to nullify an act of Congress.[356]

The new Governor of the Territory, the incoming Surveyor General, and the Chief Justice of the Supreme Court were persuaded to join the effort to sell the Maxwell Grant by late June. They would cover for the foreign

---

[356] Murphy, Lawrence R., *Lucien Bonaparte Maxwell,* Chap. 8, "The Sale of the Maxwell Grant," p. 168.

buyers who were not yet authorized to own land in New Mexico or Colorado.[357] William A. Bell, General Palmer's friend and colleague, was likely a member of the group purchasing the grant. He visited Maxwell and toured the grant with him,

when gold mining there first began.[358]

Governor Pile was himself a "second choice" for Governor. He was a former colonel of infantry, a chaplain, appointed a brigadier general of United States Volunteers, and a member of the Missouri Methodist Conference. In 1866 he was elected a representative from Missouri to the Fortieth Congress and served on the Committee on Union Prisoners and Military Affairs.[359]

On May 16, 1869, Charles Holly, a former Colorado capitalist living on the grant, prepared the letter to

---

[357] Pearson, Jim Berry, *The Maxwell Land Grant*, Chap. Three, "Maxwell Sells the Grant," p. 49.

[358] Bell, William A, *New Tracks in North America. Also, Lucien Bonaparte Maxwell*, Chap. 6, "The Cimarron Indian Agency," pp. 128-129 and 153.

[359] *Biographical Directory of American Territorial Governors*, Thomas A. McMullin and David Walker, Meckler Publishing, Westport, Connecticut. (115606-S, Doc. 147, 71-2—3)

New Mexico's surveyor general, T. Rush Spencer. Once the application for a survey was made, Jerome Chaffee, Denver banker and politician, joined Chilcott and Holly to option the estate. Lucien and Luz Maxwell granted the three men the option on May 26, 1869.

Santa Fe was 440 miles from Denver and the location of the Kansas Pacific was the primary concern of New Mexico's businessmen. The newly named railroad anticipated building to Fort Lyon just southwest of Kit Carson, Colorado.[360] The road asked for right-of-way for forty miles on each side of its tracks. It would involve 24,000 square miles of public land. The right- of-way would begin at Lawrence, Kansas and extend southwest to the boundary with Mexico near Guayamas, on the Gulf of California. The plan was submitted two years before.

When the Central Pacific Railroad and the Union Pacific Railroad met at Promontory Point, Utah the entire

---

[360] Lamar, Howard R., *The Far Southwest*, Chap. 11, "The Centennial State," p. 243. Also, Brayer, H. O., "Denver & Rio Grande Railway," 1869-1870, p. 25.

town of Santa Fe rejoiced. Wire service both east and west from Santa Fe was assured, and *The Santa Fe New Mexican* became a daily newspaper. Dependence on the erratic and expensive wire service from Denver would be replaced by a service directly connected to both coasts.

At the same time in Colorado, William Blackmore saw the promise of the Sangre de Cristo in its ability to bring the Colorado and New Mexico territories a railroad. Lambard, a director of the Union Pacific Railroad, estimated the land's value based on the coming railroad and wrote Blackmore of the forecast price. He thought a report from Professor Hayden, a world-renowned Rocky Mountain geologic expert, would be adequate to sell the grant at the present price.[361]

Blackmore named the northern half, Trinchera. It was the site of the San Luis Valley, the vicinity first seen by the geologist, Professor Hayden, in 1864. The area was

---

[361] Brayer, H. O., *The Spanish-Mexican Land Grants*, "The Costilla Estate: 1843-1870, p. 76, note 36.

ideal for cattle and sheep raising, promising a ready market. It was also near the new railhead. Hayden, at Blackmore's request, and payment of $10,000, made a geological survey of the Sangre de Cristo in October 1869.[362]

Blackmore believed the Dutch investment bankers might be interested in the Trinchera property. The terms of his contract confined both himself and Lambard to the Trinchera Estate. Costilla was the sole agency of Morton Fisher. The Dutch banking house was wary of the Costilla investment and asked for specific guarantees. They questioned the authenticity of title to the Sangre de Cristo and wanted the U. S. Congress to incorporate the property as well as Colorado's legislature. They also wanted proof of the agricultural and mineral potential Blackmore's booklets claimed. Despite the unusual and demanding stipulations, Blackmore was able to get the bankers'

---

[362] Santa Fe *Daily New Mexican*, 10/19/69, p. 1, (item), and p. 3. "A U. S. Assay Office for New Mexico," p. 2, col. 1.

provisional commitment in late 1869. The measure was argued on the floors of Congress for many months.

In Cimarron, the morning of Virginia Maxwell's arrival, strangers were gathered in the street. Officers from Fort Union stood near the fence just off the front yard. Lucien observed his own people, the mill workers, the carpenters, his house servants, primos, amigos, jockeys, Indians; all looking down the road for signs of the coach.

At last, the dust storm from the six horse-team could be seen and the coach came into view. It stopped before their house, a signal honor, only observed for dignitaries, and Maxwell strode forward to lift her from the step.

The crowd roared with delight and clapped their hands. She wore a handsome traveling suit, her hat perched neatly over her dark hair, a roll of the hair wound at the back of her neck. Luz followed Lucien and clasped her tightly. Virginia turned toward her admirers as her brother and sisters greeted her with hugs and kisses.

She waved at friends over the heads of her younger sisters. Her father led her to her new apartment. She stopped him at a little distance, clearly overwhelmed. She placed her hands beside her head and stared at the octagonal building with the glass windows near the street. It was as if she was a mannequin in her father's shop window.

Behind them, men brought down the remaining trunks and carried them inside. There, she began to call out the names of those friends, servants, and family who would receive her special attention with a gift. When someone outside was rewarded, they were brought inside.

Finally, the moment came to give her father his gift. She called for him to come and receive what she had for him. He came forward, had with him the old, deposed chief, Kaniache, whose hobby was American clothes.

Shunned by his tribe, he had followed Maxwell closely for months. His clothing nearly matched Maxwell's.

Virginia reached inside the open trunk and lifted the lid of a hat box. She drew out a black silk hat and started to give it to him. He drew back in shock, his arms raised as if to accept it, his fists suddenly tight.

He shouted, "Who in the hell do you think I am!" He took the hat, pulled it down over the head of old Kaniache, wheeled him around, and kicked him all the way down the room, into the hall and out into the street, leaving the poor girl on the floor sobbing as if her heart would break.[363]

It was July in Washington when Wertheim and Gompertz, Dutch bankers, requested Congress to consider approval of the U. S. Freehold Land and Emigration Company's incorporation. It was unprecedented. Debates

---

[363] Prince Papers, Historical Notes & Events, "Maxwell Land Grant," Box 14020, Folder 8. NMSU, *The Raton Reporter,* July 1872, from an earlier address to the Kiwanis Club, given by M. W. Mills, a former Maxwell attorney.

continued for four months before its resolution. The act passed the House and Senate with an amendment. It permitted a railroad to lay its rails over the public domain from a convenient point on its possessions to connect with one of the Pacific railroads.[364]

On July 27, 1869, the Colorado Freehold Land and Emigration (Limited) was incorporated in London.[365] This company succeeded the one Fisher originally founded in 1868. Its capital stock was £300,000 in 15,000 shares of £20 each. It would assume the subscription pledges of the former organization. The new company aimed for the purchase of the northern half of the land grant. "Emigration will be directed to the most productive districts of Colorado and other States and Territories of the United States." Trustees and shareholders were almost exclusively Americans.

---

[364] Brayer, Herbert O., *The Spanish-Mexican Land Grants*, Vol. I, "The Costilla Estate, 1843-1870," pp. 83-85.
[365] Ibid., p. 76.

When August arrived, an Army officer was placed in charge of the Cimarron Indian Agency. Captain Alexander Keyes performed an inspection tour and did an inventory. Despite his age, Lucien believed him to be efficient. His duty was a new assignment for the Army. The agency's Indians were about to arrive home from their summer hunt. Among the shortages, one item was particularly alarming: blankets. On hand were only thirty-nine, and there were 1,300 natives soon to return to the premises.

There was no precedent for solving the problem. Keyes called on Lucien Maxwell. They decided to ask the former agent, Erasmus Denison, a civilian living in Santa Fe, for advice. Maxwell accompanied Keyes to the capital. The outcome of the trio's conference was that if the goods were withheld, a war would likely break out when the Colorado Indians would join their brothers.

There were no military forces in the area. Keyes must contact his superiors in Colorado. The Indians arrived in mid-September. They asked for their clothing, tents, and blankets. Keyes wrote headquarters. What was on hand were knives, forks, and beaver traps, nothing useful, he explained.

He asked, "I would respectfully inquire if there is no possibility of my getting more blankets, and of a better quality than those I have? They are really in need of them," he wrote."[366]

The answer came back from the Indian Affairs Commissioner. If the Utes would go to their Colorado reservation, they would "find provision made for their care and comfort at that place; and until they do so, it is not the intention of the Department to furnish them with articles of any description."

---

[366] Murphy, Lawrence R., *Lucien Bonaparte Maxwell*, Chap. 6, "The Cimarron Agency," p. 143.

On July 20, a surprise announcement came from the Treasury Secretary, George Boutwell. The first payment on the public debt had come due. Boutwell happily announced that an additional $6,000,000 was found.[367] When asked for the source, he stated that it came from miscellaneous sources. He would elaborate no further.

Congress was in bitter debate for over five months on whether the remaining $356 million in "greenbacks" still in circulation should be redeemed. The topic may have affected the gold market because President Grant was known to have the intention of selling gold. The gold price plunged from 162 to 135, ruining many speculators. The September 24 date became known as "Black Friday." Somewhat later, on October 26, 1869, the *Daily New Mexican* carried an item concerning the gold market. It read, "Gold is creeping down among the twenties again. We guess that the gold gamblers and national robbers of

---

[367] Santa Fe New Mexican, 7/20/69.

Wall and Broad Streets have made their last grand raid, the late panic was their final gasp. *God grant it.*"

In Cimarron, Keyes was dismayed that his recent appointment was already threatened. He turned to Lucien for help. The pleas of the Indians were not heeded until December 7 when Lucien wrote a long letter to his friend, Brigadier General William S. Grier at Fort Union. "I am able to state . . . . . that unless prompt measures be taken to anticipate & prevent an outbreak, it will be *sure* and *terrible*." He had known Grier for nearly twenty years. The discontent of the Indians was alarming and dangerous to the whole neighborhood. Troops were needed. Only the immediate stationing of a "military force of cavalry" at Cimarron could prevent war. Lucien continued, "I trust for the sake of humanity that this warning and entreaty shall be heeded and acted upon immediately."

Grier at once forwarded the letter to his commanding officer, General George W. Getty. On

December 13, Getty ordered a hundred cavalry forces to Cimarron "to be prepared in case the Utes and Apaches should terminate their present attitude by active hostilities."

The additional blankets appeared at once. Agent Arny at Abiquiu received orders to buy an additional 450 blankets and deliver them to Cimarron forthwith.

Lucien's survey advisors continued to offer further evidence of the grant's boundaries as authentic. They could provide witnesses. There were mounds erected in the 1840s, still standing, which could be identified by "lawful witnesses as yet living in this vicinity." Everyone including Congress in approving the patent, Mexican officials at the time of donation, knew that the grant was larger than eleven square leagues. It soon became clear that the Secretary of the Interior was not expected soon to render a formal decision authorizing the survey of the grant. At this time Chief Justice Joseph Palen arrived in New Mexico.

A hearing was conducted at Santa Fe in August. Its purpose was to collect materials to be sent to Washington. Among them was "an authenticated copy" of the original sketch map showing the grant boundaries. There were two letters believed to be Maxwell's with copies of documents from the Santa Fe archives.

On September 3, Wilson acknowledged receipt of the documents at the Interior Department sent by the Maxwell Grant advisors. He wrote back that Spencer must not re-start the survey until the Secretary of the Interior rendered a formal decision authorizing it.

Influential lobbyists were sent to Washington to work for a favorable decision.[368] At the time Jacob D. Cox was Secretary of the Interior. He was an advocate of civil service reform. His opinion, written on December 31, intimated suspicion of big business. He focused on the claim that Congress created a new grant without limiting its

---

[368] Murphy, Lawrence R., *Lucien Bonaparte Maxwell*, Chap. 8, "The Sale of the Maxwell Grant," p. 183.

size. His decision to reject the survey would apply to all Mexican colonization grants in the future.

Relations between Maxwell, the Cimarron reservation, and Fort Union were close. Maxwell's ranch, and his role as government contractor, served Fort Union with beef and agricultural products. Until the end of war, at least a thousand civilian men were employed at Fort Union.[369] A community surrounded the fort. William Moore, the sutler and contractor at Fort Union, and William Kroenig of another successful nearby ranch, lived at Fort Union and were Lucien's friends.

Even in winter many visitors came to the area, some curious about developments around Elizabethtown and the mining camps. Most of the town's residents had returned to the more populous towns of Trinidad, Pueblo, and the village surrounding Fort Union, for the winter.

---

[369] Murphy, Lawrence R., *Lucien Bonaparte Maxwell*, Chap. 7, "The Greatest Gold Producer on the Globe," p. 152.

However, someone visited the Apache agent, Captain Keyes, and reported of him to the Colorado *Tribune* in January. That person stated that he had seen "Capt. Keyes who claims to be agent for what are known as 'Maxwell's Utes' and a few Apaches. He has goods and makes issues to them. He is young and sweet on Maxwell's daughter. The milk in the cocoanut is satisfactorily accounted for," the letter stated.[370]

In Colorado, ex-Governor Gilpin sought to confirm gold deposits on the Sangre de Cristo Grant, land located mostly in Colorado, reaching into New Mexico, and bordering the Beaubien-Miranda Grant as well. He brought in several other interests to develop the grant for sale and arranged with a mining expert and his team to assess the value of the estate. A crew of ten men accepted the assignment.[371] The ex-governor was under pressure to pay taxes on the land. He had paid roughly 40¢ an acre on the

---

[370] Ibid., p. 144.
[371] Brayer, Herbert O., *William Blackmore: The Spanish-Mexican Land Grants of New Mexico and Colorado*, p. 67, Denver, 1948.

estimated one-million-acre property purchased from the remaining Beaubien-Miranda heirs.[372] Gilpin counted on the property's production in mineral resources until settlement could be affected.

The *Gazette* newspaper was sold in Santa Fe to the latest Grant appointee, the Territorial Assessor, Alexander Sullivan. In the first issue of *The Santa Fe Weekly Post*, people learned that a gala was held for the retiring *Santa Fe Weekly Gazette* editor. The affair was described in its first issue on September 2. The paper would be Republican and partisan, but independent of cliques. Mr. Sullivan assumed a sanctimonious role, inferring *The Daily New Mexican's* editors had a private agenda and he would be the people's watchdog.

The *Daily New Mexican* offered a rejoinder which did not suit him. In October, Sullivan wrote that: *A certain ring of demagogues in this city and Territory misrepresent*

---

[372] Ibid., "The Costilla Estate," Chap. 2, p. 67.

and malign all who are not in the ring, for the same purpose that the real villain cries "stop that!"- viz - to hide a dirty record. . ."[373]

The Weekly Post's editor announced on September 1 that John Watts was leaving the next week for Washington to complete the arrangements for the Santa Fe National Bank. All capital had already been paid in and a temporary organization was formed. On October 1, the paper continued its attack on the *New Mexican*. Sullivan's position as assessor was withdrawn in December.

A war was clearly stated between the two competing "Republican" newspapers. *The Daily New Mexican* was launched in October 1869 when reduced rate telegraph service east and west became available to the public.

It was mid-summer when Steve and Sallie Elkins' second daughter arrived. Then, sometime between August

---

[373] Santa Fe *Weekly Post*, 10/1/69.

and November Steve Elkins was quietly reinstated as District Attorney. It was early November when the *Weekly Post* announced that the couple were leaving for the East. "Mrs. Elkins takes the trip with especial view of improving her health."[374] They were expected to return by December.

The unusual comment appeared on November 4, 1869, under items concerning the travels of the Territory's citizens. Family news, and family members' health issues, were not subjects normally printed in public journals of the era. Steve Elkins would be absent for several weeks to attend to his wife's health concerns.[375] Elkins' experience when challenged by Governor Mitchell in 1866 was still fresh in his mind. He had also challenged federal interests in rejecting Heath. It was dangerous to leave the Territory without prior leave. It was also dangerous to insist on equivalent justice. In this instance the majority supported him, and rules apparently were waived in the case of his

---

[374] Ibid., 9/6/1869, p. 1, col. 2.
[375] Ibid., 11/6/69, p.1, col. 2.

wife's medical emergency. The news item was likely not criticized because the motive for leaving was not his personally, but explained by a family illness which was critical.

Sallie's medical problems were not known in the community but were clearly a result of childbirth. She had delivered a baby girl in July.

On July 1, Tom Catron opened his private Santa Fe law office. He would cover for Steve in matters concerning the new baby and Sallie's recovery.

The Maxwell team received Secretary Cox's decision to reject the land grant claim on January 2, 1870. The next working day Watts wrote a reply on behalf of Maxwell and asked to withdraw the request for the survey and deposit. He then privately contracted with Griffin to complete the survey.[376]

---

[376] Ibid., p. 181.

Chapter Fifteen: "New Mexico All Right"

January 1870 – October 1870

John Watts and Jerome Chaffee left for the east coast in December to build a case for the validity of the Maxwell Grant to present to the prospective buyers. Chaffee was Colorado's incoming Congressman. He was also the president of the 1st National Bank of Denver when the new option was being written for the Maxwell Grant sale in January 1870.

Wertheim and Gompertz made a second provisional contract to market the mortgage bonds of the Costilla Estate. The contract would be effective when Congress passed the company's incorporation.[377] The Colorado territorial incorporation occurred on February 14 in the Denver Secretary's office. George Clark, David Moffat, and George Randolph covered for the foreign owners.

Dr. Bell's promotional book, *New Tracks in North America,* was published in London sometime in early 1870. It was designed to put the nearly two-million-acre grant in a favorable light. Many of Bell's notes from his work with General Palmer on the survey were used to compile the booklet.[378] It was available before the grant's expected purchase on April 30. John Collinson was listed as co-author with Bell, and he would be the visible figure as a part of the syndicate making the purchase.

---

[377] Brayer, Herbert O., *William Blackmore and the Spanish-Mexican Land Grants,"* The Costilla Estate", p. 81.
[378] Ibid., 182.

The company was organized under New Mexican laws and held temporarily by local citizens. Territorial laws did not specifically authorize foreigners to hold real estate. The home ranch of 1,000 acres, another 15,000 acres, a one-half interest in the Montezuma, one-sixth of the Aztec, eight quartz lodges, six placer claims, and several lots in Elizabethtown and Cimarron City were exempted.[379] Collinson and Chaffee worked together in London to raise the capital and organize the Maxwell Land Grant and Railway Company.

The Secretary of the Interior was so incensed over the presumption of ownership that he shortly afterward instructed his department members to regard the entire grant as public land open to settlement under United States law.

The reservation Indians were not wanted by the English syndicate. Another location would be sought for

---

[379] Pearson, Jim Berry, *The Maxwell Land Grant*, Chap. Three, "Maxwell Sells the Grant," p. 49.

them. Colorado and New Mexico began a determined effort to absorb the Cimarron agency's Indians in their territories. Each wanted their businessmen to share in the lucrative contracts Maxwell had held for so long.

Lucien joined the promotional team selling his grant. He traveled to New York, Boston, and Philadelphia to talk to prospective buyers. His hunger for the sophistication his daughter observed in St. Louis grew proportionately. His spending habits became more lavish and impulsive. It was said that in New York he purchased four pianos for his home. These had to be shipped to New Mexico at great expense.

Virginia and Lieutenant Keyes were sympathetic with the intent of the tribes to remain on the grant. They anticipated adequate food and clothing for the residents. The younger Indians became restive, not knowing where their home might be. Virginia missed the friends she made at school in St. Louis. There were no contemporaries at

Cimarron. Her connection to Alexander Keyes was natural for a young woman of nineteen who craved the company of others her age. They both knew her father would not allow them to be married, but their purpose was set for it. A major obstacle was the difference in their religion. Secondarily, they feared to be the object of his wrath.

Virginia and Alexander intended to find the opportunity to marry during her father's frequent absences in support of the grant's sale. In January, Keyes requested a transfer from the Cimarron agency's management. He stated that his assignment had become public knowledge and undue gossip resulted. He was told a replacement would arrive in April. They took precautions to conceal the arrangement. Virginia could not get the cooperation of a priest. She conspired with Mrs. Rinehart, the miller's wife, to find a protestant minister. Reverend Harwood agreed to conduct the ceremony.

March 30 was ration day. Hundreds of Indians crowded around the mill yard to receive their meat and flour. Virginia left the main house in late afternoon to meet Alexander. She had prepared the third-floor room for the event. It was carpeted with buffalo robes. Alexander was waiting. Mr. and Mrs. Rinehart served as witnesses and a Methodist service was conducted. The Rineharts signed the marriage certificate and Virginia returned to the kitchen of her home. Luz asked Virginia where she had been.

"I went down to see the Indians and I got weighed," she answered. "Guess how much I weigh?"[380]

The arrival of Alexander's replacement agent was delayed, and the couple waited until mid-May to leave.

On April 6, 1870, the president of the Kansas Pacific Railroad wrote a letter to the citizens of New Mexico. It was intended for publication in the *Santa Fe*

---

[380] Murphy, Lawrence R., *Lucien Bonaparte Maxwell*, Chap. 6, "The Cimarron Indian Agency," p. 147.

Daily New Mexican to call attention to the advantages of rail traffic the Kansas Pacific offered. Respectfully, he told the people that his railroad always appreciated the importance of their trade. He stated that the Kansas Pacific could not at present compete for the Santa Fe Trail route due to the distance from the railroad's business terminus to its chief distribution points.[381]

Mr. Perry offered several charts showing distances from key points such as Sheridan, Colorado to St. Louis, and the savings for wagon trains in freighting at present government rates. Sheridan was the end of the Kansas Pacific line in Colorado. The government rates were $1.15 per 100 pounds and 100 miles. The Butterfield mail contract was canceled May 11, 1869, when the Central Pacific and the Union Pacific met in Utah.[382] The coach cost of mail delivery was $1100 per mile. By railroad, the cost was only $200 per mile.

---

[381] Santa Fe *New Mexican*, April 12, 1870, p. 1, col. 3.
[382] Ibid., 5/16/69, p. 2, col. 3.

New Mexico's Union Democrats were in disarray. Pratt was the only survivor. They suffered many setbacks in 1869. Their losses began in November 1868 with the death of Frank Higgins, Governor Mitchell's district attorney appointee of 1867. In November 1868, Charles Clever renounced his party, asking to be a "people's" party candidate supporting the Grant administration, in hopes of saving his Congressional seat.[383] James Collins' death in June 1869 delivered another stunning blow. Tom Catron, a former Confederate officer, announced himself a Republican. He was named to the legislature from Dona Ana County in 1866 and made District Attorney for the Third District the following year. He served as Attorney General in 1870. On February 4, 1870, President Grant nominated Herman Heath for U. S. Marshal.[384]

The *Daily New Mexican,* wrote of the *Post*'s editor, "A. P. Sullivan, 'editor and publisher' of the Santa Fe *Post,*

---

[383] Ibid., 11/10/68, p. 1, col. 1, "Clever as a Republican."
[384] Santa Fe *Daily New Mexican*, 2/5/70, item dated from Washington, p. 1, col. 4.

has gone to Washington, in the interest of the anti-administration party of New Mexico, composed of copperheads and self-styled-for-the-sake-of-office republicans and sore heads, who affiliate and use what influence they have for the interest and benefit of the democratic party of the Territory . . . he only lacks ability and discretion to be dangerous."[385]

Following the telegram sent in April 1870 to the Senate Judiciary Chairman by Republicans and Democrats alike, Heath was finished in New Mexico, and the census began. There would be two-hundred-fifty deputy U. S. Marshals working to compile the figures.[386]

The promotional material on the Maxwell Grant was ready for distribution in London early in 1870. In the booklets the authors described William Griffin as a "United States Government Deputy-Surveyor." The promoters avoided mentioning that the official survey had been

---

[385] Ibid., 7/7/70, p. 2.
[386] Ibid., 3/30/70, p. 1, col. 1.

canceled. Watts and Chaffee continued to build their case for the validity of the grant to present to prospective purchasers. Watts promoted his credibility and professionalism. He named his many offices in New Mexico, and described the grant as "good, valid, and perfect according to the laws of said territory."[387] It was misleading at least since the size of the grant was all that was in question.

Maxwell's deed read "2,000,000 acres of land 'more or less.'" The buyers needed assurance that New Mexican laws would specifically authorize their ownership of the grant. They finally agreed the land could be held nominally by well-known authorities. An Amsterdam syndicate of bankers financed the Maxwell Grant's sale. Their collaboration became clear in a transaction of June 13, 1870, when 7,000 first-mortgage bonds of £100 each

---

[387] Murphy, Lawrence R., *Lucien Bonaparte Maxwell*, Chap. 8, "The Sale of the Maxwell Grant," p. 182.

were conveyed to the trustees in a trust deed for eleven twelfths of the Grant.[388]

Once the documents were signed, and the money delivered, Brunswick was the messenger to take the papers to Luz for her signature. A telegram was sent to Luz saying, "New Mexico all right." That telegram was the signal for her to sign the deed and turn it over to the company's representative, Mr. McFarland. Relieved of what had become a terrible burden, by May 2, Maxwell set out for home with either $600,000 or $750,000 in cash. All was carried out, and the deed recorded in the Elizabethtown courthouse by July 23, 1870.[389]

Three prominent New Mexicans were chosen to incorporate the new company in Santa Fe. The men who came forward were already associated with the Maxwell Grant's sale: Governor William A. Pile, Surveyor General

---

[388] Pearson, *The Maxwell Land Grant*, Chap. Three, "Maxwell Sells the Grant," Chap. Three, "The Maxwell Land Grant," p. 58.
[389] Murphy, Lawrence R., *Lucien Bonaparte Maxwell*, Chap. 8, "The Sale of the Maxwell Grant," p. 185.

T. Rush Spencer, and attorney John S. Watts. While Lucien was in New York, the company's articles of incorporation were acknowledged. It was May 12, 1870, and signed by Territorial Secretary Wetter.[390]

When Lucien returned home in early June, he quickly learned of Virginia and Keyes' elopement, their wedding conducted on the third floor of his mill by a Protestant minister. He raged for a week, searching for Reverend Harwood to kill him. Fortunately, there were those who warned the pastor. Lucien had sworn that if anyone dared ask for Virginia's hand, he would kill the man. Harwood was conveniently absent. Now, she had been swept away from him because of his own short-sightedness.

It was not until late July that Lucien was able to accept that Virginia was gone. He signed over his Cimarron property to the Maxwell Land Grant & Railway Company

---

[390] Ibid.

on September 7, 1870. John Collinson, the Maxwell Company's incoming president, prepared to set up the property's office in the ranch home. He notified a friend from England, John L. Reed, that he would like for him to serve as vice president and chief executive officer. It was none too soon.

On September 3, Lucien Maxwell called a meeting to organize the First National Bank of Santa Fe. It was conducted at his home in Cimarron. The only person present from Santa Fe was W. W. Griffin, the surveyor of the Maxwell Grant. He had not yet completed his unofficial mapping of the grant. The rest of the group, besides Maxwell, were Charles Holly, Henry Hooper, John Watts, and Lucien's son, Peter.[391]

The previous December, Maxwell signed the letter to the Comptroller of the Currency applying for a federal charter. Maxwell alone provided the $150,000 capital for

---

[391] Ibid., Chap. 9, "Reflections on a Frontier Life," p. 189.

the new enterprise. At the September 3 meeting he distributed among the five members present, Henry Hooper, ten shares, Charles Holly, two hundred shares, John Watts, ten shares, and his son, Peter, ten shares.

The attendees voted to issue stock certificates bearing "impressions of the bank's president," Lucien Maxwell. John Watts, then the Territory's Chief Justice, moved "that certificates of stock to the amount of two thousand shares be procured and have [Maxwell's] photograph engraved thereon." Maxwell signed many of them in blank. Also ordered in the meeting was that the bank officers demand the Bank be designated as the U. S. Depository and that the bank procure on the best terms possible the use of the U. S. Depository in the Palace of the Governors in Santa Fe for banking purposes."[392]

Local citizens and miners alike grumbled about foreigners when Maxwell prepared to leave. The company

---

[392] Walter, A. F., *The History of Banking in New Mexico Before 1900*," Speech given before the Newcomen Society on May 23, 1955.

agents and officials who attempted to force expulsion notices were helpless in the face of armed and determined mobs. Land company officers continued to manage the property as if there were no question concerning their title to the estate. The Secretary of the Interior, Columbus Delano, assured the company that the act confirming the Grant to Beaubien and Miranda was equivalent to a patent.

To encourage the public's confidence in the new owners, the Justice of the Peace, Judge McBride, was asked to speak to the disgruntled residents. A meeting was called for October 1 at the Cimarron courthouse. A crowd gathered early. The meeting proceeded quietly while many questions were asked by those attending. McBride answered honestly, listening to their protests. He responded that there was no legal recourse at present. They could not remain without eventually being arrested. Money had been exchanged and Lucien was satisfied.

Although the discussion was orderly, the miners were firm in arguing that those who worked the mines and tilled the soil had stronger claims than either the English or the Indians. They demanded a United States patent be produced, an authorized survey conducted, and the boundaries of the grant clearly defined. The crowd broke up and hung around the courthouse, talking and complaining. The mood grew more intense as dark approached. Outside, torches began to be lit.

The gathering mob turned toward the home of Judge McBride. Other torches were lit and thrown on the Judge's porch. The house went up in flames.[393]

Steve would carry out his role as U. S. Attorney. Steve and Judge McBride quickly determined the law must be called on for help. They must ask Santa Fe authorities to send for the military. An appeal was telegrammed to Santa Fe. Governor Pile was in the southern district, but Secretary

---

[393] Murphy, Lawrence R., *Philmont*, Chap. IX, "The Colfax County War," pp. 117-118.

Wetter sent word to Fort Union for troops. He then issued a proclamation "authorizing and requiring" local county officials to organize posses, arrest lawbreakers, "maintain peace, and protect the lives and property of citizens."[394] In turn, he asked for the military at Fort Union to intervene. General Getty called up a force of 100 men to leave at once for Cimarron. It was two a.m. before peace was restored.

The reservation Indians became demanding and confrontational. The new Cimarron agent who followed Captain Keyes was Captain W. P. Wilson. At first Wilson found the Indians quiet and moved to Fort Union for companionship. When the tribes learned of Maxwell's departure their tempers flared. A tribal Indian was shot while breaking into Maxwell's store. They threatened violence and Agent Wilson called for help from Santa Fe.

---

[394] Ibid. Also, Santa Fe *Daily New Mexican*, 10/28/70; Santa Fe *Post*, 10/29/70, "The Elizabethtown Riot," p. 1, col. 4; Pearson, Jim Berry, *The Maxwell Land Grant*, Chap. Four, "The English Syndicate in Trouble," p. 63.

W. F. M. Arny heard of the problem and rushed to Cimarron to investigate. It was nearly ration day. He called a conference with the chiefs. They told him that San Francisco, who acted as tribal attorney for the Apaches, was drunk and shot himself accidentally. However, the Indians told him the agent moved to Fort Union and was at the reservation only when annuities were distributed. They let it be known they allowed Maxwell to live on their land. They would not let a British company take possession. They would "clean out the country."[395] Authorities were called in to provide temporary provisions.

When Lucien heard of the Indians' insistence that they owned the land, he knew it was time to leave. Collinson had repeated the offer for the property when he returned. It consisted of the 1,000-acre ranch, the buildings, a store in Elizabethtown, merchandise worth $50,000 from his three stores, his stock, all farming utensils, twenty

---

[395] Murphy, Lawrence R., *Philmont,* Chap. VIII, "Redskins and Britishers," p. 109-111.

wagons, his mining claims and leases, all for $50,000 cash and $75,000 to be paid in one year.

In a meeting with Steve, Lucien gave the company a warranty deed for the listed properties and accepted a mortgage deed to secure the $75,000 promissory note on September 7 at ten per cent interest. After his arrival home, the animals were turned over to the company within two weeks. Steve rejected a hundred horses, but the mules, two hundred cows, oxen, and yearlings were included in the arrangement.[396]

Collinson began posting signs throughout the grant property that people holding mining claims, or right to work them, were to report to him by September 10, 1870, in person. If not, they must write a letter giving a full statement of the claim. "All persons not reporting will be regarded as trespassing and will be ejected.[397]

---

[396] Murphy, Lawrence R., *Lucien Bonaparte Maxwell*, Chap. 9, "Reflections on A Frontier Life," p. 194.
[397] Pearson, Jim Berry, *The Maxwell Land Grant*, Chap. Four, "The English Syndicate in Trouble," p. 63.

Ownership asserted, Collinson began to establish a newspaper, lease property, and negotiate a contract for mail delivery. Collinson and Elkins may have thought Editor Sullivan's loss of office might mean his income could stand a boost. Elkins and Sullivan arrived on September 22. The contract Sullivan signed that day provided him with a minimum of $500 in advertising and a guaranteed subscription of 500 copies. A rental building would be furnished for no more than ten per cent of the cost. Sullivan promised to produce a twenty-four-column weekly newspaper in Cimarron. The first issue would be ready on October 1.[398]

On the same day, Collinson wrote his first lease with the U. S. Mail contractors, Barlow, Sanderson, & Barnum. The contractors agreed to pay four dollars annually for four years to build a half-acre station near Crow Creek for the stage route between Santa Fe and the

---

[398] Ibid., p. 55.

railroad terminus. The grant company gave the mail contractor an exclusive right to sell goods and whisky and fund a hotel or an eating place on the lease. In return, the mail contractor would purchase grain and food for all stations on the grant and issue free passes to the land company executive. Collinson further contracted with Barlow Sanderson & Company giving his promise to furnish stables, grain, food for eight animals, and board, for a stock tender at the Cimarron station for $2600 a year.

The next lease, made somewhat later, was to Henry Porter, the telegraph wiring contractor who rented the Cimarron store from the company for $1200 annually. The company would receive five per cent of sales over $4,000 and sold him all the store's stock at St. Louis prices, plus freight.[399]

It was now October and the population had dwindled. Collinson wanted a hotel for guests arriving in

---

[399] Ibid., p. 56.

the area, possibly to buy land. Henry Lambert's hotel moved from Elizabethtown to Cimarron where the county seat resided.

The reservation Indians continued to be troublesome for the new owners. There were rumors that their contract for provisions would expire on the first of the new year. Agent Wilson requested transfer and the new agent, Charles Roedel, a Presbyterian nominee, would not arrive
until late in the year.[400]

At year's end Secretary Cox resigned. It was reported that he protested the President's bowing to political patronage instead of asserting his determination to exercise civil service reform. Cox had ruled against at least one other large mineral claim by capitalists to accumulate extensive land holdings. The General Land office of the Interior Department now questioned whether the Maxwell

---

[400] Murphy, Lawrence R., *Philmont*, Chap. VIII, "Redskins and Britishers," p. 111.

Grant was possibly a valid claim or public land open to settlement. Secretary Columbus Delano succeeded Cox in 1870.

The Denver and Rio Grande Railroad was chartered in New Mexico in February 1870. All major authorities in New Mexico signed the chartering papers in the Territorial Secretary's office.

The coming year would present many rival issues: railroads, riots, and competition from the Maxwell Grant's Colorado sister grant, the Sangre de Cristo's Costilla Estate.

Chapter Sixteen: Politics, Riots and Railroads

January 1870 – January 1871

In January Delegate Chaves introduced several bills in Congress to provide for Indian tribes. He also called for a bill to regulate the salaries of the Territorial Supreme Court Judges. In

February, he introduced a bill to define the northern border of New Mexico. In March he asked

Congress to support Pueblo education. There were nineteen pueblos and seven-thousand Pueblo people. Three Pueblo chieftains requested that Congress might provide teachers for their people. After much pressure was applied, his amendment in favor of the Pueblos was passed.[401]

In late January, Delegate Chaves presented the Enabling Act for New Mexico in Congress. It provided for a state constitution. The procedure required the legislature to authorize the people to write a constitution and arrange for a general vote on statehood to be taken in all precincts. The success of the proposition depended upon the census to some degree since the population in the area would dictate the number of representatives the Territory would be allowed in Congress. The people of New Mexico were concerned that their cooperation might lead to higher taxes.

---

[401] Santa Fe *Daily New Mexican*, 3/17/70.

In late February the proposed convention on statehood was addressed in an issue of the *Weekly Post* in which Editor Sullivan charged that it was a political "swindle" to suggest that any Democrat would be allowed to co-operate in the State movement. The *Daily New Mexican* replied that Sullivan intended his paper to influence Republicans to believe that the party meant to shut out Democrats from participation in the matter.

At present, Delegate Chaves could only introduce bills and take part in discussions of territorial matters in Congress. New Mexico had more citizens than the other territories, but most were below the poverty line. Local officials argued that enactment would secure the liberal concessions usually made by the federal government in favor of public schools and internal improvements.

The legislature proposed a convention on the constitution, the first step in statehood application. It was set for June 6 at Pena Blanca. After an early meeting on the convention, the *Daily New Mexican* complained that Editor Sullivan presumed to be the Republican leader while seated beside the most prominent Democrat in the Territory. The editors of the *Weekly Post* protested immediately.[402] The spat between the *Weekly Post* and the *Daily New Mexican* continued through the legislative session.

At the same time, it was a known fact that Sullivan hired only Democrats and attended meetings seated with Democrats.[403] His continual attacks on the efforts to pass statehood cost him the loss, once again, of his Collector's office. On March 24 George A. Smith was named U. S. Collector for the District of New Mexico. Smith apparently did not arrive, and Byron Daniels' name soon appeared in the newspapers as the new U. S. Collector. Sullivan's dismissal spurred his efforts as a dissembler in other matters as the year commenced.

---

[402] Ibid., 2/22/70, "The State Question," p. 1, col. 1.
[403] Ibid.

In late April *The Chicago Evening Journal* reported that New Mexico, under the new name "Lincoln" would likely be approved for statehood. It further stated that the Territory, although a constant drain on the federal economy, was rich in mineral wealth. It would soon benefit from the arrival of the Southern Pacific Railroad. It but needed to be rid of Indians and to have the advantages of railroads. Similar comments from other newspapers were expected throughout the country in the coming months. Four territories had applied, and all would likely be approved, among them Colorado and Wyoming. The issue would be considered until July when Congress was ready to close.

Colorado was favored in Congress with many influential lobbyists. The owners of the Sangre de Cristo lobbied Congressmen from their respective states until the spring.

Consideration of the foreign company's incorporation measure in Congress was unprecedented. It would be debated for four months. It was amended and permitted a railroad to lay its rails over the public domain from a convenient point on its possessions to connect with one of the Pacific railroads. The measure had to pass both the House of Representatives and the Senate. It would also confirm certain legislation in Colorado pertaining to incorporations. The main route of the New Mexico railroad would run from the New Mexican northern border to El Paso in Chihuahua, Mexico. General Robert C. Schenck, a member of the House Ways and Means Committee guided the measure through the House.[404] A branch line would run to Denver and connect New Mexico directly to the East.

The Maxwell Grant's production was being credited elsewhere to fulfill other objectives. In February, Professor Hayden wrote to William Blackmore asking him to

---

[404] Ibid., p. 85, fn. 56.

transmit an enclosed letter to Morris Bloomfield, the assayer for the Maxwell Grant. Blackmore asked Bloomfield to provide Professor Hayden with information concerning the operation and land at the Maxwell mines. He asked about the water production from the Big Ditch. Bloomfield reported it as 600 inches. Hayden was forwarded a thorough description of the area of "about 60 miles" and given the precise latitude and longitude, the height above sea level, and many other salient details. He was told that the mint returns "do not credit us with that much, for the reason that much of the gold sent away goes to Denver in Colorado, where it is then reported as 'Colorado Gold,' and more that is reported as 'Montana Gold.'"[405]

Bloomfield told Hayden of the labor cost and the average amount earned daily among the independent miners' claims. The abundance of timber was described. He

---

[405] Ibid., "Appendix B," pp. 345-350.

included the operation costs and production report of a claim which was the most expensive to open.

When the water supply in the Big Ditch began to fail in August, one claim reduced its work force from ten or fifteen men to three. The men worked day and night. Bloomfield supplied the cost of water per inch from the Big Ditch and enclosed a table of the company's water rates. The number of miners and tradesmen employed for every hundred inches of water to the mines was also provided. Two mills were operational, and the amount of money generated in the previous year from the 15-stamp mill was reported as $200,000. It began to be used in November 1868. The second mill of 30-stamps had not been in use long enough to report on it.

Bloomfield also supplied Hayden with such other features of the Maxwell mining property as the cost of goods needed in the area to feed these people. He was told that for every dollar of gold removed, it cost several dollars to produce it.[406]

The owners of the Sangre de Cristo lobbied Congressmen from their respective states until the spring. It was March 7 when Senator Anthony introduced the bill to incorporate the Freehold Company. There was much adverse opinion of the bill, but it was sent to the Committee on the Territories where it did not have a formal hearing and was opposed. It was sent to the Senate with an adverse report. Senator Anthony intervened and had the bill sent again to the Committee on Territories in March.[407]

The next Congressional matter was related to regional land development and the promise of a railroad to draw settlement from countries likely to send emigrants into the Arkansas and Moreno Valleys where the rich gold deposits were found.

---

[406] Ibid.
[407] Brayer, Herbert O., Vol. I, *The Spanish-Mexican Land Grants*, "The Costilla Estate," pp. 83-85.

New Mexicans followed the progress of General Palmer and the Kansas Pacific Railroad. In fact, as early as February 28, 1870, Palmer advertised through *The Daily New Mexican* for freighters to carry ties for the Kansas Pacific. They would travel from the end of line, turn off at Trinidad, and go via Pueblo to the Kiowa tie camp. There, they would haul ties to the railroad grade west of Kit Carson.[408] These ties would be used to complete the Kansas Pacific to Denver. During the spring of 1870, the Kansas Pacific moved toward Denver. A new wagon road was opened to Fort Reynolds to ease the movement of supplies and equipment to Pueblo.[409]

Former Maxwell Land Grant and Railway Company's brief President, William Palmer, was forced to step up his drive to reach Cheyenne for the last leg of the Denver road. He laid the final fifty miles on August 15. Free of his contract to complete the road, he was now able

---

[408] Santa Fe *Daily New Mexican*, 2/28/70, p. 1, col. 1.
[409] Brayer, Herbert O., *Early Financing of the Denver & Rio Grande Railway,* 1869-1870, p. 24-25.

to develop his own plans. He went east to prepare for his wedding and discuss the proposed railroad with his friends in Philadelphia.

Palmer described the Monument Valley tract Governor Hunt acquired for him in 1869 to his fiancée in March 1870.[410] It would be the target of his first stop on the north and south railroad from Denver. The draft of a prospectus for a colony was drawn by a specialist from the east. It was sent to Dr. Bell to make inquiries among British investors to test interest in such an undertaking. The financial plan was conceived as a subscription project to be presented to Palmer's friends in the east. Most of the land was acquired from the U. S. government at $1.25 an acre. The plots already taken were acquired for from five to ten dollars an acre. A large part was paid for in agricultural college scrip said to have cost eighty cents per acre.

---

[410] Brayer, Herbert O., *Early Financing of the Denver and Rio Grande Railway,* 1869-1870, p. 21, fn. 30.

Hunt agreed, for a fee, to purchase the land to build a colony. The land was near Pike's Peak. The area had a desirable mineral spring with a fine farm and grazing land. It was ideal for a health and recreation resort. Their venture would be called "Fountain Farms Trust."[411] The members would contribute to a fund for land purchases. The enterprise faced certain legal problems. Palmer decided an independent company might build the "North and South" railroad to skirt the problems involved in combining the railroad with a subscription land development.

Keeping the plan secret would avoid raising land prices, so that a preliminary company was established: the Rio Grande Railway and Telegraph Company was drawn and filed in New Mexico in February. Palmer was not yet free of his Kansas Pacific contract.

As early as January 29, 1870, the *Rocky Mountain News* pointed out the importance of the new narrow-gauge

---

[411] Ibid., pp. 17-18.

road to Denver. *The Denver News* countered with criticism of the narrow- gauge feature. The railroad's promoters immediately responded with "An Address to the People of Central and Southern Colorado." They explained that the demands of a railroad in mountain country requiring branch lines to the mines were the same in Europe. The narrow-gauge was extremely successful in similar regions there. This feature represented economy and was assuredly the safest means of transportation in conditions such as those in Colorado.[412] It was expected this line would serve New Mexico.

A network of business combinations was developing between the speculators in Europe and the Coloradans bent on selling southwestern undeveloped land. The success of the enormous enterprise hinged on railroad construction. At the same time, Congress had denied further land grants to railroads. The grants had proven

---
[412] Brayer, Herbert O., *William Blackmore: Early Financing of the Denver & Rio Grande Railway,* "Financing the Railway, 1871," pp. 54-57.

disastrous. They were used to sell off the adjoining lands for profit and create adjacent towns with no supporting industry. The process became called "town booming." The railroads soon defaulted while the promoters profited.

William J. Palmer proposed his own independent network of railroads and businesses designed to develop the entire region. It began with a complex of a single major railroad and seven branches which would provide business returns to the entire region.[413] It has become known as "phase capitalism." William Blackmore would become involved in the vast enterprise when he subscribed to Palmer's program and connected his private investment group to the railroader's venture of 1871.

The railroad enterprise avoided association with land grants by requesting right-of-way from Congress rather than a request for land. Each of the new companies to be founded were separate construction companies. Each

---

[413] Brayer, Herbert O., Vol. II, *Early Financing of the Denver and Rio Grande Railway*, p. 29-30.

had different members of Palmer's organization apply for financing. They appeared to be presidents of the separate companies. Palmer had the advantage of knowing where the most valuable properties were located and would be able to acquire these lands to generate some profits along the time-consuming process of railroad construction.

While Maxwell's new grant option was being signed in New York in late April, the entire team of six Sangre de Cristo owners appeared in Washington to lobby for the Congressional bill to incorporate the U. S. Freehold Land & Emigration Company.[414] The company was already established in London.

The company's purposes were stated in a manner to appeal to those interested in settlements of foreign emigrants in the territories of Colorado and New Mexico. The incorporators intended to survey, lay out and establish wagon roads, railroads, and other means of transit.[415]

---

[414] Brayer, Herbert O., Vol. I, *The Spanish-Mexican Land Grants*, "The Costilla Estate," pp. 78-88.
[415] Santa Fe *Daily New Mexican*, 6/14/70, p. 1 col. 2.

In Denver, the group of Coloradans who served as incorporators for the U. S. Freehold Company included Charles Lambard and Jerome Chaffee. This incorporation was part of a plan to finance the intricate undertaking that Blackmore and Fisher had originally filed in London, the Colorado Freehold Land Association, Ltd.[416]

The lobbying conducted by the Sangre de Cristo owner's group was successful in getting the support of Senator Henry B. Anthony of Rhode Island. He introduced the bill to incorporate the United States Freehold Land and Emigration Company. When the bill came up in Congress, it was referred to the Committee on the Territories and submitted to the Senate in an adverse report. It was then moved toward an indefinite postponement.

Senator Anthony succeeded in having it recommitted to the Committee on the Territories. Debate

---

[416] Brayer, Herbert O., *William Blackmore: The Spanish-Mexican Land Grants*, "The Costilla Estate," p. 70.

was heard for four months before the House and Senate approved the measure on July 8, 1870.

A new contract was made which superseded the previous agreement of 1869 giving Blackmore and Lambard of the Sangre de Cristo interests a liberal amount of the proceeds of the sale of the "Land Mortgage Bonds".[417] On July 14, 1870, Morton C. Fisher deeded the 500,000-acre Costilla Estate to the land company for $500,000. The accolades went to Blackmore.

Blackmore examined Fisher's booklet promoting the grant and commissioned a travel author to write a concise and attractive booklet on Colorado. These resources likely inspired the one developed by Chaffee, Wilson Waddingham[418], John Collinson, the English real estate investor, and William A. Bell. They marketed the

---

[417] Ibid., p. 85, fn. 56, and p. 86.
[418] Ibid., "The Vigil and St. Vrain Grant, 1871-1877," p. 126, fn. 3. Also, Remley, David, *Bell Ranch*, Chap. 3, "Wilson Waddingham," pp. 67-124. Waddingham was a speculator of the first order.

Maxwell Grant. Collinson was previously associated with Dr. Bell, General Palmer's former survey photographer.

Unlike the advances being made in Colorado, New Mexico's oldest and most successful mining company had run onto major problems. On March 9, Steve advertised for a company bookkeeper.[419] On March 18, former Governor W. C. Rencher succeeded Elkins as the company's resident agent. For a short time, Elkins remained as company attorney.[420] An advertisement for the sale of stock in the New Mexico Mining Company appeared in the *New Mexican* on April 16.

Michael Steck was at his native home in Pennsylvania in 1869. The greatest part of his wealth was tied up in the mining company's stock. In April 1869 he began farming on the old family acreage. He bought farm machinery. He had built a fine home in Muncy, Pennsylvania. He and Lizzie now had two daughters. When

---
[419] Santa Fe *Daily New Mexican,* 3/9/70, p. 2, col. 3.
[420] Ibid., 3/18/70, p. 1, col. 3.

he learned of the company's plight, he visited former Judge Brocchus and attempted an appointment in New Mexico as governor.

The advertisement for the 354 stock shares were for sale for non-payment of assessments. Four days later the owner of the stock was named. Payment of the owner's assessment could satisfy the debt, if paid in cash: $900. The sale would take place on May 18 on the Public Plaza in Santa Fe between 11 a.m. and 1 p.m.[421] The outcome of the sale was not announced. Members were being assessed for the annual taxes of the company since there were no earnings. The situation became more critical, and Colonel Anderson was dismissed as manager.

The stockholders were deceived. Many wanted the company sold. Many others failed to pay the assessments and allowed the stock to be sold at public auction.

---

[421] Santa Fe *Daily New Mexican*, 4/16/70, p. 1, col. 3.

Colonel Anderson had employed Steck's directions but did not keep a careful estimation of the ore reserves. A twenty-five-stamp mill was purchased, and a large work force employed, over three times the men formerly working at the mine. There were also sixteen administrative personnel. Problems setting up the stamps occurred, and the treasury was emptied in the attempt to double the mill's capacity.

Abraham Rencher, a former Governor and major stockholder, used his influence to have his son appointed the new manager. The directors fired Anderson and hired the son, also editor of the Santa Fe *Democrat*. The result was not profitable. Dr. Steck's suggestions for improvement had no effect. The directors attempted to sell the company. Steck held considerable stock and remained hopeful.

In the spring, the people of Santa Fe were concerned with matters in the capital and were unconcerned with Maxwell's grant sale. On April 2, 1870, *The Santa Fe Weekly Post* accused Librarian Ira Bond and Governor Pile of destroying public documents. The documents had not been catalogued and placed in airtight containers. Bond complained of the legislature's failure to make an appropriation to preserve the library. The two officials tried to order the storage area to provide a room the Attorney General could occupy.[422]

On April 6, Bond issued a statement in the Santa Fe *Daily New Mexican* that several knowledgeable members of local Mexican families examined papers and books being considered for destruction. Those that were deemed useless were left on the dirt floor of an adjoining and unused room.[423]

In mid-April, the *Daily New Mexican* reported a loud public outcry over the records' destruction. One week later, Bond posted a notice, "All persons having any of the

---

[422] Santa Fe *Weekly Post*, 4/2/70.
[423] Ibid., Santa Fe *Daily New* Mexican, 4/6/70, p. 2, col. 1, "Letter of Ira Bond, Librarian," Territorial Library.

papers recently removed from the Palace in their possession, are satisfied that they were removed by mistake as to their value; and all such persons are requested to return them at once to the Library."

The issue would not die quietly, and the *Post* quickly capitalized on citizen's concerns. A public meeting was held on the matter and reported on April 16. Grant owners were responsible to prove the ownership of their lands, provide maps and thorough descriptions of their properties, give evidence of the recognition of the Mexican government, and submit any formal documents related to their right to the land.[424] The matter had grave political effects.

Sullivan's charges against Governor Pile were not limited to the problem at the library's archives. The editor also charged Pile with trying to buy himself a seat in the Senate for dividing offices evenly with the Democrats for

---

[424] Santa Fe *Weekly Post,* 4/2/70, Santa Fe *New Mexican,* 4/16/70, p. 1, 4/23/70, p. 1.

passage of the statehood act.[425] Sullivan responded to a column in the Santa Fe *Daily New Mexican*. He stated the author was not qualified to speak of Republicanism since his remarks "were very bad grace coming from a Quantrell raider."[426]

Throughout July the *Santa Fe Weekly Post* hammered the *Daily New Mexican* with attacks on its attitude toward statehood and the "fusion" movement, as Editor Sullivan interpreted it. Sullivan perceived the governor was a "bolter, looking after his own personal career interests." He charged that the Republican leadership did not elevate statehood above party concerns. He likened Governor Pile to Governor B. Gratz Brown of Missouri, a secessionist who departed from his Republican Party and favored the restitution of former Confederates.

During the legislative session Steve Elkins and his partner, Tom Catron, had contributed their time to the

---

[425] Santa Fe *Weekly Post*, 10/1/70, "The Governor's Defenders," and "Conspiracy Most Foul," p. 1, cols. 1 & 2.
[426] Ibid., 7/9/70, Item, p. 1, col. 1.

writing of the Constitution. When a committee of the legislature, aided by local attorneys, including Steve Elkins, drew up the Constitution, the work had been an unusual coalition of Democrats and Republicans. Despite the successful coalition, Sullivan and the *Weekly Post* charged that the Constitution was the "laughing-stock of Congress."[427]

Sullivan's own choice as a "model Constitution" was the one designed by the state of Illinois. He declared he was in favor of the state movement and noted that an editor at *The Daily New Mexican* was hostile to the movement at first. That editor, he said, stated that the distribution of offices was a "minor consideration." Sullivan believed that statehood had become

the tool of a ring of office seekers in both parties who were doing all in their power to destroy the Republican Party.[428]

Amidst the clamor of the political parties' battles, suddenly, Maxwell's New York grant sale resurfaced when

---
[427] Ibid.
[428] Santa Fe *Daily New Mexican*, 7/9/70, "Consistency," p. 1, col. 3. Also, articles in *Post* from 7/2/70 and 7/23/70.

it was learned that he was on his way home with either $600,000 or $750,000. New Mexicans also soon heard that Lucien Maxwell was leaving the Cimarron country. During his absence in New York his son placed a bid to purchase Fort Sumner, now in the newly designated Lincoln County, about 90 miles south of Cimarron. The cost to bid on the land was $5,000.

Peter did as he was told. However, on April 26 *The Daily New Mexican* published that "in a few months" public land in New Mexico would be for sale. They learned the acquisition of government property required special arrangements to secure title to the land. Lucien would own the buildings, but not the land beneath.[429] The amount of land was nearly 14,000 acres. He had purchased only the buildings. The land had to be transferred from the War Department to the Department of the Interior. He had not secured title to the 13,645 acres beneath the buildings.[430]

---

[429] Murphy, Lawrence R., *Lucien Bonaparte Maxwell,* Chap. 8, "Reflections on a Frontier Life," p. 191.
[430] Ibid., Chap. 8, "Reflections on A Frontier Life," p. 194.

The Maxwell's soon found that no action could be taken on his petition until February 24, 1871. At that time, Congress would enact a special bill declaring the land for sale. Lucien wrote that he wanted a private non-competitive sale for a minimum price of $1.25 an acre. He was told that an 1858 statute prohibited the preemption or homesteading of abandoned army posts.

The reservation land had to be appraised and offered at public auction for no less than its estimated value. He appealed that he and more than one hundred settlers had moved to the fort before the passage of the special act. They considered that land title would result from their ownership of the buildings, but his plea was ignored.[431]

Between April and June Congress considered an amendment from the Committee on the Territories to change New Mexico's name to "Lincoln". The proposal did

---

[431] Ibid., pp. 194-196.

not excite a favorable response in the Territory. Those people questioned about the change answered that the President's name was respected and loved but the Territory had a unique heritage that should not be ignored. A new territory might take on a beloved President's name, but the legal records of the Territory, the courage and patriotism of its people in the Civil War, merited saving its name.

The issue was tabled in the Committee on the Territories just before the close of the Congressional session. The issue effectively closed the effort to field a vote on statehood. It would have to wait for at least another year.

A meeting of the new Maxwell company was held in Cimarron on May 18, 1870. The Board of Directors for the first three months included: John Watts, William A. Pile, General Palmer, John Pratt, W. A. Bell, and Miguel Otero. The Board elected General Palmer the temporary President, Governor William A. Pile, Vice-President, and J.

C. Reiff, Secretary. The officers would serve for the transition period.

The next meeting of the company was held on June 13. The articles of incorporation chartered the company to operate for 49 years with a capital stock of five million dollars.[432] At this meeting President Palmer and Secretary Reiff conveyed a trust deed for eleven-twelfths of the grant to Thomas A. Scott and Samuel M. Felton. They were appointed trustees for 7,000 first-mortgage bonds of £100 each. The bonds must be redeemed by a drawing at par July 1, 1895. They were payable at London or Amsterdam in £700,000 or 8,400,000 Dutch guilders.

The interest was fixed at seven per cent every January and July, free of U. S. taxes. John Collinson was elected company president.[433] The financiers were likely part of a joint venture between banks in Great Britain with Wertheim and Gompertz.

---
[432] Pearson, Jim Berry, *The Maxwell Land Grant*, Chap. Seven, "Maxwell Sells the Grant," p. 50.
[433] Ibid.

The lack of money was a concern of all, perhaps a bit more in New Mexico than in most areas of the country. There was a perpetual shortage in the Territory. On February 7, 1870, the Supreme Court ruled in the *Hepburn v Griswold* legal tender case brought from the Court of Appeals of Kentucky, that the decision of the lower court was sustained. Contracts made before the legal tender law could not be discharged in U. S. dollars.

Citizens' concerns for the return of coin to currency and the retirement of greenbacks were addressed in a short announcement in early March. The Santa Fe *Daily New Mexican* carried an item on the status of gold. "The decision of the Supreme Court and the sudden tumbling down of gold, is rapidly bringing the whole country to a specie basis . . . quite a number of persons are paying their debts and some of the eastern cities are paying their bonds and interest in gold or its equivalent – we hope for a speedy return to specie payment."[434]

On March 4, gold was announced at the lowest reached since August 1862: 112 ½. The drop was attributed to the weakness of foreign exchange.[435]

On May 28, 1870, Palmer, Colonel Greenwood, and Captain Schuyler organized and incorporated *The Southern Colorado Railway.*[436] Their intention was to build to Kit Carson, then to Fort Lyon on the Arkansas, and to continue through the Arkansas Valley to Pueblo. The same day a serious competitor appeared for the southern route. This group consisted of Kansas Pacific officials and Denver promoters. They called themselves *The Colorado and New Mexico Railway Company.* They had two routes in mind. They would proceed from the Kansas Pacific terminus at Kit Carson to Fort Lyon, then Las Animas, and to Albuquerque. The second route was planned for a line from Fort Lyon to Las Animas, and then to Pueblo.

---

[434] Ibid., 3/8/70, p. 1, col. 2.
[435] Ibid., 3/9/70, p. 1, col. 2. From New York, March 4.
[436] Ibid., p. 25.

In early June *Kansas Pacific* officers, John D. Perry and James Archer of Denver visited Pueblo, Colorado and stated that their railroad would be "pushed to completion during the coming fall and winter."

In Santa Fe just after the New Year began, Mr. Little, U. S. Depositary, announced that the Comptroller of the Currency had authorized the First National Bank of Santa Fe to begin business.[437]

Several years before, in 1867, the national banking system was introduced. It helped to standardize regulations on loans, deposits, bonds, and securities. When Lucien Maxwell received his bank charter, the bank was entitled to $241,000 as New Mexico's pro rata share under the new national bank currency bill.[438] That could be added to his own capital share of $150,000. New Mexicans could finally deposit their money locally, get loans, and accrue interest on their deposits. They would no longer have to travel to

---

[437] Santa Fe *Daily New Mexican*, 1/3/71, p. 1, col. 2.
[438] Santa Fe *Weekly Post*, 7/23/70, "National Prosperity," p.1, col. 3.

Colorado to do their banking or use the local federal depository where interest rates were not competitive.[439]

At the end of July 1870, the Santa Fe *Post* carried a letter from the office of the Comptroller of the Currency addressed to each member of Congress concerning the distribution of money apportioned to provide additional banking facilities in each state and territory. It asked for a report of the amount of capital needed in each district, where it was needed, the estimated population and business of each place, as well as the amount of circulation that would meet the actual demand.

The Comptroller added that it might be necessary for him to call on Congressmen to provide information on the character and standing of the parties applying for authority to organize banking associations.[440]

---

[439] Ibid., p. 1, col. 3.
[440] Santa Fe Weekly *Post*, 7/30,70, p. 2, col. 2. "Banking Facilities," from the Treas. Dept. Office Comptroller of the Currency, Washington, D. C., July 18, 1870.

Despite such bleak economic reports, and rumors of bribery in congressional circles, money appeared to be available for railroads. Financial arrangements were being made for the *Denver and Rio Grande Railway* between England and Europe's financial backers, Palmer's Philadelphia support, William Blackmore, William P. Mellen, Robert Lamborn, Governor Alexander Hunt, and Captain Schuyler. Palmer was named company president.[441] Construction would not begin until the next year.

At nearly the same time, the Congressional *Globe* published on June 2 that the U. S. Freehold Land and Emigration Company asked Congress to give the right of way over public land for a railroad. It would cross the company's lands and continue to the nearest railroad. The company was said to own about a million acres of land in Colorado and the same in New Mexico. It was stated in open Congress that twenty-thousand emigrants were

---

[441] Ibid., p. 30

expected from Holland. The local newspaper asked: Where are the lands of the U. S. Freehold Land and Emigration Company situated?"[442]

All the earmarks of a Wall Street speculative swindle applied to the Maxwell Land Grant sale, *The Santa Fe Daily New Mexican* observed.[443] Short of a miracle, its debt was overwhelming.

Promoters of the bond sales pool in England were Wilson Waddingham, Chaffee, Chilcott, and Holly. They had been in England promoting the grant and establishing a syndicate to purchase it.

The *Daily New Mexican* stated that Editor Sullivan was working with and on behalf of the Governor's enemies.[444] Troubled rumblings, like approaching hoof-beats, came late in the year when Sullivan's *Weekly Post* carried a rumor that Governor Pile and President Grant had recently met.

---

[442] Ibid., 6/14/70, p. 1, col. 1.
[443] Ibid., 8/9/70, p. 2.
[444] Ibid., 9/30/70, p. 2.

Someone knew of the Governor's request to receive the original appointment he sought in Brazil.[445]

Complaints of Steve's appearance at Judge McBride's speech before disgruntled citizens at Cimarron plagued his office in Santa Fe as U. S. Attorney. He consulted with Chief Justice Palen and resigned as U. S. Attorney resulting from the Elizabethtown riot.[446] He would favor his position as officer and attorney for *The Maxwell Land Grant & Railway Company*. He could not continue in two opposing positions at once. He was concerned for his family and was deeply involved in the Santa Fe community.

Sallie's medical condition continued. She left for Missouri in late September, accompanied by Tom Catron. They returned by November 1.[447] The previous urgent visit in September 1869 indicated this was a flare-up of the same problem which warranted further care. Steve's business

---

[445] Ibid., 10/19/70, p. 2, col. 2, "President Grant and Gov. Pile."
[446] Santa Fe *Weekly Post*, 10/12/70, p. 1, col. 2.
[447] Ibid., 11/4/70, Local Briefs, p. 1.

concerns demanded his presence in the Territory. A relatively recent arrival, S. M. Ashenfelter, Esq., assumed the U. S. District Attorney position for District One at Santa Fe.[448]

On the Maxwell Grant, the Cimarron Squatters Club would not recognize the right of *The Maxwell Land Grant & Railway Company* to collect rents from mining claimants.[449] The issue was validity of title. They demanded a patent from the company.

There were at least two legal documents which could be in conflict: the first, the decision of Jacob Cox ordering Surveyor General Spencer to claim only twenty-two leagues. Opposing it was the original deed from Maxwell stating the grant's size as 2,000,000 "acres more or less," and Commissioner Delano's answer to the Maxwell Land Grant's officers. The act confirming the

---

[448] Ibid., 11/26/70, p. 1, col. 2, Local Briefs.
[449] Santa *Fe Daily New Mexican.*, 1/2/71, p. 1, col. 2.

Grant to Beaubien and Miranda itself was equivalent to a patent.[450]

The squatters' club decided to employ an attorney and begin a lawsuit on March 31. They would test the validity of the Maxwell Company's claim. They staged mass meetings in front of the county courthouse to collect funds and demonstrate strength.[451]

An article entitled, "Governor Pile: A Grave Political Delinquency" appeared in the *Weekly Post* on October 11. Sullivan pointed to the Constitutional election scheduled by the legislature for the first Monday of October, 1870. The Governor was required to issue his proclamation for a general election thirty-days in advance. He had not done so. Sullivan's article continued to maintain that the Governor, to advance himself politically, attempted to "fuse" with the Democrats of New Mexico.[452]

---

[450] Pearson, Jim Berry, *The Maxwell Land Grant,* Chap. Four, "The English Syndicate in Trouble," p. 62.
[451] Murphy, Lawrence R., *Philmont*, Chap. IX, "The Colfax County War," p. 118, fn. 2, p. 233, 9/10/70-4/21/71.
[452] Ibid., 10/22/70, p. 2, col. 3.

The editor focused on the 1870 legislature as an illegal session. Congress decreed that the territories could manage their affairs in bi-annual legislative sessions. Sullivan stated that the present members of the lower House would serve in the House again the next session.[453] The members of the legislature, nevertheless, voted a large subsidy for *The Moreno & Rio Hondo Railroad*. Its distance was announced as forty-seven miles and was expected to be complete by June 1, 1871.[454]

In Colorado, when Palmer returned from the east in October, another railroad contender was waiting: the *Denver and New Mexico Southern Railway Company*.[455] This company had designated the same route as the proposed *North and South Railway*.

Wilson Waddingham, a real estate speculator known to Palmer's group, visited Palmer on October 24.

---

[453] Ibid., 12/18/70, p. 2, col. 1, "The Legislature."
[454] Santa Fe *Daily New Mexican*, 1/30/71, p. 1, col. 2.
[455] Brayer, Herbert O., *Early Financing of the Denver and Rio Grande Railway*, Vol. II, 1869-1870, pp. 26-27.

When asked to invest in the enterprise, he was enthusiastic. His cash investment was $50,000 and he authorized Palmer to sell his Maxwell Grant stock while he was abroad on his honeymoon. Palmer reported to Mellen that Waddingham's investment was worth a quarter of a million dollars. It was enough to finance the preliminary Denver and Rio Grande organization. Two days after Waddingham and Palmer met, the General was prepared to file the articles of incorporation of *The Denver & Rio Grande Railway Company.* A day-long meeting elected officers and *The Rio Grande Railroad and Telegraph Company* of New Mexico was then merged with the new Colorado corporation. The leader of the competing group filed a formal notice of dissolution the same day.

William Palmer was in Europe on his honeymoon when he and William Bell made a call on William Blackmore at his country estate near Croyden.[456] Many

---

[456] Ibid., pp. 41-42.

investors sought him out since his successful sale of the Costilla Estate bonds of the United States Freehold Land and Emigration Company to the Dutch firm of Wertheim and Gompertz. That day the two entrepreneurs would test their own facility for persuasion. They covered the founding of the Denver and Rio Grande enterprise, describing its potential, and outlining the program for establishing a "pool" to finance its construction. They encouraged Blackmore's interest in founding colonies, pointing out the projected road would enter the San Luis Valley. It would be near, or even cross, the lands of the United States Freehold Company. Blackmore's enthusiasm was ignited, and a plan began to be formed.[457]

Like so many other intentions, this one would prove to be entirely impractical.

---

[457] Ibid., pp. 43-45.

Chapter Seventeen: Steve Elkins

January 1871 – September 1871

It was March when Steve read of a Santa Fe connection to the new cattle trade business at Cheyenne. A former Santa Fe resident, Mr. McAuliffe had apparently made a profitable purchase of Lucien Maxwell's 4,000 heads of cattle the previous year.[458] He had taken a cue from Lucien himself, Kit Carson, and Uncle Dick Wootten. These older

---

[458] Santa Fe *Weekly Post,* 3/4/71, p. 1, col. 1, "Local Briefs".

New Mexicans had made their first fortunes delivering animals to market.

McAuliffe was only one sign of improving market conditions. Steve was headed to Las Vegas to attend District Court.[459] While there he would attend a meeting of the Moreno and Rio Hondo Railroad. He would have to contend with Will Dawson, *The Cimarron News* editor. At the last meeting of the railroad interests, Dawson spoke disparagingly of the Maxwell Company's prospects for a railroad. Steve didn't care about whose railroad might come into the Territory, just how soon?

Sallie was concerned about Steve's frequent trips to Cimarron. He was worn out from traveling.

His own concern was for Sallie and the children. He would not have them live at Cimarron. If the residents had a problem with him, it was one thing, but he would not put his family in danger. His secondary concern was banking.

---

[459] Ibid, 3/11/71, p. 1, col. 2

New Mexico needed money to fund schools, roads, bridges, and public buildings. A railroad was crucial to moving coal and other heavy minerals. Coal was abundant on the grant. When business boomed, the bank could contribute to the general economy. Loans could be made, partnerships established, and incorporations formed.

So far, the business climate was generally improving. A new method of water extraction was being tested by the Artesian Well & Mining Company. They announced their solvency and gave an accounting of their costs and expenditures in a public statement. Lehman Spiegelberg and Sam Ellison were company leaders, men who could claim successes in previous attempts. Spiegelberg was a long-time merchandizer and financier of many projects. The artesian well business would serve the placer mines across the Territory.

The Atlantic & Pacific Railroad promised the 35th parallel route. Its land grant of several years previous would be a forty-mile strip of land across New Mexico and Arizona.

The census announcement at the end of January confirmed that New Mexico's population led those of other territories. The only discouraging company was the New Mexico Mining Company. Their production level did not justify the expansion of its staff.

When Steve returned to Santa Fe, the *Daily New Mexican* announced that the National Bank of New Mexico would soon be in operation.[460] Steve had to replace Ashenfelter as District Attorney. Ashenfelter was unable to stop the Comanchero trade on the Llano Estacado and cite the proper legal authority. He returned to Santa Fe to oversee the challenge to Lucien Maxwell's 1st National Bank of Santa Fe as well. He had assembled a new bank application. Their own bank was recently authorized by the Treasury Department to begin business. Steve had adopted

---

[460] Ibid.

the New Mexico charter of an earlier territorial bank. Their officers would be outstanding members of the Santa Fe community.[461] He had forged a union between leading Democrats and Republicans over the bank matter.

There were other assurances the Territory was on a progressive course. The Atlantic & Pacific Railroad was on schedule.[462] In 1866 it had received a forty-mile land grant across Arizona and New Mexico. It promised the railroad crossing on the 35th parallel which William J. Palmer sought for the Kansas Pacific.[463]

What information was available at a Las Vegas meeting on the proposed Rio Hondo Railroad would address concerns about drilling for water across settler's lands. Some authorities may have been alerted and could provide useful data. Disgruntled citizens were easily

---

[461] Ibid., 3/23/71, p. 1, col. 3.
[462] Ibid., 1/16/71, "The Atlantic & Pacific Railroad, p. 1, col. 1 and 1/26/71, p. 1, col. 1.
[463] Lamar, Howard R., *The Far Southwest*, Chap. 18, "Politics and Progress," p. 401.

deceived. The reality of the plan, and the million-dollar financing budget it needed, had to be explored.

On January 30, 1871, the Territory's population appeared in an article of the *Daily New Mexican* giving the ranking of each state and territory. New Mexico led the territories with a population of 86,245. Pueblo Indian Agent Arny would later qualify the number further. The total number of wild Indians in New Mexico indicated there were 4,278 wrriors; 5,326 women, 4,745 children, a total of 14,349 natives. These Indians were not included in the official census.[464]

On April 1, the *Weekly Post* published a letter from Delegate Chaves to Senator Trumbull, Chairman of the Senate Judiciary Committee. It had been sent the year before, on March 4, 1870. The letter had recently been published in the Elizabethtown *Argus*. Delegate Chaves' letter was a complaint of the actions of the Santa Fe Bar

---

[464] Santa Fe *Daily New Mexican*, 1/31/71, p. 1, col. 2.

Association.[465] According to Chaves, the members of the Bar wrote the Judiciary Committee an objection to the confirmation of H. H. Heath who was nominated for Territorial U. S. Marshal. Chaves noted that he had not been sent a copy of the parties who signed the letter opposing Heath's confirmation.

Delegate Chaves provided a biography of several members he considered the leaders of the movement against Heath. He first condemned Steve Elkins. He stated that Elkins had avoided the draft in the war, his father and brothers were in the Rebel Army, and he was a Seymour and Blair man, Missouri Republican "bolters." Chaves said that he had Elkins removed last spring, but his successor became ill and resigned.

Chaves then pointed to former Chief Justice Benedict who was "completely demoralized from the use of ardent spirits." The Delegate had just learned that Benedict

---

[465] Santa Fe *Weekly Post,* 4/1/71, p 1.

was recently called to court to explain why he should not be struck from the Roll of Attorneys. There were other statements denouncing Benedict. Chaves named other Bar members who also denounced Heath.

There were rumors that such a letter was circulating in the halls of Congress, but it was likely hoped it would not be known in the Territory until the election was over. A majority was needed to support Chaves even though most people likely recognized the man's attraction to villainy.

There was little that could be done to counter the charge. It would only create further disturbance and open a greater gap between the party's factions. Publishing the letter only three weeks before the convention was part of Sullivan and the Democrat's strategy to destroy Republican party unification. Who could the Democrats possibly put forward who would command a presence in Washington?

The county delegate election conventions began in Santa Fe on April 12. They met at the Probate Court on

Wednesday at four o'clock. Elkins called the packed convention room to order. W. W. Griffin was made permanent chairman. Griffin was a political unknown, but a familiar and congenial figure. The permanent organization was formed, and A. P. Sullivan moved for a committee of five to appoint delegates to the Territorial Convention. The committee was composed of a mix of regular Republicans with Sullivan, the rogue Republican. They were unable to agree and responded with two separate reports. The first report was not affirmed, and the second was read. Sullivan and two known Democrat committee members signed one report. These men had been on the Democrat ticket in the previous election.[466]

The report of known loyal Republicans was affirmed, then signed by Elkins and William Manderfield, *The Santa Fe Daily New Mexican* editor. Sullivan's faction went into the street to collect supporters but failed to do so.

---

[466] Santa Fe *Weekly Post*, 4/8/71, p. 1, cols. 5-6.

The Santa Fe county convention adjourned with eight Republican delegates who satisfied the majority. The counties were in conflict over the revelation that Delegate Chaves had denounced several of the Republicans' most prestigious members.

Afterward, Jose Sena, whose wife's family were prominent party members in San Miguel County, asked Steve to attend their nominating convention. Elkins would take his wife, and Tom Catron would join them. Sallie could visit her friends in Las Vegas.

The Santa Fe *Daily New Mexican* revealed that the rule of political ethics was in effect. The friends of the candidate could attend and assist in the proceedings of a convention. They were bound by its action although unfavorable to their candidate.

The Post assisted in organizing the proceedings. It moved for a committee of five to be appointed to nominate delegates to the convention. Sullivan made himself its chairman. He insisted on having six delegates for his candidate. The convention adopted the report of the minority rather than his own, and he repudiated the whole proceedings. He called for a convention to be held within thirty-six hours after the minority report was issued. None of these developments were reported to *The Daily New Mexican*.[467]

Editor Manderfield charged that Sullivan was deemed by "the President as a person unfit to hold the responsible position of Collector of New Mexico, despised by all Republicans as a traitor and disorganizer, a beggar upon our streets for the necessary means to support his bankrupt concern and relieve him from the pressing claims of creditors . . . ."[468]

The San Miguel County meeting revealed that Delegate Chaves had raised the ire of the members by naming a young man from the east to West Point earlier in

---

[467] Santa Fe *Daily New Mexican*, 4/19/71, p. 1, col. 1
[468] Ibid.

the year. Chaves' latest blunder turned the entire Republican county members against him. Sena declared himself a candidate for Delegate opposing Chaves.[469] They considered that Chaves' letter's denunciation of the bar, was reason enough to be rid of him. Steve counseled otherwise. Unity was needed and there wasn't time to groom Sena to go against Chaves.

Jose Sena's wife's family were the de Bacas, the most prominent and influential family in San Miguel County. They wanted to see Chaves defeated and someone else named as the Republican Congressional candidate. Jose Sena was nominated. He was attending the meeting and was willing to run for the office. He was respected by all as the legislature's translator since the war ended. He was also Santa Fe County's sheriff.

While Steve was meeting with the Las Vegas delegation, he was called out and informed his house in

---

[469] Santa Fe *Weekly Post,* 4/8/71, p. 2, cols., 6-7; Santa Fe *Daily New Mexican*, p. 2, col. 1.

Santa Fe had been robbed. He and Sena left at once. Steve left to collect his wife from her visit with the Dold family, their local friends.[470] Tom would stay to placate the other angry members. As Santa Fe County Sheriff, Jose needed to accompany Steve. Jose left immediately for Santa Fe, Steve and Sallie following.[471]

The Dold family had an ambulance and a relative who could take the couple home. Once home, Steve discovered the burglars obtained entrance through a window. The couple took stock of their losses and offered a reward for the return of much of their belongings. John Pratt suspected the invasion was more than robbery, likely intentional destruction based on political malevolence. Many flowers and minor losses were not items destroyed by someone intent only on financial benefit.[472]

---

[470] Ibid., 4/15/71, p. 1, col. 3.
[471] Ibid.
[472] Santa Fe *Daily New Mexican*, 4/12/71, p. 1, col. 1.

The necessity to move was evident. They needed to be in town where authorities were near enough that such an attempt to enter their home would never happen again.

Steve attended the Colfax County Convention which Editor Sullivan attempted to disrupt. In it, the public was encouraged to have confidence in the new grant owners. Judge McBride was invited to speak to calm the disgruntled residents. A crowd gathered early. The meeting proceeded quietly while many questions were asked. McBride answered honestly, listening to their protests. There was no legal recourse at present. They could be arrested. Money had been exchanged and Lucien was satisfied. The miners were firm in arguing that those who worked the mines and tilled the soil had stronger claims than either the English or the Indians. They demanded a United States patent be produced, an authorized survey conducted, and boundaries of the grant clearly defined. The crowd broke up and hung around the courthouse, talking and complaining. The mood grew more intense as dark approached. Outside, torches began to be lit.

The gathering mob turned toward the home of Judge McBride. Other torches were lit and thrown on the Judge's porch. The house went up in flames.

Steve would carry out his role as U. S. Attorney. Steve and Judge McBride quickly determined the law must be called on for help. An appeal was telegrammed to Santa Fe. Governor Pile was in the southern district, but Secretary Wetter sent word to Fort Union for troops. He then issued a proclamation "authorizing and requiring" local county officials to organize posses, arrest lawbreakers," maintain peace and protect the lives and property of citizens." In turn, he asked for the military at Fort Union to intervene. General Getty called up a force of 100 men to leave at once at Cimarron. It was two a.m. before peace was restored.

The Indians at the reservation became confrontational and demanding. When the tribes learned of

Maxwell's departure their tempers flared. A tribal Indian was shot while breaking into Maxwell's store. They threatened violence and Agent Wilson called for help from Santa Fe.

W. F. M. Arny heard of the problem and rushed to Cimarron to investigate. He called a conference with the chiefs. They told him that San Francisco, who acted as tribal attorney for the Apaches, was drunk and shot himself accidentally. They let it be known they allowed Maxwell to live on their land. They would not let a British company take possession. They would "clean out the country."

News of Lucien Maxwell's golden grant and its many resources, his ever-growing wealth, percolated through the eastern states and Europe throughout 1869. The news circulated in Eastern papers and multiplied as reports of the Sangre de Cristo's sale price followed.

While Steve and Sena were in Las Vegas, Lucien Maxwell, supposedly establishing his bank in Santa Fe, announced a horse race challenge. He would sponsor a race against his champion mare, "Fly." The news was a shock to all. The Republican Territorial Convention would meet in only nine days. The First National Bank had not yet opened. His bank, the first in New Mexico, was about to open, and he was urging a betting event. It was soon reported that a wag in Kansas City who knew Lucien Maxwell, and was also in banking, took his race challenge, printed on First National Bank stationery, and tacked it in his bank with the heading "Banking in New Mexico."[473] The problem was that Lucien Maxwell was not averse to horse racing and gambling, an unsuitable image for a banker.

News from Colfax County was reported several days later. On April 13, a riot took place at Cimarron between employees of the Maxwell Land Grant Company

---

[473] Murphy, Lawrence R., *Lucien Bonaparte Maxwell*, Chap. Nine, "Reflections on A Frontier Life," p. 200.

and independent miners.[474] Governor Pile rushed to the scene. Citizens and miners had formed a Squatters Club.[475]

Around forty Englishmen arrived in Cimarron several days previous. The Englishmen were armed on the 18th and took possession of the Maxwell Company's property. Major Wightman, the superintendent, broke down the door to the mine shaft through a funnel connection at the Montezuma Mine to begin work. The mine was divided in ownership between the Maxwell Company and "Big Jack" Cazart, an independent owner.

It was later reported that a band of Maxwell Company employees marched into the mine and began to work. No amicable settlement was made on the entry matter and work had been suspended for the winter.

The shaft's opening to the Montezuma was on the eastern side owned by Cazart. The mine was eighteen miles

---

[474] Pearson, Jim Berry, *The Maxwell Land Grant,* Chap. Four, "The English in Trouble," p. 63.
[475] Murphy, Lawrence R., *Philmont*, Chap. IX, "The Colfax County War," pp. 117-118.

from Cimarron. The local miners learned of the early entry by "foreigners" and made haste to arm themselves at Cimarron. They marched to the mine, some breaking off to construct a gallows on the route. Wightman heard of the coming mob and had a guide lead him through the mountains to Cimarron. The twenty-six company men, with an assayer, had been issued six-shooters. The men remained hidden until the next morning when Governor Pile and troops arrived. The Governor issued a proclamation published on April 21.[476]

In response to lawlessness and violence, the authorities of Colfax County, the Sheriff, his deputies, the Constable, and Justices of the Peace, were to collect arms, the employees to return the same to the company. All unlawful and riotous combining together [of persons intending to resist or obstruct the peaceable possession and

---

[476] Santa Fe *Weekly Post*, 4/22/71, "Correspondence: Trouble in Colfax County, An Insurrection at the Mines," p. 2, col. 3. Also, Murphy, Lawrence R., *Philmont*, Chap. IX, "The Colfax County War," pp. 117-118.

working of all mines lawfully owned or claimed] by any person or company within said county is strictly forbidden." All persons must "submit their personal claims to property and their personal grievances or injuries to the decision of the courts whose duty was to decide such questions and administer impartial justice to all."[477]

The Governor remained for several days while tempers cooled, and the mob accepted the presence of military authority.

It was no longer a secret. The Maxwell Company was so desperate for labor that it sent to England for miners to work the Montezuma Mine. The English miners were soon sent home.

Several days later Congressman Chaves stopped in Cimarron to learn the latest news on his way from Missouri to Santa Fe to begin his race for Congress once again.[478]

---

[477] Santa Fe *Daily New Mexican*, 4/21/71, p. 1, col. 1, "Proclamation."
[478] Ibid., 4/22/71.

On April 22 it was published that the First National Bank of Santa Fe would soon open at the Fernando Delgado building on the plaza.[479] Two days later the *Daily New Mexican* reported that the stockholders of the National Bank of New Mexico would be holding an organizational meeting that afternoon. Citizens watched anxiously for the outcome of the stand-off between opposing banks.

John Watts had made a sudden trip to Washington in early April and returned on Tuesday, April 24, the day before the Bank of New Mexico announced its organization.[480] Stockholders of the new bank were: President, Jose L. Perea; cashier, William W. Griffin; Directors; J. L. Johnson, Manuel A. Otero, Thos. B. Catron, S. B. Elkins, and Jose L. Perea. The release boasted that all the "stockholders and officers are well known in our community as being men of undoubted integrity . . ." The bank's paid-up capital was $100,000. Unsaid was that the

---

[479] Santa Fe *Weekly Post*, 4/22/71, p. 1.
[480] Ibid., 4/25/71, p. 1, col. 2.

team of stockholders represented both Democrats and Republicans. They had assembled a non-partisan directory of officers and directors.

On Wednesday, *The Santa Fe Daily New Mexican* predicted that Editor Sullivan would "bolt" the Republican Convention, although he had denied it vehemently.

The much-anticipated Republican Territorial Nominating Convention finally arrived on April 29. The meeting began at 11 a.m. After the call to order, Steve Elkins nominated Salvador Armijo for temporary chairman. A. P. Sullivan nominated Anastacio Sandoval. Armijo received the greater number of votes and the meeting proceeded in the same manner, Sullivan countering each move with one of his own. The credentials committee was challenged but reported permanent officers unopposed.[481]

The resolutions included one offered by Steve Elkins calling for a voice vote in the decision of the entire

---

[481] Ibid., 4/29/71, p. 1, col. 1; ibid., 5/1/71, cols. 1-2, "The Territorial Convention."

assembly for Delegate. A. B. Sullivan was questioned as to the validity of his assumption of the four votes of Dona Ana County. He was permitted to be recognized since the votes would not change the outcome of the convention. The resolutions echoed the policies of the Republican Party, but Elkins added a further resolution supporting New Mexico's admission to the Union at as early a date as possible.

The chairman ordered a permanent organization be led by Tom Catron. The action reflected Sullivan's suggestion of a Territorial central committee. Such means would provide for distribution of documents and call meetings in a unified and competent manner. Four members were named with two secretaries also appointed.

Steve had invited Jerome Chaffee, Colorado's representative, to speak up for the joint resolution of New Mexico and Colorado for admission to Congress. Chaffee's presence at the convention was not regarded as acceptable by many.

The resolutions were presented in the afternoon session. One resolution was read which called for one of the supporters to receive the ballots for each candidate named. The representative would also announce the totals for his candidate. The resolution was not adopted. Elkins offered that the vote for delegate would be decided in a roll call by voice vote. The compromise was adopted.

Steve added a resolution that the convention unanimously be in favor of the admission of New Mexico into the Union as a state and the delegate nominated use his utmost efforts to secure the enabling act at as early a date as possible. The resolution passed.

When the nominees' names were read, Elkins moved for Chaves, and Sullivan for Sena. A vote of the sixty-seven delegates determined the winner was J. F. Chaves. Forty-four voted for Chaves and twenty-three for Sena. Chaves accepted the invitation in a brief speech.

Candidate Sena accepted the outcome and pledged his support for Chaves.

On May 2, 1871 the *Daily New Mexican* announced, "The stockholders of the National Bank of New Mexico have organized with the following selection of officers: President, Jose L. Perea; Cashier, William W. Griffin; directors, J. L. Johnson, Manuel A. Otero, Thos. B. Catron, S. B. Elkins, and Jose L. Perea." These were all well-known and trusted men of the community. Their founding capital was $100,000. The newspaper stated the bank would no doubt do a safe and successful business.[482]

When the daily paper made the pronouncement, Charles Holly knew the First National Bank of Santa Fe could not survive. The array of prominent citizens associated with the National Bank of New Mexico was too strong to challenge. Holly was from Colorado and Maxwell had not appeared for the First National's opening. Their

---

[482] Ibid., 5/2/71, p. 2, col. 1.

insistence that the Federal Depository must close was a lost cause. The few days they were open only a few individuals crossed their doorway. Maxwell failed to attend a meeting called on May 3.[483] There had been no meeting of bank stockholders and directors since the bank organized. Holly recommended Maxwell sell out to Elkins and his colleagues. Maxwell was bitter. He had faced several losses since his closure of the Cimarron properties. He finally appeared in Santa Fe on May 10, but it took much persuasion to turn over his stock shares to the Elkins faction.[484]

On May 1, *The Daily New Mexican* carried the news that J. F. Chaves was the Republican candidate for Delegate. On May 13 the newspaper admitted that it did not favor Chaves' election but would abide by the convention. They attributed their choice of another to Chaves' writing the Heath letter and thereby considering the claims of an

---

[483] Walter, A. F., *The History of Banking in New Mexico Before 1900*, Speech before the Newcomen Society, 1955, p. 19.
[484] Ibid.

individual above those of his collective constituents. The paper would do all it could to heal dissension in the ranks.[485]

Much had transpired during the preparations for the Territorial Convention and citizens sighed with relief that they could return to civic concerns.

On May 17, Maxwell released all but ten shares to the Elkins crowd. Holly also held ten shares. Elkins was elected absentee President and Jose L. Perea, also absent, Vice-President. W. W. Griffin was elected Cashier with a monthly salary of $100.[486] Their bank opened on Santa Fe's plaza. They adopted the name of the original bank: First National Bank of Santa Fe. The bank's money was delivered in February, in heavy snow, when "a large sum of money" consisted of $125,000 in currency, in denominations of fives, tens, twenties, and fifties.[487]

---

[485] Santa Fe *Daily New Mexican*, 5/13/71, p. 1, col. 1.
[486] The Newcomen Address of Mr. A. F. Walter, delivered on May 23, 1955, pp. 18-20.
[487] Santa Fe *Daily New Mexican,* 2/20/71, p. 1, col. 1.

The paper recommended the First National Bank's ability to handle government vouchers and checks on the Depository without further charge than the current rate of exchange, now three quarters of one per cent. This was a transparent reference to the advantage the First National Bank held over the Federal Depository.

By May 22, the First National Bank of Santa Fe announced several innovations as well as its increased capital of $150,000. They would issue blank check books and certificates of deposit. Their bonds were steadily increasing in value.[488]

In Indian matters, Colonel Pope was confirmed as New Mexico's Superintendent of Indian Affairs. W. F. M. Arny was appointed by President Grant as agent for the Pueblos in the Territory.[489]

---

[488] Ibid., 5/22/71, p. 1, col. 1.
[489] Ibid., 1/16/71, p. 1, col. 1, 1/26/71, p. 2, col. 2, and 1/19/71, p. 2, col. 2.

Chapter Eighteen: The Snake Sheds Its Skin

May 1871 – February 1872

It was widely known that Mr. Sullivan was deeply in debt and the *Daily New Mexican* continually sent him barbs on the subject. As much trouble as he was to Republicans, he was still able to receive an appointment on May 27 as Santa Fe's Postmaster.

Editor Sullivan took aim at those who would enter the Union with any sully of treason or the remotest sympathy with it. It could only be said that the sole official in New Mexico with provable Confederate loyalty in the war was Tom Catron to whom the inference had to be made.[490] Catron was part of the team of local attorneys who advised the legislature on the writing of the Constitution.

On July 9 another attorney advisor on the Constitution was challenged. The *Post* charged that an article in the *Daily New Mexican* of the previous week was written "with very bad grace from a Quantrell raider" who presumed to talk about Republicanism. There was always a great deal of undercurrent concerning the various officials and their backgrounds. District Attorney Elkins likely had the best credentials and most reputable sponsors of any official, but those also generated the most gossip. One of the remarks made against him was that he was part of William Quantrell's outlaw band. It had likely been heard that many of his students in Cass County where he taught

---

[490] Santa Fe *Weekly Post*, 6/17/71, p. 1, col. 1.

before coming to New Mexico were members of the outlaw's circle.

Although the *Weekly Post* continued its battery of criticism of the statehood movement into late July. The governor was given the major part of the blame. Sullivan wrote that in a resolution of a statehood meeting these words were used, that party and principle should be "forsaken" [sic] and the offices *divided equally between Democrats and Republicans*. The resolutions were nearly unanimously adopted.[491]

The Democrat Convention met on June 24, but was not fully reported until the following Saturday, July 1, 1871, in the Santa Fe *Weekly Post*. The *Post* was clearly shocked that the convention chose the Las Cruces *Borderer* as its mouthpiece. The *Post* noted that the party's platform stated, *the laws passed by Congress to protect the lives and property of loyal men of the South* [were] *infamous bills*

---

[491] Ibid., 7/2/70, "The Statehood Movement," p. 2, col. 2

[and spoke of the President] *as one from whom the people have to fear the prostitution of the army to gratify his selfish ambition "to establish a military despotism on the ruins of a republic."* The Santa Fe Post added, "A candidate sent on such a platform would be looked upon as New Mexico's insult to the administration. Keep him at home." [492]

Mr. Gallegos, once before a Delegate to Congress, was nominated reluctantly by a solemn assembly of men gathered in Albuquerque for the occasion. A former priest, ousted by the strict rules of the Roman Catholic diocese, he did not speak English and required an interpreter. Mr. Sullivan, who seldom pulled punches, stated, "Mr. Gallegos may have been an active, energetic man in his time, but we think even his friends, if they be candid, must admit that his days of activity and energy are past."[493]

---

[492] Santa Fe *Weekly Post*, 7/1/71, p. 2, cols. 3-6, "Democratic Territorial Convention."
[493] Ibid., 7/1/71, p. 2, cols. 1-2.

Sometime in June Governor Pile resigned his post in New Mexico for a Venezuelan assignment. When he left, he set out for the transcontinental line at Denver. Once there, he participated in the July 29th festivities sending off the Montezuma engine when the first rails of *The Denver & Rio Grande Railway* received several commemorative spikes. As an honored guest, he drove the third spike and briefly addressed the surrounding crowd. He pointed out the need of extending the road to New Mexico. Within a month Colonel Greenwood, the Denver & Rio Grande Railway's secretary, and William S. Jackson, the company's treasurer, hosted the first excursion over the partially completed line.

In mid-July the *Weekly Post* reported that Jose Sena was canvassing for his own election in the eastern portion of New Mexico. Ten days later he appeared at a rally in the Santa Fe plaza where he was invited to speak. The event was cast as a concert by the military band but morphed into a political occasion. *The Daily New Mexican* published an editorial berating Sena for going back on his word and announcing his candidacy.[494]

In New Mexico, citizens were following the candidates for Delegate to Congress: Frank Chaves and Jose Gallegos. They were on the campaign trail and recently joined by the new candidate, Jose Sena.[495]

Frank Chaves was in Las Vegas on August 11 where it was reported that an enthusiastic crowd heard him speak. He returned to Santa Fe to say that San Miguel County was certain to vote Republican. Although the county was Sena's wife's home, Chaves did not acknowledge Sena's candidacy.[496] Sena's recent promise to acquiesce to Chaves' election was too sensitive a matter for public discussion. The *Post* did not shun the topic. Editor Sullivan suggested that Sena's candidacy would split the Democrats of Mora County and the rivalry would hurt

---

[494] Santa Fe *Daily New Mexican*, 7/26/71, p. 2, col. 2.
[495] Santa Fe Weekly *Post*, 8/5/71, p. 1, col. 3.
[496] Ibid., 8/5/71, p. 1, col. 4.

Gallegos' candidacy more than Chaves. He recognized that the Republicans would tend to condemn Sena for breaking his promise.[497]

Marsh Giddings of Michigan was expected to arrive in New Mexico to become governor soon. *The Post* hailed Giddings as a prominent and upright citizen of his state and a staunch Republican. Sullivan recommended that citizens welcome the new appointee.[498]

On August 1, *The New Mexican* wrote of candidate Gallegos that he had also once appointed a young man from Alabama to the U. S. Military Academy rather than a son of New Mexico. The article was written to counter the San Miguel County opposition published against Chaves who had recently abridged their loyalty oath. In 1857, Gallegos' appointee was a relative of the Confederacy's vice-president. Jabs at Chaves by Gallegos on this point would be countered by revealing Gallegos' own vulnerabilities.[499]

---
[497] Ibid., p. 1, col. 1.
[498] Ibid., "A New Governor," p. 1, col. 1.
[499] Santa Fe Daily *New Mexican*, 8/1/71, "Gallegos' Cadet

The Democrats held the Republicans responsible for the Territory's debt. *The New Mexican* attributed the Territory's debt to the Mitchell administration's 1868-69 legislature when the governor vetoed nearly every bill presented by the Republicans. Mitchell did not complete his term in office but left the duties to Secretary Heath who held them for the rest of the term. Heath served in mid-year during the robbery of the Federal Depository and the murder of James Collins.

Jose Sena gave a press release to the *Weekly Post* of his candidacy for Congress which appeared in an early August issue. It was stated that he would leave on his canvassing tour that same day, August 5. *The Daily New Mexican* would thereafter report him as the renegade candidate.[500]

A convention to name candidates for the legislature in San Miguel County chided Sena for having "the

---

Appointment," p. 1, col. 1.
[500] Santa Fe *Daily New Mexican*, 8/17/71, p. 1, col. 1. Also, 8/7/71

effrontery and insulting audacity to present himself . . . as an independent candidate."[501]

It was August 20 when Chaves and Gallegos spoke to a large crowd of citizens from a platform in Albuquerque. According to a news report, the Democrats forced Colonel Chaves to cut short his speech. The Republicans treated Gallegos respectfully and without interruption. Ben Stevens, Republican Chairman, tried to address the crowd but was compelled to leave the stand.[502]

A Democrat mass meeting was held in Mesilla's plaza on August 27 where Mr. Gallegos addressed a large group of followers. At the same time, the Republicans held their meeting before the home of John Lemon. Arrangements were made to accommodate both parties and local businessmen counseled cooperation. The separate meeting locations were agreed to in advance.[503]

---

[501] Ibid., 8/17/71, "The Republican Meeting at Las Vegas," p. 1, col. 1.
[502] Santa Fe Weekly *Post*, 8/31/71, p. 1, col. 1.
[503] Fulton, M. G. and Horgan, Paul, *New Mexico's Own Chronicle*, "The Forty-Seventh State," Banks Upshaw and Company, Dallas, TX., p. 320. (Account written by S. M. Ashenfelter, U. S. Attorney for New

When the meeting at the Plaza ended, over one hundred armed and mounted men from La Mesa started home. Afterward a procession formed, accompanied by a brass band. The group began a march around the plaza. The Democrats sang taunting words to the Republicans to the tune of "Marching Through Georgia." The Republicans had reached the plaza and took the song as a challenge. They formed their own chain and marched in the opposite direction, the two processions meeting each other before Reynolds & Griggs Store.

The two leaders, I. N. Kelley, a printer and a Democrat, faced John Lemon, the Probate Judge. They exchanged angry words. Apolonia Barela, accidentally or otherwise, fired a shot in the air. Excited by the shot, Kelley, who carried a heavy pick handle, struck Lemon a fierce blow to the head. Lemon fell to the ground. A Republican then shot Kelley, causing a mortal wound,

---

Mexico)

before he was then shot through the heart by another person. There was general chaos, fighting on all sides. The next ten or fifteen minutes the sharp rattle of musketry could be heard. The plaza was crowded with people and masses pushed their way toward the streets around the plaza. Several people, even small children, were severely injured by the panic-stricken crowd. Pistol shots were heard in the melee.

A store owner, James Edgar Griggs, sent a reliable messenger with his racehorse to a friend at Fort McRae to ask for troops to restore order. About ten o'clock that night a command of six cavalrymen arrived at a home on Mesilla's outskirts. One officer and a small detachment moved into the plaza. A few men of both parties assembled and joined in a request that the entire body of troops be brought in. The bugle was blown, and the remaining troops galloped in. They camped in the plaza that night. The next day a detachment of twenty men remained.

The result of the fatal encounter was nine men killed and between forty and fifty wounded.[504]

On August 28, four Treasury officers arrived in Santa Fe. They brought a half-million dollars in greenbacks from Washington to the Federal Depository. The committee of four included J. C. Poynter, S. W. Saxon, Wm. Fessenden, and F. A. Simons. They remained for several days before returning east. They undoubtedly learned of the excitement of the final days before the Delegate election and the riot in Mesilla that followed.[505]

The new governor, Marsh Giddings, also arrived on August 28, the day following the Mesilla riot. Election Day was on Tuesday, September 1. Returns began to appear in Santa Fe papers on September 5. At first, all were from Santa Fe County. Gallegos led in Santa Fe, the most Republican County in the Territory. Sena was not far

---

[504] Fulton, Maurice G. Fulton and Horgan, Paul, *New Mexico's Own Chronicle, "The Forty-Seventh State." Pp. 320-323, Banks Upshaw and Company, 1937.* From an article by S. M. Ashenfelter produced in the Silver City *Independent.*
[505] Ibid., 8/29/71, p. 1, col. 1.

behind. By September 7 the Santa Fe *New Mexican* admitted that the Democrat candidate would be elected by a majority of at least 500. In Chaves' own county of Bernalillo, he received a majority of only 34 votes.[506] The *Post* wrote that "The rule or ruin policy of forcing Mr. Chaves on the convention has brought about a result which his friends should have learnt had they known anything of public sentiment."[507]

Within several weeks the Governor returned east to bring his family to New Mexico. Tom Catron left for the east on the same stage. Catron stated that he would be absent only several weeks, returning in time for the courts in the third district.

At the same time as the violent uprising in New Mexico, in Colorado, a more civil international union of business financing and local development was taking place. It was then April 1871.

---

[506] Santa Fe Daily *New Mexican*, 9/8/71, p. 1, col. 1.
[507] Santa Fe Weekly *Post*, 9/9/71, p. 1, col. 1.

William Blackmore's Mountain Base Investment Company was his investor's fund to acquire potentially valuable land in the Arkansas Valley. He was merely an agent. His fund was not designed to develop land. The subscribers were not responsible for the groups' capital. They trusted Blackmore to invest in land wisely.

In an arrangement with General Palmer and Alexander Hunt, Blackmore negotiated the Nolan Grant with the owners, Dodson, Goodnight, and Mrs. Blake. He told them that his "friends" were ready to make a purchase of their grant land.[508] Afterward, he agreed to join the Palmer group and their Arkansas Valley Pool. The Palmer group promised to take over the Nolan Grant purchase in exchange for his participation in their investment pool. When Blackmore left for England in November, plans for the new Arkansas Valley Pool were laid out and completed

---

[508] Brayer, Herbert O., *William Blackmore: Early Financing of the Denver & Rio Grande Railway,* "Land Development Companies, 1871," pp. 88-91.

by the Palmer group. They would find other desirable properties in the valley.[509]

Now, six months later, in April, when the investment fund was in Palmer's hands, 8,426 acres were purchased for $74,295.16 or $8.81 an acre. Without direct consultation with Blackmore, the Arkansas Valley Pool was converted into the National Land and Improvement Company. Palmer and Mellon intended to purchase coal lands at $5000, the mineral springs, and an adjacent tract of 400 acres for $30,000. These lands would become Colorado Springs, Manitou, Palmer Lake, and Monument. The National Land and Improvement Company was a joint stock company meant to develop the lands.

Hunt had seen that the National Land and Improvement Company could broaden its investment base if joined with Blackmore's investors. It would take such an enlarged group to purchase the Nolan Grant and adjacent

---

[509] Ibid., p. 94, fn. 53, the option on the Nolan Grant expired in November.

properties. He suggested to Blackmore that his Mountain Base Investment Pool might profit from transferring these lands to a second organization. The second fund could use them without assuming the liability and expense of such use.

The financier was successful in linking the securities and mortgage of Wertheim and Gompertz with the Denver & Rio Grande the year before. If Blackmore had investments in the valley, he had much to gain from joining this group.

On May 1, the National Land and Improvement Company signed papers with the Union Contract Company to build such stations and townsites before their value was affected by construction and railway extension. Various protective measures were taken to manage the income of the land company and handle its capital stock to their best advantage. The English held a sixth of the total stock issue of $37,700 in the National Land & Improvement Company.[510]

On June 26, 1871 the Colorado Springs Company was formally organized.[511] Correspondence went back and forth between Blackmore, Bell, and Palmer. Blackmore was concerned for the best interests of his original pool. He felt he was insufficiently informed of the specifics of the National Land and Investment Company. He warned Palmer and Bell of his consideration of a withdrawal from the enterprise. He returned certain stock certificates to his pool members with his concerns, but he did not withdraw.

As early in the Denver & Rio Grande Railway's first division grading south of Denver, a corps of engineers surveyed for an extension to a point near Pueblo, then to the mouth of the Royal Gorge Canyon.[512] In running the survey it was often necessary to cross areas of the Nolan Grant.

Rich coal and iron lands were purchased by the company below Canon City and along Grape Creek twenty

---

[510] Ibid., p. 77.
[511] Ibid., p. 82.
[512] Ibid., p. 93.

miles southwest of the City. Then, Hunt and Palmer searched the southern Arkansas Valley, southwestern Colorado, and northern New Mexico. They noted desirable locations for further purchases. Hunt acquired many valuable tracts in the Arkansas Valley for the National Land and Improvement Company.[513]

In November 1871, Palmer's associates organized a new company, the Central Colorado Improvement Company with an authorized capital stock of $3,750,000. The CCIC would purchase lands, mineral springs, coal and iron and other mines and quarries in Fremont, Pueblo, El Paso, Bent, and Greenwood Counties. They would establish and develop colonies, towns, coal mines, and so on. They would build canals and wagon roads. The officers of the new company included Palmer, his friend Robert Lamborn, and S. F. Parrish, Blackmore's agent's brother, representing Blackmore's interests.[514]

---

[513] Ibid., pp. 93-94.
[514] Ibid., p. 95, CICC was formed in Nov. 1871, but not incorporated until 1/11/72. Blackmore was notified of the new company by

The day the railroad was completed to Colorado Springs, October 27, 1871, James C. Parrish concluded a second agreement with the Amsterdam banking house of Wertheim and Gompertz for financing the railway extension to Pueblo.[515]

The network visualized, and placed in action, included European subscriptions beyond Blackmore's original pool and Palmer's Philadelphia friends. The organization formed at the time would establish precedents which were accepted afterward to open and develop an entire region as well as build a major railroad. The Arkansas Valley Pool would raise funds to set in motion the program of the Central Colorado Improvement Company.[516]

The Denver & Rio Grande Railway's first excursion in January 1872 filled the new passenger cars with tourists bound for Pikes Peak and the planned Colorado Springs

---

telegram. His agent's brother was made an officer of the CCIC.
[515] Ibid., p. 100.
[516] Ibid., p. 96.

site. The press and public were both on hand. Behind the scenes, grading had begun for Pueblo in October 1871 when the Denver to Colorado Springs unit was complete. However, finishing touches were given to the original section before the excursions began in January.[517] Depots, loading stations, and such were built.

William Blackmore traveled on the line to Littleton[518] in August the previous year, before it reached the planned Colorado Springs site.[519] The date was when Blackmore, Mellon and Hunt first discussed their financial pools and the possible methods available to exploit them.

By the end of 1871, the Denver & Rio Grande parent company had seven construction and land development companies in its network.[520] Two were

---

[517] Brayer, Herbert O., *William Blackmore: Early Financing of the Denver & Rio Grande Railway,* "Opening the Arkansas Valley, 1872," pp. 99-100.
[518] Ibid., p. 92
[519] Ibid.
[520] Ibid., "Land Development Companies, 1871," p.98.

construction companies, four land development companies, and one a colony development company.

New properties were acquired by the National Land & Improvement Company. In this manner, considerable money was raised for the purchase and development of the Nolan Estate. The Nolan Estate funding was in William Mellon's hands.

The failure of the Kansas Pacific in 1870 to complete its construction plans left Pueblo hanging dry. The previous year Pueblo and Canon City feared a D & RG route would skirt them.

In February 1871 Governor Hunt gave an address to the citizens of Colorado. He told them financial support would be expected from El Paso, Pueblo, and Canon City.[521] In return they would receive paid up railroad stock equal to the amount of their bonds. Rumors swirled and encouraged local enthusiasm.

---

[521] Ibid., p. 104.

In March 1871 the promoters intimated the exact route was still uncertain. There was also a newly revived proposal to extend the Kansas Pacific to Pueblo. Hunt told the two towns they were not on the route, they would have to assist the railroad. Fremont County leaders at Canon City readily supported a proposal to float a bond issue of $50,000, on condition the road would be built to their town.[522]

On March 5, 1871, a mass meeting was held in Pueblo when Governor Hunt told citizens they were not on the main line of the road. It would require an additional twenty-five miles of construction to build there.[523]

On May 8, 1871 a petition was signed by one-hundred and nine Pueblo citizens for a bond election.[524] The amount of county bonds proposed was $100,000. The subscription required one-half the bonds to be delivered when the grading was completed and the balance to be turned over when the line was finished to Pueblo. There

---

[522] Ibid., p. 105.
[523] Ibid.
[524] Ibid., p. 106.

was a stipulation that the railway depot should be constructed within one mile of the courthouse square. The bond issue was voted on June 20 and submitted to the D & RG at once. No acknowledgement was made for three months. Pueblo leaders were dismayed. Committees were appointed to confer with the Kansas Pacific and the narrow-gauge road to determine their true intentions.

Governor Hunt went to Pueblo on November 23, 1871. He reported that the road would be built to Pueblo, but more county bonds were needed for the division from Pueblo to the coal fields a few miles below Canon City. Fifty thousand in county bonds or a $35,000 cash purchase of railway stock would fund the extension. An election was proposed for January 16 but was postponed to January 30. The second bond issue was approved on that date.[525]

It was January 1, 1872 when the Union Contract Company agreed to complete the new line to the Pueblo

---

[525] Ibid., p. 109.

County courthouse by July 1, 1872.[526] The stock and bond arrangement was included in the contract. A meeting of Denver and Rio Grande officers on January 30, 1872 determined that the main line of the railroad would be changed. It would go from Pueblo south to near the Purgatoire River instead of going up the Arkansas by Canon City. They must still accommodate the paying coal and iron lands with branch railroads.

The new contract was drawn by Palmer, as Denver and Rio Grande president, and Charles Hinchman as president of the Union Contract Company. This was privately done to arrange for the building of sixty-five miles to Pueblo and Canon City. There would be branches to the coal and iron mines near Canon City and to the Purgatoire River. The contractor stated the road would extend to a point ten miles below Canon City. Bonds would have to be sold to pay the extra expense. The remainder of

---

[526] Ibid., p. 110.

the extension would be done by a year after that date. The Denver & Rio Grande thereby met the requirements of their bondholders, Wertheim and Gompertz. This contract was privately signed on May 1, 1872.[527]

In New Mexico, on January 15, 1872, the Republican Territorial central committee met at a convention to elect two representatives to attend the National Republican Convention in Philadelphia on June 6, 1872. The Philadelphia Convention would nominate their candidates for U. S. President and Vice-President.[528] The party's central committee had set the local convention for January to unite the Republicans. The lost delegate election and an attack on Chief Justice Palen by the legislature's Democrats shook party resolve. The leadership apparently determined to be rid of the undermining influence of A. P. Sullivan and his associate, Henry Wetter.

---

[527] Ibid., p. 11.
[528] Ibid., "Selection of Delegates," 1/16/72, p. 1, col. 1.

Once all factions of the party appeared to be in accord, Jose Sena and his followers were welcomed and forgiven. The only prominent Republicans not in attendance were Frank Chaves, defeated Delegate candidate, and the two professed Republican printers of the *Post*, Editor Sullivan and Henry Wetter. The latter two were clearly not invited to attend.

On January 26, the *Daily New Mexican* continued its complaints of the *Weekly Post* asking that the editor "inform the public who forged the telegram to the Attorney General of the United States purporting to have been signed by Hon. Severo Baca, President of the Legislative Council."[529] The *Weekly Post* responded to the question first published on January 24, that the editor wanted to know the full name of the individual who was a Captain in Price's rebel army, and acknowledged being a traitor to his country by taking the amnesty oath before the then Chief

---

[529] Ibid., 1/26/72, p. 1, col. 1. "Yesterday's *New Mexican* says: . . ." Also, "$5,110.000," col. 2.

Justice of New Mexico. The *New Mexican* replied that it was not aware that any such person had held the office of Assistant Assessor or any other federal office, in this Territory . . ."[530]

The *New Mexican* then asked Secretary Wetter where $5,110 dollars went that was paid by him to a mercantile house in [Santa Fe].[531]

In this manner the argument continued to implicate discredit to various people with evil political and personal motives. Amidst all other revelations, one appeared which charged Mr. Sullivan with having voted all four votes of Dona Ana County in the Republican Delegate's nominating convention of April 29 the previous year.[532] It was possible for Sullivan to have done so if he held all four proxies of the absent Dona Ana delegates. However, that may have been illegal. In Sullivan's replies to the *Daily New Mexican's* charges, he began to refer to the "Santa Fe

---

[530] Ibid.
[531] Ibid.
[532] Ibid., 1/17/72, p. 1, cols. 1-2. "The Convention."

Ring," a term which insinuated Santa Fe had a Republican ring like the infamous Democrat Tweed ring of New York City.[533] In Sullivan's eyes the Republican leaders were a "cabal of Rebel sympathizers."[534]

Territorial Secretary Henry Wetter's response to charges of illegal disbursement of money appeared in the *Daily New Mexican* on January 20. The money was related to an amount received from the Treasury Department for the legitimate expenses of the Legislature. The Secretary was unable to pay the members their salaries when prior payments for supplies were made before the legislature closed. The Secretary stated that he was prepared to make a full disclosure of his accounts. The matter was ultimately resolved when Attorney General Thomas Catron paid the legislative salaries from his own pocket, together with friends.[535]

---

[533] Santa Fe *Weekly Post*, 1/27/72, p. 2, col. 1.
[534] Ibid.
[535] Larson, Robert W., *New Mexico's Quest for Statehood, 1846-1912*, Chap. Seven, "The Constitution of 1872," p. 98.

By February 1, it was revealed that A. P. Sullivan, Postmaster at Santa Fe, and editor of *The Weekly Post* owed money to Ceran St. Vrain, a prominent Democrat and owner of a large distillery at Taos. St. Vrain had since died and his son, Vicente had attempted collection of the note. St. Vrain and Sullivan vehemently denied knowledge of any part of the note, but it was in the official records of the court, July 20, 1871 in the first District at Santa Fe.[536] The debt had been contracted on October 1, 1869.

On February 12, 1872 the Cimarron *News* office burned down, destroying the building and all equipment inside. It was assumed that Sullivan's commitment to the Maxwell Land Grant Company to print their newspaper was cancelled due to the circumstances.

The fight which began in New Mexico's legislature was continued into February and March 1872 when a series of charges were hurled between Santa Fe's two

---

[536] Santa Fe Daily *New Mexican*, 2/1/71.

newspapers, both claiming to be the official Republican newspaper of the Territory. The *New Mexican* published an article on the first day of February summarizing the background of its fight with Alexander Sullivan, editor of the *Post* and Santa Fe's Postmaster. They enumerated several instances of slander Sullivan exercised over his three-year editorial career. His professions to be a Republican were unmasked and his libels exposed. Sullivan arrived in the Territory amidst the wave of Republicans who came with the new Grant administration. He held an appointment as Collector of Internal Revenue.

The Santa Fe *Weekly Post* was first published on October 2, 1869. Sullivan immediately declared himself a Republican, but independent of party politics, although he had purchased the printing equipment and location of the *Gazette*, the former Democrat newspaper. He implied the *Daily New Mexican* was a mouthpiece for party politics.

His appointment to office was withdrawn by the following March.[537]

The *Daily New Mexican* stated that during Sullivan's editorial career he was free in applying epithets to the best and most useful citizens of the Territory and on frequent occasions denounced such men and all who dared to expose his unworthiness and his service to the democracy. The *New Mexican* stated that Sullivan professed the most devoted Republicanism, while calling other party members liars, perjurers, and slanderers. ". . . . We have been the recipients of a great deal of mendacious abuse [for exposing his hypocrisy and dishonesty.]"[538]

In December 1869, the *New Mexican* charged that Sullivan, to secure the *Gazette* printing establishment, had procured the signature of Mr. Vicente St. Vrain of Mora as an endorser and security for the payment of Sullivan's note given for purchase money. The *New Mexican* then

---

[537] Santa Fe *Weekly Post*, 3/24/70, p. 1, col. 1.
[538] Santa Fe *Daily New Mexican*, 2/1/72, p. 1, col. 1.

produced the record of the district court as evidence of the transaction and a later attempt to collect it by Vicente St. Vrain. Certain forgeries on the part of Sullivan and an instance of procuring a false affidavit followed. Part of this was altered and published by Sullivan in attempting to clear his name.

Exactly when Henry Wetter became involved with Sullivan cannot be determined, but it was evident by February 1871 when complaints of their association were sent in letters to Washington asking for Wetter's removal from office as Territorial Secretary.[539] The irregularity of Wetter's ability to pay legislative salaries in January provided reason for further complaint.

January to March was the legislative period in New Mexico and a storm was brewing in the Palace walls. Few

---

[539] New Mexico's Territorial Papers of the Legislature, 1870-1871, 2/16/71, complaint of U. S. D. A., S. M. Ashenfelter against Henry Wetter, Register of the Territorial Land Office, and William Breeden, Clerk of the U. S. District Court for the 1st District, and Wetter's response, 3/15/71. Also, complaint of William Manderfield, affidavit dated 2/10/71.

New Mexico attorneys were educated in U. S. Constitutional law. They had not served as legal assistants in a law office or a court of law. The problem was brought to the attention of the public by Judge Hezekiah Johnson as early as 1864 when he owned and edited the *Rio Abajo Press*. Johnson criticized Chief Justice Kirby Benedict for admitting some candidates for the Bar who were not qualified.[540] It was now December 1871 and the matter came to a head in the Legislature.

The problem was that the law in New Mexico was the Organic Law, the Kearny Code. As a result, Benedict only quizzed candidates on what they knew of the local territorial law. Johnson pointed out that Benedict often overlooked a candidate's shortcomings and used his version of "charity" in granting legal licenses to men who were not competent to hold them. Johnson stated that Chief

---

[540] *Rio Abajo Weekly Press*, 2/26/64, p. 1, col. 1, "Law and Charity."

Justice Benedict assumed that he alone was imbued with authority to grant licenses.

He should also have been impelled to strip the feathers of those "new style turkies" [sic] who assumed the characters of lawyers practicing in the Supreme Court having "evil intentions to serve unprincipled pretenders."[541] The same could be said of the land agents who affected the authority of attorneys in acquiring and dispensing pieces of land grants.

The House assembled at ten o'clock on Friday, January 12, and reopened business with a quorum which was then conducted in an orderly manner. They met in the Palace Library since the rebellious Democrats occupied, and refused to surrender, the seat of the House Speaker. Speaker Rudolph called on the Territorial Secretary to provide a room for the House of Representatives to conduct business.[542]

---
[541] Ibid.
[542] Ibid., "The Legislature – Yesterday's Proceedings," 1/13/72, p. 1, cols.1-2; also, *SFDNM*, 2/15/72, p. 1, col. 2.

On January 13 a public letter was written, published, and distributed in the Santa Fe area to arouse citizens against the Chief Justice. It appeared as a Las Cruces *Borderer Extra* and was allegedly produced in the office of the *Post*. The *New Mexican* shortly published a response which vilified it.[543] The legislature had not yet broached the essential dilemma. The newspapers reminded them of tax reform and educational funding, but there were no complaints of poor legal practice. Attorneys were everywhere in Santa Fe, a dime a dozen. Instead of examining the problem for a solution, the legislators became embroiled in a fight with the judicial branch.

An act was introduced in the legislature to move Chief Justice Palen to the third district.[544] The matter, the *Daily New Mexican* declared, was instigated by the rebel press led by Alexander Sullivan of the *Post* and his

---

[543] Ibid., cols. 1-2.
[544] Santa Fe *Daily New Mexican*, 1/2/72, p. 1, col. 1.

associate, Henry Wetter, territorial secretary. The *Daily New Mexican* charged the two men as conspirators in stirring up legislative disunion.[545] The Santa Fe *Daily New Mexican* attacked the *Weekly Post* for inciting the Democrat members of the legislature against the Republicans to give the Democrats a majority, first in the Senate, and then in the House.[546]

The Democrats saw the opportunity to pass their favored legislation and earn the sympathy of the electorate at the same time. The *Weekly Post* never failed to mention Wetter's sacrifice to the Union in losing a leg in the war. During the turmoil, three Republicans were ejected from the Council (Senate), and several more from the House. The fight closed the legislature for a week when one of their memorials to Congress asked for the members' salaries to be increased.[547]

---

[545] Ibid., 1/8/72, p. 1, col. 1, "Nearly all rebels around town . . . ." Also, p. 1, col. 1, Wetter charged in U. S. District Court with extortion.
[546] Ibid., p. 1, "The Legislature," col. 1, "The House of Representatives."
[547] Ibid., "The House of Representatives,"

The law governing the right of the legislature to transfer judges to a different district became the issue. It involved a petition signed by one hundred forty citizens who asked to move Chief Justice Palen from the first district at Santa Fe to the third at Dona Ana. The agitators maintained that Judge Palen favored the service of certain attorneys over that of others.[548]

The Santa Fe Bar was forced to go on the defensive. Their members were primarily attorneys who had been fully accredited in the east. The cases in New Mexico were diverse. They included the exclusive right of Pueblo Indians to their land. The law included a resolution of the Indian trade problem. It included the matter of peonage. These were technical issues which required knowledge of strictly local problems as well as legal expertise in land settlements, slavery issues, and mining rights. The complainants could not understand the overlapping issues

---

[548] Santa Fe *Weekly Post*, 1/6/72, p. 1, col. 1, "Why?" Also, col. 4, "Correspondence."

of the law. In fact, many of the petitioners' signatures had been forged.[549] Governor Giddings responded with an explanatory address and a veto.[550]

Attorneys who had passed eastern states' bar exams received the most cases. They were able to write incorporations for mining claims, towns, and businesses. Laws pertaining to precedents of like cases settled in the past required reference to several books, too costly and inaccessible for novices. At its heart, the request to remove Chief Justice Palen was a matter of jealousy and vindictiveness.

In the confusion of the junta performed by Democrats for control of the legislature, the House Speaker, Mr. Rudolph, and two members of the House, were arrested and dragged into the Hall by its "minions."[551] Santa Fe County's Sheriff was a recently elected Democrat.

---

[549] Santa Fe *Daily New Mexican*, 1/6/72, p. 1, col. 1. "The list of one hundred-forty citizens . . . ."
[550] Ibid., 1/5/72, "Address of Governor Giddings," p. 1, cols. 1-2.
[551] Ibid., p. 1, cols. 1-2.

As a matter of recourse, friends of the Speaker and House members applied to the Supreme Court for a writ of habeas corpus on their behalf, to release them. The U. S. Marshal served the writ on the perpetrators of the arrest when he placed it in their hands.

In response to the mandate of the writ, the prisoners were produced in open court the next day. The court placed the prisoners in the custody of the U. S. Marshal. The decision of the Chief Justice was in conjunction with the other judges of the Supreme Court.

At the heart of Sullivan's departure from New Mexico, an article from the Pueblo *People*, a Democrat paper, questioned the *Weekly Post's* charges against Chief Justice Palen, calling them "vague." [552] The *Post* answered with a complaint of a meeting staged by the "ring" in Las Vegas following court on March 11. The Las Vegas *Mail*

---

[552] Santa Fe *Post*, 3/23/72, "Jails and Judges," and Santa Fe *Daily New Mexican,* 4/6/71, reference to Pueblo *People,* a Democrat paper which called the *Post*'s charges of Judge Palen "vague."

reported that the meeting was held without prior notice, therefore "spontaneous" and drew a large crowd.

Jose Sena was said to be the "leading spirit" and had difficulty finding a presiding officer. Speeches praised Chief Justice Palen and resolutions were read. The *Mail* stated that as soon as the object of the meeting was clear, the most respectable people left the room. "Like all the ring meetings it was gotten up without previous notice and by speeches and encomiums upon the Judge [Palen] the excitable Mexican people present were induced to commit an act on the spur of the moment [they] would later regret."[553]

Also, from the Las Vegas *Mail*, further proof of the ring's activity was given in an incident of 1860 when a saloon owner was fined $50,000 for permitting card playing in his house. The perpetrator never went to court but privately sought out Thomas Catron and "regulated him by paying the costs alone of $29.75" – of which $20 was

---

[553] Santa Fe Weekly *Post*, 4/6/72, p. 2, col. 1.

Mr. Catron's fee for conviction. The claims of the county and territory were ignored for Catron's fees. In this case, Thomas Catron did not arrive in New Mexico until 1866.

Another case was cited by the *Mail* which occurred at Elizabethtown. No date was given. It involved a court term in which a gambler was a member of the grand jury. He was allegedly taken out to one side by Catron and promised that if he would secure the reproach of other gamblers in town, his own fine and that of one of his friends would be remitted.

These two incidents were the responses to the Pueblo *People's* question of the vague charges against Judge Palen.[554] The Santa Fe *Daily New Mexican* rejoiced at Sullivan's departure.[555]

On March 8, 1872, Thomas B. Catron was confirmed as U. S. District Attorney of New Mexico.[556] At nearly the same time Sullivan and Wetter were removed

---
[554] Ibid.
[555] Santa Fe *Daily New Mexican*, 4/3/72, "At Last," p. 1, col. 1.
[556] Santa Fe *Weekly Post*, 3/15/72, p. 1, col. 1, "Local News."

from office in March 1872.[557] Sullivan delivered his final blow to the Republicans. He inferred Steve Elkins and Tom Catron were Rebels and one a member of Missouri's outlaw band in the Civil War, Quantrell's Raiders, mentioned in a *Weekly Post* article of April 6, 1872. He suggested that Elkins was "too careful of his 'dogskins' to go into the Rebel Army."[558]

Elkins was a Union officer in 1861 and 1862 before going to New Mexico in September 1863.[559] He was also a Union spy in Missouri.[560] The object of his surveillance were his students in Cass County, Missouri. Several of these students were personal friends of his family, among them Cole Younger, a known member of Quantrell's band.[561]

---

[557] Santa Fe Daily *New Mexican*, 4/9/72, p. 1, col. 2.
[558] Santa Fe Weekly *Post*, 4/6/72, p. 1, col. 1.
[559] Brayer, Herbert O., *William Blackmore: The Spanish-Mexican Land Grants*, Vol. I, "The New Mexico Land Grants, 1871," p. 167, fn. 52.
[560] New York *Herald,* 25 April 1909, New York ed. p. 2, Sunday Magazine Sect., "Cole Younger's Story." His Union officer status confirmed by Herbert O. Brayer, *The Spanish Mexican Land Grants*, p. 167, fn. 52.
[561] *The New York Herald*, 25 April 1909, Sunday Magazine Section, Interviews of Stephen B. Elkins and Cole Younger, pp. 1-2, "How Cole Younger Saved the Life of Stephen B. Elkins and A U. S. Senator Paid the Debt He Owed the Bandit."

Elkins' own father and brother were in the Confederate Army, his father an officer.

Sullivan left on the eastern coach on Monday for the States. He was charged with embezzlement.[562] The remainder of the newspaper's issues through July 2 were likely written, gathered, and published by Mr. Wetter. Former Secretary W. F. M. Arny was restored to the office of Territorial Secretary in his place.[563]

Although foreign investment in Colorado and New Mexico was not faring well, the 1st National Bank of Santa Fe was thriving. Its rates competed favorably with the Federal Depository and many business loans were being made. Several new buildings were being remodeled in Santa Fe and the city was considering construction loans for needed bridges.

An announcement in February 1872 from Washington stated that the Treasurer held as security for

---

[562] Santa Fe Daily *New Mexican,* 7/26/72, p. 1, col. 1.
[563] Ibid., 4/9/72, p. 2, col. 2.

national bank circulation $372,389,450 and for public deposits, 154,320,000. National bank circulation outstanding in February was $330,404,946. The National Gold Bank circulation outstanding was $579,400.[564]

On August 27 it was reported that three gentlemen from Washington were in town on business connected with the Treasury Department and the Federal Depository. The officers seemed well satisfied with the business being conducted by the branch house at Santa Fe. It was considered an honor that Santa Fe had the only "such Treasury among the Territories." The *New Mexican's* editors were told that the depositories in Arizona and Washington Territory had been discontinued due to the malfeasance of their officers.[565]

---

[564] Ibid., 2/22/72, p. 1, col. 2.
[565] Ibid., 8/27/72, p. 2, col. 4.

Chapter Nineteen: The Financial Wizard

September 1871 – October 1872

It was storming the evening William Blackmore arrived in Taos, unusual for September. His slicker and sou'wester shed the onslaught and he shook the drizzle from his beard. Such conditions were commonplace in London.

He was about to depart from his usual business plan and engage several industrious agents to scout their prospects for opportunities he might find advantageous. In such cases he was extremely cautious before committing significant amounts of investment capital. The "front money" in these would secure the agents' loyalties.

Inside the taproom Lucien B. Stewart sat at the bar expecting him. He hung his rain gear on the coat tree and joined Stewart. They had met once before on his last trip to Costilla. They moved to a table and ordered grogs. They spoke of the Cieneguilla Grant. Stewart co-owned the estate, a 150,000-acre tract, with four other men. He was a Prussian land speculator. He was sent by his partners to approach the English promoter about a possible purchase of their grant. The group had determined its price would be $40,000. Stewart unfurled the map. They studied it while their drinks were served. Blackmore agreed to consider the proposition.[566]

The next morning Theodore Wheaton, a Santa Fe attorney, politician, and prominent land speculator called

---

[566] Brayer, Herbert O., *William Blackmore: The Spanish-Mexican Land Grants*, Vol. I, "The New Mexican Land Grants, 1871," p. 148.

on Blackmore. The two men discussed grants in both New Mexico and Colorado. Wheaton was familiar with the grantees or heirs of many of these properties. The solicitor was enthusiastic and retained Wheaton for one hundred dollars on account. Could Wheaton keep him advised by mail of the status of the grants whose local owners he knew personally?[567]

Blackmore was overwhelmed with the New Mexican land grant field. He learned the activity was even greater than he expected. Much time and a large amount of investment money was spent taking interests in several grants near Costilla. His New Mexican agents continually reported to him the prices asked for these properties.

That afternoon the solicitor obtained a cart and driver to visit the office of the Surveyor General in Santa Fe where he could obtain further information on the various land grants he might choose for investments.

---

[567] Ibid., p. 149.

The fifty-six-mile trip took them four hours and they arrived at suppertime. At Santa Fe, Blackmore was directed to the land office of the Surveyor General just off the Plaza. He was charmed by narrow and dusty streets traveled by trudging midget burros. These donkeys were tethered in Burro Alley. The firewood venders padded their backs and sides to carry every kind of product, but most often wood bound for domestic ovens. In fact, these tiny creatures, with their long draping ears bore nearly all goods to the market-house under the porch roof at one corner of the street.

Trees circled the plaza where on one side the single-story adobe government center, ranch style, long and rambling, occupied a block of frontage. It was called the "Governor's Palace." Stores filled all other plaza buildings. Freight wagons continually unloaded goods in the busy thoroughfare. Nearby, the white-washed Fort Marcy headquarters buildings made up the major real property of the old town. The quartermaster depot, barracks, and stables surrounded the parade ground filled with ambulances, wagons, and several cannons. At a distance the cathedral's towers were evident over the commercial roofs.[568]

A short time later, Blackmore met Charles Clever, the recent congressional delegate, also a Santa Fe attorney. Clever had acquired an interest in several grants through his representation of their claimants. Blackmore arranged to join Clever in the purchase of half of the estimated 500,000-acre Los Luceros Grant. The land lay between Taos and Arroyo Hondo. Congress had confirmed the grant in 1869. The promoter copied the title documents for the property and assigned Clever the duty of investigating the possibility he might purchase the entire estate.[569]

When Blackmore finished his work in the land office he talked with other local officials before turning

---

[568] Ibid., pp. 149-150.
[569] Ibid., pp. 150-151.

back to Taos. The attorney-politician joined him on his trip to confer with Lucien Stewart.

Once in Taos, Captain Smith H. Simpson and several other associated land speculators approached him concerning Los Conejos, a large unconfirmed land grant on the western side of the Rio Grande. It was opposite a town site the Englishman and Gilpin proposed on the border of New Mexico and southern Colorado. The promoters claimed the grant was thirty-five miles wide and eighty to ninety miles in length. It was well watered and its soil rich. Blackmore promised to examine the property. He also asked for full information on the title and selling price which should be sent to him for consideration.[570]

The northern New Mexico land office at Elizabethtown interested him. He had received good information on the Maxwell Grant from them nearly two

---

[570] Ibid., p. 151.

years earlier.[571] He cherished the idea of owning a piece of the gold mine district. He arranged to travel there.

The trip to Elizabethtown was fifty miles by wagon. They passed through fir and pine covered forest bordering steep and rocky cliffs before descending into the Moreno Valley. When he arrived, he found the rough-hewn clapboard buildings and tents of a typical mining town. It was located on the foot of a rock-strewn hillside, abutting a glacial moraine over Moreno Creek. The men who worked the stream for gold numbered in the hundreds. They used sluice boxes or gold pans. They ignored passing strangers.

The hotel on the hillside was a two-story rough board building. Blackmore soon found the land office and became occupied with copying title documents and making notes on former Spanish and Mexican land grants. He met John T. Graham in the land office.[572] Graham was a land speculator and canny merchant, the owner of a nearby

---

[571] Ibid., p. 145.
[572] Ibid., p. 152.

sawmill. He had purchased interests in several unconfirmed grants.

The Cebolla Grant was around 150,000 acres and north of Taos. Graham recommended it. Blackmore conferred with Graham over several days and agreed to an arrangement for an interest in the Los Luceros, Cebolla, and Mora Grants. Graham would hold an interest in the Cebolla and Mora Grants and would sell half his interests to Blackmore. He would join Blackmore in Taos when Blackmore would meet with another prospect.

The return to Taos provided the world traveler with a chance to observe the Fiesta of San Geronimo. An extremely colorful affair, he could see every variety of the local residents. Tall Pueblo Indians wore grey blankets around their waists or over their shoulders. Half-naked Apaches and northern tribesmen rode fearlessly through the dusty streets. All around him were Yankee traders, teamsters, and miners who tramped from saloon to tavern.

Blackmore stood back for a while and observed the unusual procession. He made notes in his diary. He was not customarily distracted for such a long time.

Before leaving Taos on October 3, 1871, Blackmore engaged George Muller to purchase an interest for him in the Maxwell Grant and some of the available interests in the Luceros property. Muller was given a draft on his New York bankers, Brown Bros., & Company, for one thousand dollars.[573]

Wheaton wrote him of the New Mexico Nolan Grant. Blackmore again considered the property too expensive and advised Wheaton to negotiate further.

The arrangement made with Stewart committed Blackmore to a payment of three hundred dollars to the investor and agent. As agent, Stewart told him he must have the deed for half the Cebolla estate executed by October 7. The expense included Stewart's service as his

---

[573] Ibid., p. 153.

agent for one year. Before leaving the Cebolla Estate, Blackmore observed Stewart bargaining with the widow of one of the claimants. The agent ended the brief exchange by paying the woman thirty-five dollars for her one-tenth interest in the property.[574] She was able to sign his papers.

Four hundred dollars was given Graham for expenses in handling the land program they had outlined. Both Graham and Stewart accompanied Blackmore on a short tour of several grants they represented. Stewart and Graham would have to work out a suitable arrangement on the Cebolla Grant independently.

On October 16, Graham notified Blackmore of the availability of the Los Luceros Grant. Colonel Samuel Smoot, owner of an undivided interest in the Mora estate, a valued agricultural community grant, was in the capital at the time Blackmore arrived. Telegrams must have passed

---

[574] Ibid., p. 154.

between Blackmore and Graham because the latter appeared in Washington by December 6, 1871.

Several conferences transpired between Blackmore, Graham, and Colonel Smoot which yielded a contract for Smoot's interest. Blackmore agreed to pay the Colonel five thousand dollars within two months. The Englishman estimated the 138,000 acres of Mora would sell for a shilling an acre for a total of £6,900. He realized that one dollar in gold an acre would yield £27,500. His profit was ample on an expected investment of between five and eight thousand dollars.[575]

Colonel Smoot was on hand and offered an undivided interest in the Mora Estate. After several conferences on terms, Blackmore and Graham signed a formal contract for the purchase of Smoot's interest in the grant. Blackmore agreed to pay the colonel five thousand dollars before the expiration of two months. He also agreed

---

[575] Ibid., p. 156.

to remit the balance in sixty days. Unknown to Blackmore, the grant was guaranteed to be not less than 138,000 acres and Smoot's total interest was one fifth what had been purchased for the pool. Further, Smoot held no part of the grant in his own name. The whole of the pool was being held undivided in Elkins' name. The pool consisted of Elkins, Catron, Smoot, Darling, and Surveyor General Spencer.

On a return trip to Washington, Blackmore sought out Senate and House members of the public lands' committees on land grant confirmation legislation.

Blackmore was bound for London on December 13, 1871. He had acquired 125,000 acres, or half of the Cebolla Grant, five hundred thousand of the Los Luceros Grant, and one hundred thirty-eight thousand acres of the Mora Grant. Other major grants he held interests in were: the Agua Negra, the Rio Grande, the Rio Colorado, the Mora, the Conejos, the million and a quarter acre Ojo del Navajo

Grant, the half-million-acre Tierra Amarilla, the three hundred fifty-thousand-acre Preston Beck Grant, the one hundred-fifty-thousand-acre Cieneguilla Grant, and many smaller tracts.[576] Information would be sent to him on each one.

It was after Blackmore's departure for England that Palmer, Mellon, and associates agreed to transfer the Colorado Nolan Grant to another company, the National Land and Improvement Company. Palmer telegraphed Blackmore an explanation of the sudden move after his departure for England. He assured Blackmore that the interests of the National Land and Improvement Company were of the greatest concern, and nothing would be sacrificed.

When Blackmore arrived in England, he received Dr. Bell's draft of the proposed Arkansas Valley Company and the planned program of the Central Colorado

---

[576] Ibid., p. 148.

Improvement Company. He was disturbed and got in touch with James Parrish. They discussed the program and Blackmore wrote Bell on January 8 that he could do nothing until he received more information. It was necessary to know about the land purchased and sold, the prices, mode, and time of payment, a map of the lands, and a report of company affairs with a copy of the trust deed. He insisted that the first pool must not be sacrificed to benefit the Arkansas Valley Pool.

The solicitor informed Bell that he was sending copies of his letter to all the directors and trustees as well as Palmer. He included the English subscribers, Parrish, Lloyd, Potter, and Colonel Bridges.[577] Writing to Lloyd on February 16, 1872, he stated that ". . . at my age I cannot afford to wait for the development of the larger scheme, and I certainly see no good reason for the proposed transfer.[578]

---

[577] Brayer, Herbert O., *Early Financing of the Denver & Rio Grande Railway,* Vol. II, "Opening the Arkansas Valley," p. 123.
[578] Ibid., p. 123, fn. 43.

Behind the misunderstanding was the steady fall in the rate of exchange of gold specie. It was necessary to peg the English subscriptions to the improvement company bonds at £190, instead of £186. The company would presently lose £4 on every English subscription of $1000.[579]

Despite Blackmore's continued insistence that his pool's lands should realize nearly $10,000,000, he did not withdraw the original Mountain Base Investment Fund.[580]

These arrangements to build the branch lines and develop the coal property must be accomplished without turning the sum in bonds over to the Union Contract Company. To meet their obligations to the bondholders, the railway promoters created a new contract with the Central Colorado Improvement Company which, on paper, owned a great deal of land, coal and iron mines, water rights, etc. along the Arkansas Valley Division's adjacent properties.

---

[579] Ibid.
[580] Ibid., p. 129, fn. 53.

A complex agreement made by the Central Colorado Improvement Company handled the mortgage and railway bonds in return for its obligation to make haste in building the Arkansas Division. They would also transport all necessary coal to each railroad for thirty years.[581]

News of the Denver & Rio Grande Railway's schedule to arrive in Pueblo came to New Mexico in the first week of February. The town of Pueblo subscribed aid to the railroad's construction. A majority of 434 citizens voted in favor of issuing the bonds and the county was expected to give a hundred and fifty majority. The residents were also preparing to secure a broad-gauge road through the Arkansas Valley.[582]

The English investors could lose their entire investment in the venture, as well as the anticipated profits. They were taking property already mortgaged to secure bonds of the National Land and Improvement Company

---

[581] Ibid., pp. 112-113.
[582] Santa Fe *Daily New Mexican*, 2/6/72, p. 1, col. 1, courtesy of the Colorado *Chieftain*.

and allowing it to immediately become security for a second issue of bonds by the Central Colorado Improvement Company.

In early March 1872, Surveyor General Spencer reported on many properties requesting surveys.[583] A great part of his report was devoted to the status of land grants. He announced that land grants had daily increased in importance due to the approach of numerous railroads. Also, the purchase of one grant by a foreign company had made sales of land grants increase.

More of these grants have been registered in this office during the past [year] than during the ten years previous, and since 1851 not a single one had been adjudicated by the surveyor general until within the last twelve months. A number of these grants recently registered or already on file in the office have been called up for adjudication by the parties interested, and five of

---

[583] Ibid, 3/9/72, p. 1, cols. 1-2. "Surveyor General's report. The surveyor for these land grants was Robert B. Willison.

them have been acted upon, which together with others as may in the meantime be decided, will be transmitted in time for the action of the next Congress. Of the whole number now on file in the office, but fifty-two have been called up for action. A much larger number, it is believed, remain to be filed. No claims so far have been spurious or forged as far as could be determined.[584]

No small number of these involved the name of William Blackmore who purchased a great many interests in 1871.

The Maxwell Grant grappled for its existence. On March 13, 1872, Lucien Maxwell received final payment of principal and interest in the amount of $87,500 on the $75,000 note of September 1870.[585] One hundred-ninety-two-thousand five hundred was due on 140 bonds to be drawn June 15, 1872. John L. Reed was still the Maxwell Company's president. It was at first deemed advisable to

---

[584] Ibid.
[585] Murphy, Lawrence R., *Lucien Bonaparte Maxwell*, Chap. 9, "Reflections on A Frontier Life," p. 194.

borrow enough money at ten percent interest from John Collinson, former president, and other bondholders who called themselves the "Anglo-American Association."

Ownership of the valuable ranch property made another bond issue possible. The arrangement on this first mortgage of the Home Ranch property secured 2,750 £100 bonds bearing seven percent interest. The coupons were to be paid in May and November at Amsterdam in 1875, the capital redeemable in 1892. A write-in was set to open at Amsterdam on November 26 against 75 ½%. The company's annual interest payments alone amounted to $350,000.[586]

The Maxwell Company was not alone in its struggle for survival. In neighboring Colorado, on May 24, 1872, it was announced in Costilla County that the Sangre de Cristo would be sold in a public auction for $29,000, its unpaid

---

[586] Ibid., p. 58.

back taxes.[587] The sale would take place June 3, 1872 at ten o'clock.

The Maxwell Land Grant & Railway Company was facing serious financial trouble. The promised European settlers of Wertheim & Gompertz had not materialized. When new settlers came from abroad, they settled on the prairies. The bankers did not recruit and ship citizens from Holland. Open rebellion by the miners against the Maxwell company threatened its extinction. By 1872, Colfax County's gold production was only one-fifth the territory's gold. Two years before, the county turned in sixty percent of the territory's total gold production.

Back in Colorado, on March 2, 1872, Blackmore returned all the membership certificates issued to Lloyd, Potter, Bridges, and Mrs. Hamp. Dr. Bell received them for the National Land and Improvement Company. He was emphatic that the Mountain Base transfer was without his

---

[587] Santa Fe Daily *New Mexican*, 4/24/72, p. 1.

associates' approval. He said, "I cannot consent to accept 190,000$ in paper as suggested by General Palmer for what is expected to be worth 5,250,000$."[588]

The Arkansas Pool was a critical piece in Palmer's land funding program. The Pool contained two ten thousand-acre tracts on the north side of the river next to Pueblo. It included the townsites of Alamo and Labadie. There were also two thousand acres of coal land on two creeks below Canon City and six hundred acres for a townsite "adjacent to the coal mines" which would be called "Labran."

Another townsite tract near Canon City included fourteen hundred acres with the ditch head site at the mouth of the Arkansas Canon. Three hundred twenty acres southwest of Canon City held "a mass of pure magnetic Iron Ore." The Nolan grant of 48,000 confirmed acres was nineteen miles long and thirty miles broad. The pool hoped

---

[588] Brayer, Herbert O., *William Blackmore: Early Financing of the Denver and Rio Grande Railway,"* Vol. II, pp. 130-131.

that it could claim an additional 322,000 of the grant's original 370,000 acres. Also, ten thousand acres of land composed a colony tract which lay on the railroad route between the Nolan Grant and the coal mines.

A bond and stock agreement would pay the National Land and Improvement Company for the Central Colorado Improvement Company's purchase. The original cash cost of the land plus seven percent interest would make their annual payment about $300,000. It was based on the date of the original purchase by the National Land and Improvement Company. Revenues were expected to be adequate to pay excellent returns and retire the company's obligations when due.

The Union Contract Company set to work in March 1872 when the railroad construction was complete at Pueblo. They met the schedule by April 15 and began construction of the Arkansas division to the mouth of Coal Creek, only seven miles from Cañon City. Construction camps were set up to house and feed the men. The work of laying out the Labran townsite had begun in January. It was reported that common laborers were paid $2.50 to $3.00 per day and were boarded for $6.00 weekly.[589] The Fort Union civilians and former Army laborers were traveling to Canon City to work rather than work the nearby gold mines. The Maxwell Company was being boycotted!

On April 17, 1872, Senator Thomas Scott introduced a bill in Congress for the Denver & Rio Grande to be granted right-of-way through public land from Denver to El Paso. It was granted with two provisions. The railway had to complete its line to Santa Fe in five years from the act's passage. At least fifty miles was required to be built each year until the line was complete.[590]

On April 30, 1872, Blackmore joined Senator Henry B. Anthony on a visit with President and Mrs. Grant

---

[589] Brayer, Herbert O., *William Blackmore: Early Financing of the Denver & Rio Grande Railway*, Vol. Extension and Development," p. 145.
[590] Ibid., p. 157.

at the White House in the evening. All was well in the Capitol.[591]

At the time Blackmore was challenged by General Palmer's alterations to the agreement on the land companies supporting the railroad, another matter arose. The financier was forced to confront Governor Gilpin and his associates on the Sangre de Cristo's agreements for his commission to be paid in large tracts on the Trinchera Estate. The property in which Blackmore held title was in part a five-thousand-acre tract where he had placed his brother, Henry, in a sheep operation on the lower Culebra land. However, the promoter held no formal title to the tract. Although Fisher authorized transfer of title, Gilpin had not acted on it. Blackmore's attempts to gain Colonel Reynold's authority or deed were refused.[592] Fisher left further action to Blackmore.

---

[591] Brayer, Herbert O., *William Blackmore: The Spanish Mexican Land Grants*, "The Costilla Estate," Vol. I, pp. 116-121.
[592] Ibid., p. 117

In Washington, the promoter made two appointments with Gilpin for his authorization. The first was postponed, the second cancelled. On a third attempt, Blackmore learned that Gilpin had left for New York an hour after promising to meet him the next morning.[593]

Blackmore wrote Gilpin demanding to know how he intended to meet his obligation to convey the property according to the contract. He threatened court action if the conveyance was not signed in one month. Gilpin signed the papers following a meeting with Henry Blackmore on May 24, but without Reynolds' signature. William then notified Fisher and requested a deed for his additional 2,500 acres without delay. These acres had been promised in a separate agreement in 1870. The promoter then urged Fisher to seek an immediate partition of the whole property.

Blackmore referred to the Trinchera Estate since this property still belonged to the original investors Gilpin,

---

[593] Ibid., pp. 117-118.

Fisher, Reynolds, Hartshorn, and Hitchcock. These men had placed their interests in the Colorado Freehold Land & Emigration Company Ltd. Bonds had been issued, but like the Costilla Estate's development, there was no growth indicated. Taxes were mounting, and delinquency would result in a tax sale.

Governor Gilpin was unable or unwilling to resolve the issues with the native grant settlers. At the same time, the anti-land grant movement continued to fester. The populist Press and political opportunists began to take advantage of the situation.[594]

The Denver & Rio Grande line was completed to Pueblo on June 19 in the early morning before a jubilant crowd marking an important event for the Santa Fe Trail and the Arkansas Valley.[595]

The situation changed by October. The extension of the Denver & Rio Grande and the proposed land

---

[594] Ibid., p. 119.
[595] Ibid., p. 110.

development by the CCIC caused an explosion of growth in Pueblo. Palmer reported that Pueblo was six times its size before the railroad arrived. The corporate limits of the town were extended in every direction, but property values rose accordingly.

One of the first projects was a large hotel to accommodate visitors and potential buyers. A canal was begun and would be completed by December 1872. Agricultural areas were planned to manage food supplies for the explosion of people.

On October 19, 1872, the Pueblo County Commissioners ordered the first issue of bonds for $100,000 signed and delivered to the railway. The County Clerk was authorized to provide a receipt for the same amount of railway stock which the railway attorney, Mr. Stone, delivered to the county officials.

In November 1872 the railroad promoters laid out the new town of South Pueblo. They surveyed and platted six thousand business and residential lots within the town. Adjoining lands were subdivided into villa and farm lots much like Colorado Springs. Half were sold at once, the remainder held for future sales. Allowance was made for increasing valuations.[596]

At the end of 1872 the money market was tight. It was becoming difficult to market the mortgage bonds of the railway. There were few reasonable incentives to buy the bonds unless steps were taken to place the common stock on a dividend paying basis, and in such an instance there would be serious limitations.[597]

The railroad's obligation to build the depot on the north side of the Arkansas River and within a mile of the courthouse still stood. Nevertheless, when the D & RG was certain it owned the 48,000 Nolan Grant property, a bridge

---

[596] Ibid., pp. 140-141
[597] Brayer, Herbert O., *William Blackmore: Early Financing of the Denver & Rio Grande Railway*, "Extension and Development, 1872," p. 162. See also p. 126, fn. 49 in "Opening the Arkansas Valley, 1872." All of the figures given in these reports were based on whether the program would succeed. They were promotional figures meant to entice people to join their subscriptions.

was built between north and south Pueblo. Then, a depot was built on the railroad's townsite.

Chapter Twenty: Comanches and the Texas Cattle Trade

February 1872 – December 1872

Early in February 1872, a party of fifteen Cheyenne were seen going down the Arkansas River on foot, leading their horses. Thirty-five well mounted Ute warriors followed them closely. Settlers along the route were persuaded to cook for these two groups. Interested observers decided that the Ute were escorting the Cheyenne out of their buffalo range and away from their horses. It was certainly unusual.

Four months later, a great many Cheyenne traveled north from New Mexico and crossed the Arkansas River about forty miles below Fort Lyon. They were clearly on the lookout for the Ute who were likely hunting buffalo in eastern Colorado.

By June 19, 1872, in southeastern Colorado, the Denver & Rio Grande Railway had reached Pueblo. The Colorado Ute reservation was around 200 miles from the railroad. In September, the Utes were fighting amongst themselves over the disposition of lands.[598]

It was May 26, 1872 when a large band of Kiowas roamed the high plains in search of buffalo. They were also on the lookout for the Utes. Around 300 Kiowa suddenly appeared before eighteen members of San Juan Pueblo on the Rio Grande. There were three Mexicans with the

---

[598] *New Mexico Historical Review* XLVI: 4, 1971; Taylor, ____, "Plains Indians," pp. 316-317.

Pueblos. The site where the Pueblos were camped was at the Cimarron Cutoff where it crosses Carrumpaw Creek. The Kiowas attacked the Pueblo party so that the twenty-one took refuge in a cave. The Plainsmen attacked all day until nightfall when they withdrew. The bodies of the fallen were taken, including two chiefs. The Pueblos stayed in the cave for two days, uncertain all were gone. They finally reached Mora on their route home.[599]

It was a portent of trouble ahead. At almost the same time, in southern Arizona there was an Apache attack at Apache Pass and another in the Prescott area where Apaches had begun stealing stock and settlers' provisions. Locals wrote the Arizona newspapers that General Crook and a good cavalry unit was expected to "bring to a close the hollow truce." It was because of the problem in halting illegal Indian trading which Singleton Ashenfelter could

---

[599] Santa Fe *Daily New Mexican*, 3/12/72, p. 1, col. 2.

not prosecute that President Grant named Tom Catron U. S. Attorney for New Mexico in March of 1872.

The Union Contract Company needed cash to purchase lands for stations and townsites while the company was surveying for the Denver & Rio Grande Railway. This would enable the railroad to get the land before the value shot up and became too costly. Palmer and Bell transferred the Mountain Base Pool into an old and idle company incorporated in Pennsylvania in 1866. It had been designed to improve lands for emigrants. The Palmer company rewrote the by-laws and formally reorganized the company in April 1871. They used it to make a contract with the Union Contract Company. "Friends" of the road had already purchased a large quantity of such lands and property at rates below the present value. The National Land & Improvement Company received the funds of the Mountain Base Pool to purchase these lands. Blackmore's investment pool became a limited liability company, or joint stock company by this means.[600]

In December 1871, Dr. Bell had outlined the plan for the Arkansas Valley Pool. It was a method of raising money for effecting the program of the Central Colorado Improvement Company. It was planned to issue 10-year 6% gold bonds for a total of $1,500,000 of which $825,000 would be used for the construction of a railroad from Pueblo to the mouth of the Arkansas Canyon. It would provide for the purchase of land, including the Nolan Grant, and the balance of $375,000 would be used as a development fund.

The military at Fort Union was alert for trouble on the eastern border. Troops were sent out to patrol between Texas, and New Mexico near Fort Bascom. This was on the edge of the Staked Plains separating Texas and New Mexico. The Comanches and Kiowas as well as some

---

[600] Brayer, Herbert O., *Willliam Blackmore: Early Financing of the Denver & Rio Grande Railway,* "Land Development Companies, 1871," pp. 92-95.

Arapahos lived on the Texas side of the border. They let their often-stolen cattle graze on the Llano Estacado, the Staked Plains, Indian Country.

Colonel John Irwin Gregg and three companies of the Eighth Cavalry were ordered to march from Fort Union and patrol along the Canadian River. A guide and a packer accompanied them. Complaints of cattle thieves at Fort Sumner took them south, but no criminal activity was detected.

John Hittson, a prominent Texas cattle rancher, prepared for the annual Comanche cattle raids by visiting other nearby ranches. He secured power of attorney from his neighbors to represent them in civil court and recover their stolen cattle. He had counseled with Colonels Gregg and Granger the year before when New Mexican courts failed to prosecute in the sale of stolen cattle.[601] The Fort Union authorities told Hittson they would support him in

---

[601] Pueblo Colorado *Chieftain,* 7/11/72.

his efforts to retrieve his herds.[602] In March 1871, Colonel J. I. Gregg learned of traders moving toward the plains with large quantities of goods. Major Clendenin, Fort Union's commander, reported many burros and carretas directed toward Comanche country. The military did not interfere, concerned for their own safety.[603]

Hittson went to Denver. He hired and armed sixty men and sent them to New Mexico. He also recruited James Patterson of Denver to assist him. Patterson owned a large southeastern New Mexico cattle ranch on the Pecos. He had sold cattle to Fort Sumner when the Navajo still occupied the Bosque Redondo. Patterson sold his spread to John Chisum in 1867 and continued to sell beef to the government from other properties he held in New Mexico.

---

[602] *The Third Fort Union: Construction and Military Operations,* Part Two, 1869-1891, Chap. 7. Also, Fort Union, NM, A Historic Resource Study – National Park Service, Leo E. Oliva, 1993. "Fort Union and the Frontier Army in the Southwest." Also, *Rocky Mountain News*, 4/29/73. Annual Report of the Secretary of War, 1872, p. 151. Testimony of former Army office, R. S. Mackenzie.
[603] Ibid.

Together, Hittson and Patterson hired another 150 men and sent them to the southern Territory.

One of the men hired was H. M. Childress of Coleman County, Texas. Between 1867 and 1871 he drove an average 2500 head of cattle annually to Abilene. Childress was hired to lead the posse seeking stolen cattle throughout farms and ranches in the eastern Territory. They collected 4,000 to 6,000 head of cattle with Texas brands.[604]

When the area ranchers learned the Texans' cattle were being driven from New Mexico, Pribert and Kirchner, the primary Santa Fe meat market owners and ranchers, obtained writs of replevin preventing their cattle from being driven from the Territory until the courts had decided their proper owners.[605]

Texas raiding of New Mexican ranches suspected of purchasing their cattle persisted. Trouble with the Indian

---

[604] Santa Fe Daily *New Mexican*, 8/7/72, p. 1, col. 1.
[605] *New Mexico Historical Review*, Vol. XXXVII, October 1962, pp. 243-259. Kenner, Charles, "The Great New Mexico Cattle Raid - 1872," p. 243-259, p. 254, fn. 35.

tribes continued as the railroad drew nearer. Washington ordered Secretary Arny to gather the Ute Indian tribe at Cimarron for a council to be held at Pagosa Springs in August.[606] Commissioners would be present there to locate the tribe on a reservation suitable to them. The region at the headwaters of the Rio Las Animas, Baker's Park, and the tributaries of the San Juan River had been determined to be ripe for settlement and mining. The Secretary of the Interior had appointed the commissioners to negotiate with the Utes to remove them in favor of hardy pioneers who would develop the land to be productive.[607]

Reports of Apache raids in southern New Mexico had been ongoing since February.[608] The problem was with Cochise, the Apache chief. In April it was published that Cochise and his tribe had one month to submit and go to the reservation. They would be turned over to the military

---

[606] Ibid., 6/28/72, p. 1, col. 1.
[607] Santa Fe Daily *New Mexican*, 7/10/72, p. 1, col. 1. Also, 9/26/72, p. 1, col. 1.
[608] Ibid., 2/16/72, p. 1, col. 1, "Letter from Silver City."

at month's end.[609] Reports of murder and robbery dragged on into mid-May from Arizona.[610]

Several days afterward, in reporting the incident in the *New Mexican*, the newspaper upbraided the local citizens for tolerating the participation of so many territorial citizens in the long-known traffic in stolen cattle. New Mexicans had too long turned a blind eye in the trading with Comancheros. "We allude to that unholy and barbarous traffic which has so long been carried on between the cattle dealers of New Mexico and the Comanche Indians of Texas and Northern New Mexico . . . ignoring the *modus operandi* of obtaining "cheap cattle" from Texas."[611]

Later revelations indicated that stealing and robbery were being practiced by "certain capitalists" who enlisted the aid of Indians. "These men hire ignorant creatures to go

---

[609] Ibid., 4/1/72, p. 1, co. 1.
[610] Ibid., 5/16/72, p. 1, col. 1. Also, 5/17/72, p. 1, col. 1, "Southern Apaches."
[611] Santa Fe Daily *New Mexican,* 9/26/72, p. 1, col. 1.

out and meet the Indians on the plains and bring or take the stolen stock to market where bona fide purchasers become the sufferers. This kind of traffic is what has led to the Texan raids in San Miguel and other counties in New Mexico."[612]

The recent trouble had begun in the spring of the previous year and the *New Mexican* wrote of it in June 1871. The article reminded New Mexicans that the trade was illegal and citizens without the proper license or authority of law were going into Indian country. These citizens gave whiskey, powder, and trinkets to the Indians for their stolen stock. It had been the common practice for many years. Also, the Indians sold the cattle to local farmers as well as the best meat markets in the Territory. The Comancheros, mostly mixed breed Indians, were agents for the Comanches. The Comancheros lived among

---

[612] Ibid., 8/9/72, p. 1, col. 1. Also, 9/26/72.

the villagers, but their primary means of support was the ill-gotten gains from cattle sales.

In 1871, the Texas ranchers had finally made headway with the authorities and were aided by the military. Colonels Granger and Gregg of Fort Union encouraged Hittson's men whose case in Santa Fe court had previously fizzled. Captain Randlett and the 8th Cavalry captured a pack train of twenty-three burros loaded with powder, lead, cloth, and trinkets. The train was destroyed in obedience to orders. The animals were killed, and twelve prisoners were captured with a Comanche squaw who served as a guide to the Comanche camp. Ten Mexicans were also taken. They claimed to be residents of Santa Fe, San Miguel, and Mora.[613]

The following day Captain Randlett captured five hundred and ten head of cattle which came from the Comanche country. The trading party escaped excepting

---

[613] Ibid., 6/5/71, p. 1, col. 1, "More Captures from Comanche Traders."

one man. He was held at Fort Bascom in charge of military authorities.

Early in 1871 the Army approved Hittson's raids and supplied the Texas raiders with ammunition from Fort Union.

In April it was announced in New Mexico's newspapers that the bill introduced earlier in Congress would now allow proceedings for grant claimants to try the validity of their claims. A jury would consider the facts and a court of equity would determine the titles to the land. The cost of surveys of these grants would be borne by the government. Several important matters would be examined when considering the plaintiff's rights to such claims: 1) Did any other person claim the same land? 2) The quantity and boundaries had to be specified. 3) A map had to be provided which conformed to U. S. Surveys. 4) Had the grant been formally authorized by a Congressional act or any U. S. authority? 5) The boundaries must be declared.

Petitioners for confirmation meeting the requirements named could present to a district attorney, chief or associate justice the papers stating the nature of the claim, the date of the grant, concession, warrant or order of survey, and must name the parties to the claim. Two years were given to make the claim. An appeal could be filed within one year of decision. The decision of the Supreme Court would be final.[614]

The care and safekeeping of the archives remained a problem for the Territory. The *New Mexican* reminded the public of the need to conserve such a valuable library of fragile documents and maps. The papers should be sorted, filed, and kept in air-tight containers. They were now left to the land grant owners to pay privately for their care.[615]

The difficulty which developed in June was that the office of the Surveyor General was vacated due to the unexpected death of Surveyor General Spencer.[616]

---

[614] Santa Fe Daily *New Mexican*, 5/2/72, p. 1, col. 1.
[615] Ibid., 9/27/72, p. 1, col. 1.
[616] Santa Fe Weekly *Post*, 6/22/72, p. 1, col. 1.

Surveyor General Proudfit would not arrive until sometime after his appointment on August 20, 1872.[617]

A great deal of energy, planning, and advertising went into the Territory's preparation for the June 16 statehood election. Each district held public meetings to discuss the matter, with varying results. Much depended on the attitude of local leaders in the eventual outcome.

In Bernalillo County, Frank Chaves chaired the first meeting on May 28 and the resolutions were adopted according to the rules of order.[618] The assembly resolved to adopt the Constitution and demand admission as a state.

Steve Elkins, a strong proponent of the measure, was invited to speak. His presence signified that peace had been made with Chaves.

In Santa Fe County, the meeting was held on the same day and in the same manner. On June 3 the *New Mexican* carried an article on why the state constitution

---

[617] Santa Fe Daily *New Mexican*, p. 1, col. 1.
[618] Santa Fe Daily *New Mexican*, 5/14/72, p. 1, col. 1.

should be adopted. In summary, it stated that a state government would be beneficial to have a voice in Congress, to enforce their just rights, to ensure railways, have a ready market for the Territory's products, protect its interests, and induce prosperity. However, almost two weeks later, and after the election results were counted, at least three Santa Fe county precincts voted against it.

Statehood failed to pass by a large margin. On June 11 it was announced that the time was too short in which to make returns and thereby many counties did not set up voting areas. On June 11, the *Daily New Mexican* attributed the poor showing to the general belief that Congress would not admit New Mexico.[619] Many rejected the election for its expense. It was thought that only one-third of eligible voters participated and was over before election day.

The climax of the Comanche and Comanchero cattle trade occurred in late September.

---

[619] Santa Fe *Daily New Mexican*, 6/11/72, p. 1, col. 1.

After August 1, 1871, the military learned they had no legal authority to support or give aid to the Texans. Colonel Granger directed the troops at Fort Bascom to "take no part in the matter . . . except to prevent bloodshed if possible."[620]

A party of Texans arrived in Loma Parda, New Mexico on the 22nd or 23rd of September. They went to the corral of one local resident and demanded their cattle. A great deal of noise prompted a neighbor, Mr. Seaman, the police chief, to rush into the midst of the argument and to shout for the intruders to "Come on!" Seaman then presented his revolver in the face of the group's leader, Mr. Childress. Childress' associate, immediately behind him, shot Seaman in the head, killing him instantly. Another local resident attempted to intercede between the Texas hired posse and Seaman. Toribio Garcia was also killed.

---

[620] Oliva, Leo E., *The Third Fort Union: Construction and Military Operations: 1869-1891;* Part Two, Chap. 7, "Fort Union and the Frontier Army in the Southwest," A Historic Resource Study – National Park Service, 1993. Footnotes 75 and 76.

In nearby Mora County, Hittson was advised to negotiate with Vicente Romero and his family who were leading residents. He approached Romero tactfully and they agreed to a pact. They kept it a secret that Romero was paid for his lost cattle. Romero advised his people on the smaller ranches to be courteous and release the cattle with Texas brands. However, a few ran the cattle into the mountains and slaughtered them rather than allow them to be taken away.[621]

On September 12, 1872, a peace council composed of a group of commissioners went to the Kiowas on the Texas border and took gifts of canned fruit and other desirable foods to entice the Indians to call off their raids.[622] It was reported that the attempt at conciliation was met with insolence and the party returned at once.

Shortly afterward, Indian agent Lorenzo Labadi met with Steve to ask if he would be interested in representing

---

[621] *The Colorado Magazine*, XI, May 1934, vol. 69.
[622] Santa Fe Daily *New Mexican*, 9/12/72, "A Peace Council . . . in Indian territory," p. 1, col. 1.

John Hittson in court. Lucien Maxwell had lost many cattle in his herds as well. Peter Maxwell had an appeal in court to have the Pecos ranch mapped and they had no time for another case. He had deposited $2500 in the Santa Fe Land Office to get a deed to the former military property. Steve told Labadie he would see if he could manage to handle the case which might take a considerable amount of time. He didn't tell Labadie, but Sallie was declining and he intended to stay at home with her as much as possible.

Steve decided to consult with Judge Palen. The cattle rustling case involved too many parties. There were the Comanches, the Comancheros, the people of Loma Parda, Hittson, and the other Texans, and Santa Fe's leading meat marketers. Ashenfelter had lost the U. S Attorney's office the year before over his inability to prosecute. He didn't want Tom to be caught up in another power play. Sallie was dying. He had to be home with her as much as possible. There would have to be a negotiation.

Palen agreed and all parties were called in to resolve the matter. After a month of meetings, the case was resolved. A compromise was reached in which all parties would have to share more blame than profit.

At home, Steve and Sallie accepted her own solemn and hasty departure. Medical alternatives no longer offered a relief from an agonizing end. They wept together. On October, she lapsed into a coma.

The case of Pribert and Kirchner against Hittson was announced on October as settled out of court. Some months later the accused killers of Seaman and Garcia were arrested but escaped jail and were not brought to justice.[623]

Governor Giddings called a public meeting on September 30 to inform citizens of a plan of operation to induce and expedite the construction of railroads in the Territory. The meeting was conducted in Council chambers. It was intended that all sections of New Mexico

---

[623] Oliva, Leo E., *The Third Fort Union: Construction and Military Operations: 1869-1891;* Part Two, Chap. 7, fn. 77.

should be covered. Several railroad companies were considering construction to the west and at least one to the south. The railroads named were the Atlantic & Pacific, Texas Pacific, Denver and Rio Grande, New Mexico and Gulf, and the Atchison Topeka & Santa Fe. The last-named road was thought to be on the route to join with an extension of a branch of the Kansas Pacific near Fort Lyon, Colorado. After the completion of that extension it was uncertain what the Kansas Pacific would do.

A committee of nine was appointed by the governor. Its consensus would state the meeting's aim. The purpose was to give a full and proper presentation of facts concerning the value of New Mexico's resources. A report to this effect should be provided these prospective railroad companies. The resultant facts related to the economic desirability of railroad construction in New Mexico should be made available to the railroads. Included in the committee of nine men was a chairman, a recording secretary, and a corresponding secretary. The group would prepare, point out, and forward their findings to the proper railroad officials and corporations.

The committee should call public meetings to relay propositions received from these railroad companies. It should also call meetings at such times as needed to discuss railroad matters. It should gather information and solicit action from other parts of the Territory to aid and hasten railroad construction.[624] The comments indicated that much had been learned from observation of the difficulties being experienced in Pueblo with the Denver and Rio Grande officials. Among the resolutions presented that evening was one which stated that owners of land grants in New Mexico would make important concessions to persuade the railroad officials to build through their grants.[625]

On October 30 Philip Elkins was in Santa Fe to support his son, Steve. Sarah Elkins, familiarly known as

---

[624] Santa Fe Daily *New Mexican,* 10/8/72, p.1. col. 1.
[625] Ibid.

Sallie[626], died on October 27.[627] A funeral service would be conducted on the following day. Although a cemetery plot was opened in Santa Fe, it was known that her bier would be taken to Missouri for burial.[628]

Two months later railroad officials began arriving in Santa Fe to study New Mexico's promotional material. These men were invited to attend a reception which included the president of the Council, Tomas Cabeza de Baca of Las Vegas, a land grant owner who raised sheep and cattle. Perhaps prompted to remark on the effect of the railroads on the Territory, he spoke candidly, "We don't want you damned Yankees in the country. We can't compete with you, you will drive us all out, and we shall have no home left us. We won't have you here."[629]

---

[626] Twitchell, Ralph E., *Leading Facts of New Mexican History*, Vol. II, "New Mexico During the Civil War," p. 401, fn. 327.
[627] Keleher, William A., *The Fabulous Frontier*, Chap. Five, "Thomas Benton Catron," p. 135. Also, Santa Fe *Daily New Mexican,* 10/30/72, "Funeral," p. 1, cols. 1-2.
[628] Santa Fe Daily *New Mexican*, 10/28/72, p. 1, col. 1.
[629] Lamar, Howard R., *The Far Southwest:1846-1912*, Chap. 6, "The Santa Fe Ring, 1865-1885," p. 143.

These remarks were apparently made to David Bryan and J. N. Atchison of San Francisco. They represented the Atchison Topeka & Santa Fe Railroad. They were visitors at the Exchange Hotel on December 3, 1872.[630] The date would have been during the opening of the New Mexico Legislature. De Baca considered the railroad an interference with his wool business. Rails would restrict free grazing, even on his own land.

In New Mexico, one civic leader, Elias Brevoort, a businessman in Santa Fe, former Army officer, and mail contractor, spearheaded a campaign for a railroad to the Cimarron Country. Plans were drawn up with a surveyor for a projected rail line from the Arkansas Valley to Santa Fe, then across three rivers, the Vermejo, the Ponil, and the Cimarron. The surveys were conducted to Cimarron. The promoters recognized that if the route were run through the canyon to the Moreno Valley, they could also reach the rich

---

[630] Santa Fe *Daily New Mexican*, 12/3/72, Item, p. 1, col. 2.

Taos Valley. During this survey period William R. Morley, a young railroad engineer who had recently joined the Maxwell Company, became a part of the Arkansas Valley and Cimarron team.[631]

Steve Elkins' arrangements to leave New Mexico for Missouri and Sallie's burial took several days. Shortly after Sallie Elkins' death, the annual meeting of the Maxwell Land Grant and Railway Company announced that new officers were elected for the coming year. John Collinson presided for the Board of Directors. S. B. Elkins was named president, W. R. Morley, a railroad engineer, vice-president, R. H. Longwill, an Elizabethtown doctor, H. M. Porter, and A. J. B. Malagay, new directors. Morley, Longwill, and Porter, were named executive officers. H. M. Porter had purchased the former Cimarron store from the company. Morley was finance committee chairman. His annual report offered brilliant prospects for the company's

---

[631] Pearson, Jim Berry, *The Maxwell Land Grant*, Chap. Four, "The English Syndicate in Trouble," pp. 57-59.

future operations. Only Steve Elkins' temporary absence was noted.[632]

On November 7 the Santa Fe *Daily New Mexican* had forecast the re-election of President Grant. No one reported any surprise at the expected outcome. The same issue announced that Steve Elkins had left for the states and would be absent until spring. Two days later an article appeared confirming that a hundred buildings were constructed, and several bridges repaired during the year.[633] The plaza was renovated, and the town's general appearance was greatly enhanced. The improvements were undoubtedly due to bank loans. City streets and plank sidewalks were not forgotten. There were no signs of the tight money market the Denver and Rio Grande Railway was experiencing.

---

[632] Ibid., 11/6/72, p. 1, col. 2, "Arkansas Valley and Cimarron Railway."
[633] Ibid., 12/9/72, p. 1, col. 2, item.

Chapter Twenty-One: The Treasure
May 1872 – November 1872

On May 1, 1872, the directors of the Central Colorado Improvement Company authorized President William Mellen to execute a mortgage for $1,500,000. It would cover all company property presently owned, or to be acquired, to secure its ten-year 6% gold bonds.[634]

Between February and May 1872, William Blackmore prepared three general pamphlets outlining the legal background of the Spanish and Mexican land grants

---

[634] Brayer, Herbert O., *William Blackmore: Early Financing of the Denver & Rio Grande Railway*, Vol. II, "Extension and Development, 1872," p. 137.

in New Mexico. He provided the history, boundaries, and potentialities of the Cebolla Grant. This was written by Newell Squarey, assistant manager of the Costilla Estate. It was lithographed and published by Blackmore. Blackmore owned half of the Cebolla Estate of 250,000 acres by January 25, 1872.[635] The Luceros and Mora Grants' pamphlets and two maps were also prepared and duplicated. Early in the year two short pamphlets were designed to give force to the question of the land grants' legality.[636]

Addressing location, one map Blackmore created was dramatically colored to accentuate the size and location in relation to the rest of the region. The other map was nearly identical to a map of the territory previously distributed by the General Land Office.[637]

---

[635] Brayer, Herbert O., *William Blackmore: The Spanish-Mexican Land Grants*, Vol. I, "The New Mexican Land Grants," p. 152.
[636] Ibid., 176-177.
[637] Ibid.

Each pamphlet contained a list of private land claims in the New Mexico Territory submitted to the Surveyor General for confirmation together with a copy of the official report of the Committee on Private Land Claims of the U. S. Senate. This item displayed a great many New Mexico grants which had been recommended by the U. S. Senate for confirmation. The list included the Luceros Estate which Blackmore owned with Charles Clever, John Graham, and Frederick Muller.[638] A total of almost half of the latter property of 1,000,000 acres had been purchased by January 1872 for $16,000, or seven cents an acre.[639] It adjoined the town of Taos.

Blackmore lobbied in Congress in 1871 for passage of "The Western Lands Improvement Company." It was a bill designed to obtain a national rather than territorial authorization for the Spanish and Mexican land grants. Wertheim and Gompertz previously sought the same

---

[638] Ibid.
[639] Ibid., p. 162.

security through the U. S. Freehold Land and Emigration Company's incorporation.[640] Blackmore's argument for national authorization was based on the claims made in favor of the Vigil and St. Vrain Grant before the war. It had been delayed for war concerns, then a great many parcels sold during the war. The Las Animas Grant was only a few miles east of Pueblo. Blackmore had previous experience with Las Animas from the year before in a Kansas Pacific Railroad projection for the Fort Lyon to Pueblo route in Colorado.

The promoter dealt with several attorneys and speculators in connection with New Mexican land grants. His primary interests and investments in New Mexico were with Charles Clever, former Congressional Delegate. There were six grants to be purchased, at least in part, between them. Blackmore had supplied an option payment, or provided Clever with a portion of his interest, in two of

---

[640] Ibid., p. 182. See fn. 33 on p. 186.

these. There was a written agreement on all six grants. Other grants were under consideration for purchase.[641]

The solicitor was invested to a total of nearly $100,000 in 2,070,500 acres of land in Colorado and New Mexico by the end of 1872. He had spent eight months in the U. S.[642] Blackmore was also a collector of geological artifacts and specimens. In his home was a virtual museum of these articles. His tours of the vast western terrain provided him with specimens which displayed his expertise in geology and archaeology. He was best described as an anthropologist. His thirst was insatiable. The attempt to capture the essence of this new land was evident in his collections.

The promoter's fascination with the open lands he observed was that of a man whose own landscape was limited by a density of population. Great Britain was comparable in size to Alabama and had few of the natural

---

[641] Brayer, Herbert O., *The Spanish-Mexican Land Grants*, Vol. 1, "Trust Lands Program, 1872-73", pp. 189-200.
[642] Ibid., p. 193.

curiosities of the American West. He was unconcerned with the development of the lands he acquired. That was left to General Palmer. However, Palmer could not have completed his program without the financial support of his English colleague.

Early in 1872 Blackmore began a program to create an income from his major properties. The pamphlets he drew up served as the basis of his new "Trust Lands Program." He proposed to sell interests in portions of the land grants already acquired. The three primary estates he promoted were the Cebolla, Los Luceros, and Mora Grants. He projected the values of these lands based on the arrival of the railroad and the growth of the area. He took the suggestion of a client to form a syndicate.[643]

In April that year the English solicitor's efforts faltered when the bill for incorporation of the "Western Lands Improvement Company" failed to be called up

---

[643] Ibid., p. 178.

before the adjournment of Congress. He took up temporary lodgings in New York City. The society he enjoyed in the capital must have compensated for his disappointment. His enthusiasm was not dampened.

In May, the Office of Indian Affairs contracted J. Gurney & Son, to produce a portfolio of photographs of the American Indian delegates to Washington, D. C. Images of nineteen tribes were compiled by the capitalist into ten albums which were exhibited at the Smithsonian. Alexander Gardner took the photos in his studio in Washington, where Blackmore was lobbying for his bill. In Album 1, the photos of Red Cloud and the Dakota Indians were produced for Blackmore's Salisbury Museum.[644] The exhilaration Blackmore experienced at recording these natives must have provided a great boost to his morale.

The public learned of the increase in land values in New Mexico when the U. S. Land Office announced the

---

[644] Hamber, Anthony, *Collecting the American West*, "Blackmore and Photography," pp. 219-222.

route of the Atlantic and Pacific Railroad on May 18, 1872. The route began at the Canadian River in eastern New Mexico and followed the Concha, Pecos, and Galisteo Rivers to the Rio Grande near Santa Domingo. It crossed the Rio Grande, finally turning southwest toward Fort Wingate and the territorial boundary with Arizona. Alternate sections of public land for construction purposes were stated, being 20 acres per mile. In the territories ten alternate sections on each side were allowed.

The amount of land granted the railroad was about eleven million acres, or one-seventh of the land in New Mexico. Real estate increased in value more than eleven million dollars in twenty-four hours due to the announcement of the definite route. It was stated that no lands on the road secured by a good title were affected by the grant.[645]

---

[645] Santa Fe Daily *New Mexican*, 5/19/72, p. 1, cols. 1-2.

Three-hundred-twenty-two miles north of Santa Fe, the colony of Colorado Springs was formally organized in the summer of 1871. At that time, construction was begun on the Colorado Springs Hotel, Hunt House, and the railroad depot. When work was completed the remainder of the land purchase and construction funds reverted to the National Land & Improvement Company. This amount was then transferred to the Railway Company's books.[646] The residence, business, and agricultural tracts were open for sale at drawings in March, May, and June 1872. The El Paso Canal Company, also a Palmer, Cameron, and Greenwood corporation organized in July, would supply the town with water.[647] Conditions in Colorado generally were not favorable for settlement unless the newcomer had financial resources. The colony was designed for wealthy English families.

---

[646] Brayer, Herbert O., *William Blackmore: Early Financing of the Denver & Rio Grande Railway,* Vol. II, pp. 64-65.
[647] Ibid., p. 84.

Blackmore visited Colorado Springs in the summer of 1871 when he made a comprehensive inspection tour of mines at Black Hawk and Boulder, and the two newly founded towns of Colorado Springs and Manitou near the foot of Pike's Peak.[648]

While the Central Colorado Improvement Company was progressing in its development of the Arkansas Valley property, the Colorado Springs Company was advancing two communities, the "Fountain Colony" project at Colorado Springs and the Manitou district at the base of Pike's Peak. Newspapers were advertising the colony program broadly. Also, the vice president, General Robert A. Cameron and his secretary, William E. Pabor, toured the eastern states promoting emigration to Colorado. In the winter of 1871 and 1872 they visited mid-west towns and settlements to circulate prospectuses and broadsides about the colonies.

---

[648] Brayer, Herbert O., Vol. I, *William Blackmore: The Spanish-Mexican Land Grants*, "The Costilla Estate," p. 103.

Since the railway's completion to Colorado Springs the town became a thriving community. The $20,000 Colorado Springs Hotel was completed, and fifty-five modern houses were built. Broad streets were graced with trees and a mile and a-half irrigation canal served the townsite with water from the Fountain River. Dignitaries of the original railroad pool visited the colony in July. There were 616 residential lots at Colorado Springs of the total 8832.27 acres. Four-hundred-eighty acres at Manitou were owned by the company.[649] In September seven-hundred-ninety-five residents occupied the community.

The first lands "sold" by the National Land and Improvement Company were the coal and townsite properties near Canon City. A transfer of these lands was made to the Central Colorado Improvement Company for $33,000 in six percent bonds and $187,000 stock of the improvement company.[650] There was a theoretical

---

[649] Brayer, Herbert O., Vol. II, *William Blackmore: Early Financing of the Denver and Rio Grande Railway,* pp. 150-151.
[650] Ibid., p. 153.

substantial increase in stock as well as in its receipt of the original property cost, plus seven percent interest. In 1872, the company directors claimed the colony had established about 300 houses and 1200 individuals.[651] The principal efforts of the land company were expended on Colorado Springs.

The first annual report to stockholders of the National Land and Improvement Company was issued by President McAllister on January 1, 1873, acting for the company's board of directors. The company formed an offshoot, the Colorado Springs Company, with a capital basis of $300,000 to obtain funds and acquire new property for area development.[652]

The stockholder funds, obtained through subscriptions, were used to purchase three groups of property: 1) Twenty-five tracts, or a total of 5,445.91 acres along the railway line between Denver and Pueblo; 2) The

---

[651] Ibid., p. 153.
[652] Ibid., pp. 153-155.

Colorado Springs property of one-half the colony tract of 6,012 acres plus adjoining tracts containing 2,820 acres and 480 acres at Manitou; 3) Coal and townsite lands in and near Canon City. The coal and townsite lands "sold" by the NL & IC were transferred to the CCIC for $33,000 in 6% bonds and $187,000 in stock of the improvement company.

Dividends were being withheld to allow the value of the investment to increase rather than sell the lands and securities for less than their intrinsic worth. The payments to stockholders would begin at the close of 1873.[653]

In fact, by February 1872, Colorado Springs became a thriving community. A business development was undertaken and a second canal from the Fountain River was nearly complete. When visitors of the original railway pool visited in late July 1872 a road through Ute Pass was being prepared for business in the spring with the newly opened mines at Mount Bross and Mount Lincoln. The

---

[653]Ibid., pp. 153-155.

bankers and financiers were introduced to a community of 795 persons. Private residences had increased to 159. A building was constructed to house the emigrants until they could be moved into homes.[654] The land company was forced to form an offshoot, the Colorado Springs Company, with its large capital to support further land acquisition.

The land companies aided in the construction of the Denver and Rio Grande Railway, but they also depended greatly on the railway's success. One hundred-eighteen miles of the main line, and thirty-eight miles from Pueblo to the coal mine district at Labran were divisions completed as well.

It was August 15 when Palmer and his associates filed the Articles of Incorporation of the *Canon City Coal Railway Company* in the office of the Secretary of State at Denver. This short line railroad would connect with the *Denver and Rio Grande Railway* at Labran. The branch

---

[654] Ibid., p. 150-151.

railroad would be only eight miles long. Although the grading was complete, there was difficulty in disposing of the railway and development company securities. The railway had a capital stock of $500,000 in shares of $100 each. Also, it was decided that Labran was where the line must end. The terminal depot would be on Labran's property owned by the Central Colorado Improvement Company. There was a guaranteed traffic for the railway so that investors would benefit. The Central Colorado Improvement Company was the critical component of the entire project.

The success of the colonies depended on the success of the railway. The railway promoters sought a franchise from the Mexican Congress to build a narrow-gauge system in the neighboring republic. All that blocked the way was the increased land values. However, a Congressional measure was passed in early June to grant the railway one hundred feet on each side of the track and twenty acres every ten miles for shops and stations from Denver to El Paso.

Many squatters believed the Las Animas grant invalid and the land to be in the public domain. These people deliberately settled on much of the best lands on the estate. They continued to file pre-emption applications. The Pueblo Land Office turned them away. They were told the land was reserved under a derivative claim from the original grantees.[655]

The General Land Office in Colorado would change its policy in some manner in 1873 and issued patents to the desired land to "a number of persons unknown in the country in which the claims were located." These claimants allegedly made warranty deeds to David Moffat, Colorado Assemblyman. Moffat's agent, concealing himself and whomever he represented, recorded the muniments of title at the county seat under the cloak of darkness, at night.

---

[655] Ibid., pp. 142-143.

Moffat and Chaffee were rewarded by being "given" a portion of the grant amounting to seven quarter sections, and 4,271 acres of land adjoining the West Las Animas townsite. Anti-grant feeling resulted from the entrance of political interference and settlers organized to protect their interests. There were threats against Moffat and Delegate Chaffee as well as St. Vrain and other claimants.[656]

It was announced in mid-April 1872 that *The North and South Railroad* would construct a railroad from Kit Carson, Colorado on the Kansas Pacific line fifty-four miles to Fort Lyon, the first division of the road. The second division would extend from Fort Lyon south to a point near Raton Mountain connecting with the *U. S. Central Railroad*. The purpose would be to establish a through line from Kit Carson to Cimarron on the Maxwell Grant, then to El Paso, Texas. Bonds were issued in the amount of $972,000, or $18,000 per mile.

---

[656] Ibid., p. 142.

The railroad executed a mortgage in favor of the Farmer's Loan and Trust Company of New York. It was recorded in the Bent County Recorder's Office. The mortgage covered the rights, franchises, roadbed, rails, ties, etc. together with lands for railroad purposes. The bonds would draw interest from September 3, 1871 at seven per cent per annum in gold and payable semi-annually, the payment of and interest guaranteed by the *Kansas Pacific Railway Company*. The mortgage was signed "*North and South Railway Company*, President, Jerome B. Chaffee." The promise of a railroad made to the Bondsmen, Wertheim and Gompertz in 1870 by the Maxwell Grant was, in this manner, fulfilled.[657]

In 1872, on the Nolan Grant opposite Pueblo, the Central Colorado Improvement Company constructed sixty-six buildings. One hundred and eighty lots were sold, yielding $23,262. A twenty-five-mile-long irrigation canal

---

[657] Santa Fe *Daily New Mexican*, 4/17/72, "Another Railroad for New Mexico," p. 1, col. 2.

was nearly complete. Six thousand business and residential lots constituted the prospective town proper. It was known that *The Kansas Pacific* and *Atchison Topeka* lines would cross at, or nearby, their site on the Nolan Grant. They built a hotel since there was none across the river in Pueblo.[658]

The Denver & Rio Grande Railway's depot at Pueblo was completed on the arrival of the railroad in July 1872. However, since that time the Nolan Grant transaction was executed. Construction was begun on the rival town of South Pueblo. The Union Contract Company built the bridge across the river and erected a new depot on its own property. The negative effect on old businesses and homes was profound. Those who had voted for the $100,000 bond issue and the additional $50,000 bond were incensed.[659]

No annual financial report of *The Denver and Rio Grande Railway* was printed. A report of traffic and the general results of one year of operations alone was

---

[658] Ibid., p. 141.
[659] Ibid., p. 142.

recorded.[660] No surplus or reserve fund existed at the end of 1872. All income from the completed road was required for current operating expenses and for paying the interest on the first mortgage bonds.[661] Increasing difficulty was experienced in marketing the mortgage bonds of the railway. The bonds already sold were paying an average interest of almost 11% on the amount invested. That was comparable to the established rate of 7%. Increasing the discount at which the bonds were sold would further increase capitalization, and not provide the necessary funds for future extensions.

Common stock needed to be placed on a dividend paying basis or there would be serious limitations. Markets had tightened by year's end. The only mileage completed after October 31, 1872, was the eight miles between Labran and Cañon City on the Arkansas Valley Division. Trinidad

---

[660] Ibid., p. 159.
[661] Ibid., p. 162.

was orphaned. Economic stress could easily topple the fragile pyramid Palmer and his associates had established.[662]

The financier's trust lands group interested in the purchase of the enticing Mora Grant was continually held up by a failure to divide the interests of the one hundred and seventy-three heirs and descendants of the original grantees. However, the grant was approved by Surveyor General T. Rush Spencer on June 13, 1872. If the grant purchase could be settled, it would still require the purchase of Fort Union when it was abandoned. It had been mistakenly located on the property when the Fort was built in July 1851.

The first six months of 1873 Blackmore continued his negotiations for the land grant purchases he had begun in 1871 and 1872. In March 1873, he wrote Clever and rebuked him for his failure to send promised title documents previously agreed upon between them. He

---

[662] Ibid.

demanded certain papers on the Navajo Springs Grant he had purchased from the Armijo brothers, Manuel and Rafael. Blackmore told him he would confer with him in Taos or Santa Fe in April or May.[663]

They would not meet. The arrangements between the two men failed when John Graham died suddenly before mid-year 1872.[664] Blackmore was not informed and assumed Graham was not honoring his commitment. However, Blackmore would continue to invest with other agents.

There had been a Squatter's Club on the Maxwell Grant since March 31, 1871. By June 2, 1872, they met at Charles Peterson's Store. By late 1872 the anti-grant men decided to begin a lawsuit. They collected money for some time before employing an attorney to test the validity of the Maxwell Company's claim.[665] On March 30, 1873, after

---

[663] Ibid., p. 194.
[664] Ibid., p. 211.
[665] Santa Fe *Daily New Mexican*, 4/2/73 and Murphy, Lawrence R., *Philmont*, Chap. IX, "Colfax County War," p. 118.

the Colfax County district court met at Cimarron two days earlier, the club staged a meeting in front of the county courthouse to demonstrate strength.[666] Many farmers and stock raisers had been hit with ejectment suits.

Squatters Club meetings in Cimarron and Elizabethtown openly defied the company officers to carry out the convictions. The Willow Creek miners joined the Elizabethtown miners in forcing the Maxwell Company to produce proof of its lawful authority to demand rents and eject them.

In the spring of 1873 William Morley was authorized to hire an attorney to assist him in filing and countering suits in the district courts. Frank Springer, his chosen attorney, had been Morley's fellow classmate at Iowa State College.

---

[666] Pearson, Jim Berry, *The Maxwell Land Grant*, Chap. 4, "The English Syndicate in Trouble," p. 64.

Chapter Twenty-Two: Smoke Signals

November 1872 – September 1873

On November 26, 1872, John Collinson, William Morley, and Steve Elkins appeared in Trinidad, Colorado at a meeting before a large crowd in the Town Hall. Elkins had returned briefly to support the company's efforts for the railroad. They sat quietly at the rear of the room while talk circulated around the railroad news from Pueblo. Finally, the moderator announced that representatives of the forthcoming Arkansas Valley & Cimarron Railway were attending the meeting and would tell them of new developments closer to their location.

    The three men went to the podium and were introduced. An enthusiastic round of applause followed. Steve Elkins, *Maxwell Land Grant & Railway* president, began to explain their railroad's plans. *The Arkansas Valley and Cimarron Railway* would enter New Mexico from Trinidad. They intended to co-ordinate with other railroads entering Colorado. Any of these railroads would have to file for operation under a different name to meet the requirement of Territorial law. It might involve connection with more than one railroad. At least two roads appeared to be surveying for building in the Fort Lyon vicinity. He and John Collinson were traveling East to arrange for such a connection. They hoped Trinidad would cooperate and join the effort to bring the Valley's central region into the plan to reach El Paso.

The Maxwell Land Grant men left the meeting in a great round of applause. They went outside to two different conveyances. William Morley, railroad engineer with the company for only one or two months, returned to Cimarron to manage company affairs until Steve could return.[667] Steve and John Collinson took a private coach to Pueblo. They would leave Pueblo for Kit Carson the next day. In several more days, they would take the Kansas Pacific for New York City.

Inside the meeting hall the consensus was that if the company would build a railway through Trinidad, Las Animas County would commit $250,000 in county bonds. They would obtain right-of-way for the road and any buildings required for its operation. A later meeting would be called to bring the matter to an election after further news from the Maxwell Land Grant Company who would notify them from the East.

---

[667] Ibid., Chap. Four, "The English Syndicate in Trouble," p. 59.

On December 3, *The Santa Fe Daily New Mexican* reported on an earlier article from the Pueblo *People*. It provided news to Santa Fe that Steve Elkins and John Collinson had started to England to secure the means to contract *The Arkansas Valley & Cimarron Railway*.[668] A correction was issued the next day. The men were on their way to New York City, not England. "The projected line runs from Fort Lyon or a point near there to Cimarron and is to be built by the united efforts of *The Atchison, Topeka and Santa Fe Railway Company* and the proprietors of the Maxwell Grant."

It would later be revealed that the Maxwell Land Grant Company men visited the Farmer's Loan and Trust Company, the same bank in which Jerome Chaffee placed the mortgage of *The North and South Railway* in mid-April 1872.[669]

---

[668] Ibid., 12/4/72. From the Pueblo *People* newspaper "of last week."
[669] Pearson, Jim Berry, *The Maxwell Land Grant*, Chap. 5, "The Dutch Bondholders Take Over," p. 78.

The new Maxwell Grant vice-president, William Morley, wrote Collinson in January 1873 that the squatters were still meeting but were losing strength. He wired Elkins in New York City on February 4 that he thought by spring a few suits would settle all the rest of them. Two men, Willow Creekers, settled for half of the profits on March 20.[670] However, the rest of the men were not cowed. They stubbornly refused to pay a red cent.

More ejectment suits went out from the Maxwell office. District Court began at Cimarron on Friday, March 28, 1873. The Maxwell Company had filed cases against small farmers and stock raisers. The anti-grant ranks, mainly miners, were there to get support from the angry settlers. The Squatter's Club called a mass meeting to be held at Cimarron on March 30 to raise money to contest the company's title.[671]

---

[670] Ibid., p. 64.
[671] Ibid., p. 65.

In mid-January news from Washington, D. C. reported that an investigation was being conducted of Congressmen holding stock in *The Union Pacific*'s construction company, Credit Mobilier. It would clearly reveal a great deal of corruption in stock manipulation of the largest enterprise in the nation. All who read of it wondered what the outcome might be.

Three British investors were committed to Blackmore's trust program in the amount of seven thousand pounds each. These investors were John Horatio Lloyd, J. Gerald Potter, and Roger Gadsden. The money was committed before the promoter's titles to the three New Mexico estates were completely perfected.[672] Professor Ferdinand Hayden and James Parrish also benefited from the Sangre de Cristo venture. In that transaction Blackmore acquired a large tract of land as his commission on the

---

[672] Brayer, Herbert O., *William Blackmore: The Spanish-Mexican Land Grants,* "Trust Lands Program, 1872-1873, p. 200.

property secured by Wertheim & Gompertz. If taxes were paid, he could maintain the land.

Several other grants in which Blackmore was interested with Adolf Guttman became much more expensive with the advent of the railroads. Their negotiations were cancelled. Blackmore remained interested in the 250 square mile Cieneguilla Grant which was pending confirmation. He held certified copies of fourteen deeds on this grant.[673] Cieneguilla had been approved by Surveyor General Spencer in June 1872, but final confirmation was still before Congress. The solicitor and Guttman had arranged for the possible purchase of three other grants.[674] His interest in the Maxwell Grant was another matter.

Open hostility continued between Pueblo and *The Denver & Rio Grande Railway*. The key concern was delivery of the promised rails inside Pueblo and its depot

---

[673] Ibid., p. 197.
[674] Ibid., p. 200.

near the courthouse. On January 11, 1873, the commissioners asked the District Attorney if they were bound to deliver the second bond issued on January 30, 1872. It was in the amount of $50,000. The District Attorney ruled that the county was not obligated to the railroad. The commissioners voted to withhold the bond. They were also inclined to nullify the first bond issue.

The status of the two Pueblo bond issues of $50,000 and $100,000 to the *Denver & Rio Grande* Company was still in question. The January 30, 1871 legal requirement of a register of voters had not been made prior to the election. Also, the railroad had not complied with the spirit of the contract. The commissioners voted to withhold the bonds. They further questioned the delivery of the first bond issue on May 3, 1873. They ordered the district attorney to begin legal proceedings against the railroad. On July 23 the county clerk returned the certificate of stock in the railway.

It is believed the corporation returned the county bonds. In November there would be further action in the bond return.[675]

The Denver and Rio Grande Railway Company had organized the *Mexico National Railway Company* and petitioned the Mexican Congress for a franchise to construct a narrow gauge in that country.[676] It would connect with *The Denver and Rio Grande Railway* at El Paso. In the interim of these events private property prices soared and the company sought relief from the problem of purchasing right-of-way.

On April 8, 1873, the Squatter's Club of Cimarron met and warned the Maxwell Grant men that they would protect John Lynch against ejection from his home. Matt Lynch, John's brother, an Aztec Mine discoverer, was killed in a robbery in 1871, making the brother heir to his property. The speakers were heard relative to the "evils

---

[675] Brayer, Herbert O., *William Blackmore: Early Financing of the Denver and Rio Grande Railway*, Vol. II, "Extension and Development, 1872," pp. 140-148.
[676] Ibid., p. 155.

stirring from the attempts of land speculators, home and foreign, to absorb the greater portion of the territory."

Statements were made that land speculators prevented the "settling up" and civilization of the country. The first speaker addressing the topic read letters from government officials. These pointed to speculators' activities in Colorado relative to questionable surveys and other spurious documents which enabled grants to be enlarged many times their original size. The speaker focused on the current financial condition of *The Maxwell Land Grant and Railway Company*. He noted the "magical disappearance of the Dutch guilders" which were raised to purchase the grant's claim to such an enormous acreage.[677]

W. W. Mills, the settler's attorney spoke briefly on his duty to support the settlers' rights to a "free soil." One local businessman expressed his opinion that the company had not yet proven its title to the two-million-acre property.

---

[677] Santa Fe Daily *New Mexican*, 4/11/73, p. 1, col. 2.

He stated that until it could do so the land grant must be considered public domain.

William Moore rose to recommend the organization of other clubs in the territory like the one in Colfax County which would pursue the land grant question to its conclusion.

A suit was brought against Lynch for possession by the new homeowners. The district courts of Colfax and San Miguel were asked to defer for reason of extreme prejudice. The case was moved to Taos County. In Taos County, on April 17, 1873, the court upheld the position of the Maxwell Company. Lynch was declared guilty of trespassing.

One month later, land claimed by John Lynch was sold by the company to Henry Porter and George Carpenter. Lynch would not move.

The New Mexican covered the Cimarron land grant public meeting and soon after published an editorial on strikes. It stated that it never knew a strike to benefit the workers.[678] On April 30 *The New Mexican* carried the refusal of the Squatters Club to accept Lynch's ejectment and its implication that the club would physically defend Lynch against any attempt to remove or incarcerate him.

When enforcers hired by the company to remove squatters arrived at Lynch's house, a line of club members blocked the entrances. They would not move to admit the company agents.

On April 22, the Squatter's Club informed the company that "We consider the judgment of said court to be in violation of existing orders of the Department of the Interior at Washington. And as citizens and lawful subjects of the government and administration, [we] *peremptorily refuse* to permit said defendant's ejectment, and until Saturday the 26th inst. we shall deem a word to the wise sufficient."[679]

---

[678] Ibid., 4/14/73, p. 1, col. 1.
[679] Ibid., 4/30/73, p. 1, col. 1.

On May 1, 1873, a Thursday, it was about eleven o'clock at night. Two men crept up on the ranch house where John Crowley, a pronounced enemy of the Squatter's Club, and his friend, William Parker, awoke to gunfire. Bullets were striking the house. The residents grabbed their rifles in time to find bullets ripping at the planks around the door frame. They threw the door open and fired at the flashes.[680]

Outside, a man shouted that he was hurt and needed help. The voice came from the willow grove at the house front. Crowley and Parker left the porch and slipped carefully into the trees. They found John H. Moore who had spoken out for the settlers in the recent Squatters Club meeting. He was seriously wounded, and seven empty Winchester shells lay next to him. His partner had fled. They took Moore into the house. One of the two house occupants rode for Dr. Longwill, but it was too late. Moore

---

[680] Pearson, Jim Berry, *The Maxwell Land Grant*, Chap. Four, "The English Syndicate in Trouble," p. 65.

did not live to explain the attack. The actions of the political leaders in Santa Fe were blamed. They were dubbed "the Santa Fe Ring."[681]

On February 12, 1873, in support of "hard" money, Congress passed an act demonetizing silver by omitting the standard silver dollar from the coinage. Gold was made the sole monetary standard, despite the increase in U. S. silver production. New discoveries of silver had been made in the west. Gold standard advocates feared that silver presented at the mint could feed inflation. In 1869 the Public Credit Act obligated the government to make its payments in gold. This was particularly hard on New Mexico where most of the active precious metal mines produced silver.

On January 8, it was reported in Santa Fe that *The AT & SF Railroad* was conducting a preliminary survey from the Kansas state line to Fort Lyon. The editors of the *Daily New Mexican* predicted that the railroad would not be

---

[681] Santa Fe *Daily New Mexican,* 5/10/73, p. 1, col. 1.

stopped until it reached the "waves of the Pacific" and is made the fair-weather trans-continental route of the nation.

All corners of the Territory were plagued with Indian outbreaks during the year. The Peace Commission reported in January that the Utes of Colorado and New Mexico had murdered a party of six people. They would not allow miners on their land. They either drove them out or killed them.[682]

In February, the Elizabethtown *Press* complained the Jicarilla Apaches were stealing settlers' stock and blaming the Utes of the Cimarron reservation.[683] By July, the agent reported that the Utes, excepting the old ones receiving provisions every ten days, had been absent the last two food issue days and he had been forced to throw out a large amount of beef prepared for them.[684]

---

[682] Ibid., "The Utes and the Report of the Peace Commission", p. 1, col. 1.
[683] Ibid., 2/17/73.
[684] Ibid., 7/10/73.

The Apaches, under Cochise, were raiding across the Mexican border near Fronteras. They stole stock and then returned to the U. S. and their reservation for refuge. Depredations and robberies were reported as early as May of the previous year. Relations with Mexico were threatened. Letters from Mexico complaining of the San Carlos reservation Apache's attacks had been sent to the War Department in Washington.

The Treasury agent at El Paso asked Washington for protection. He stated that the frontier may as well be given up to smugglers, as the deputy collectors were all resigning. Their lives were daily at risk from both Indians and bandits and their salaries were inadequate for the risks involved. The collector at Presidio del Norte had resigned and asked for troops to protect himself and government property until his successor arrived. The military told the press that the troops would have to force Cochise to refrain from raiding in Mexico or trouble between the U. S. and its neighbor would break out.[685]

An Apache Peace Conference was held at Camp Verde on April 6. Due to the army's rout of the Apaches in the last campaign over 200 Indians were killed, and 150 Tonto Apaches surrendered. The warriors gave up their arms and the talks began at 9:30 a.m. General Crook was in charge. The general policy was announced that "the Indians would be treated humanely. The mixed-breeds will be placed on reservations where they can at least partially maintain themselves, keep order and harmony within their own tribe."[686]

Though somewhat abated, the illegal Comanche Indian trade on the eastern border continued. The Comanches were not considered a New Mexican tribe or its responsibility, but plans were afoot to place the tribe on a reservation.

---

[685] Ibid., 5/26/72.
[686] Ibid., 4/6/73, p. 1, col. 2.

In April at Trinidad, announcement of meetings every few days were being held to discuss the policy of voting $150,000 bonds to *The Atchison, Topeka & Santa Fe Railroad* to build to their location. The fourteenth of April was set for a bond election and was expected to carry a decisive majority.

Sallie Elkins died on October 268 1872. On April 15, 1873, *The Daily New Mexican* published that Steve Elkins had returned to Santa Fe after six months absence. The news item was small, though on the first page. It would be customary that a public figure should be allowed a liberal amount of time to recover from the loss of a spouse. Friends apparently invited him on a fishing trip which was later reported.

The Navajos had been quiet. W. F. M. Arny was replaced as Territorial Secretary in mid-June. On June 20, 1873, President Grant officially nominated Arny to manage the Navajo tribe. Arny accepted. The old challenges of territorial secretary were no longer there. He planned to get the Navajo schools in proper order and advance the tribe's education. The reservation was nearly three and a half million acres and contained nearly10,000 Indians. His headquarters were at Fort Defiance, an old military post near the New Mexico and Arizona border. In 1872, their agent, William F. Hall had been able to return stolen livestock, expel whisky sellers, and maintain order. One hundred Indians had cooperated, but Superintendent Levi E. Dudley insisted that if the Indians were peaceful there was no need to expend so much money.[687]

    The tribe planted corn, beans, pumpkins, and other crops, but that winter was especially harsh and additional provisions were necessary. Snow covered the reservation two feet deep in 1872. Sheep had died by the thousands and game had disappeared. Although matters were clearly in

---

[687] Murphy, Lawrence R., *William F. M. Arny: Frontier Crusader*, Chap. 11, "Sowing the Seeds of Revolt," pp. 212-317.

crisis, and Washington was fully informed, the authorities would not relent.[688]

Despite the hardships the government would not recognize, Arny was successful in his plan to establish the Navajo police force at the Fort Defiance reservation. However, the force was ordered to be abandoned. Arny developed a system of using tickets issued as payment for labor at the agency to pay the police for their services. The Commissioner of Indian Affairs never detected the secret operation.[689]

Two weeks later, General Alexander of Fort Garland reported to the newspaper that he had gone to Cucharas. He said the Utes had since returned to their old neighborhood. He spoke with their primary chief who said they intended to stay at Cucheras. They had no feelings of hostility toward the whites but seemed sullen and closed to receiving any advice. The General decided to send troops to

---

[688] Ibid., p. 314.
[689] Ibid., p. 213.

Cucharas, a company of the Fifth Infantry. The soldiers would see that there would be no more outbreaks. Lieutenants Rice and Pope led the troops.

The Pueblo *Chieftain* reported to the *Daily New Mexican* on June 16, 1873, that Colonel Dudley, Indian Commissioner, had gone to look after the Utes, and would do all in his power to make them go back to their reservation and stay at Cimarron. "We learn that Kaniache and his twelve lodges of disreputable savages are on the Cucharas, interfering with settlers, destroying the growing crops, and causing them much trouble and annoyance." The Coloradans thought the Cimarron agent should take better care of them than he had been doing. He should be able to account to the government when he makes the next requisition for supplies. The people of southern Colorado want the Utes and Apaches removed or restrained, or they may "meet with a style of punishment that may materially decrease their numbers."[690]

New Mexicans in Santa Fe always celebrated the Fourth of July when there was enough money to pay for the planned events. This year there would be more than the usual orations at the Plaza. The Declaration of Independence was read in both languages, music was by the 15th Infantry Band, and a roaring salute was given at mid-day. In the evening there was music in the Plaza. Bonfires, torch lights, and fireworks lit up the streets almost as bright as day. General G. A. Smith of Fort Marcy coordinated the affair.[691] Steve had invited his boyhood friend, Henry Waldo to visit him at Santa Fe over the July 4 holiday and they joined the crowd that evening in celebrating the affair.

On July 10 it was learned that *The Arkansas Valley Railway*, branch railroad of the *Kansas Pacific Railway*, was under construction between Kit Carson and Fort Lyon,

---

[690] Santa Fe *Daily New Mexican*, 6/16/73 and 7/1/73.
[691] Ibid., 7/5/73, p. 1, col. 1.

Colorado. The tract to Fort Lyon would be completed and the cars running by August 1.

On July 15 the Republican Territorial Convention was organized and met. Nine counties were represented, the southern counties excluded due to their credentials arriving late. The resolutions were made by committee, and read to the assembly in the afternoon. These were accepted and unanimously adopted. The next order of business proceeded to nomination of a candidate for Congressional Delegate. Pedro Sanchez of Taos nominated Steve Elkins and the vote was called.[692] Elkins was elected by acclamation.

Since Elkins' arrival in Santa Fe, he had stayed out of sight. Several men approached him to accept the nomination for Congress, but he refused. He begged that the needs of The Maxwell Land Grant and Railway Company and The 1st National Bank allowed him no

---

[692] Ibid., 7/16/73, p. 1, cols. 1-2.

further responsibilities. However, his supporters continued to press him for a positive response. He attended the convention as a delegate from Santa Fe County, and finally consented.

The day following the convention, *The Daily New Mexican* wrote of Elkins as the Party's choice: "*He has constantly declared ever since his return from Washington last spring that he was not a candidate for the nomination and endeavored earnestly to induce the delegates to nominate another man. In this he was sincere . . . . and reluctant to accept the position . . .*"[693]

Elkins was nominated against his will and his earnest appeals. He begged that his business affairs demanded his attention as well as his duties to the bank. He agreed to give his best effort in the campaign, and if elected to do his best for the Territory in Washington.

---

[693] Ibid., 7/17/73, p. 1, col. 1, "Our Next Delegate."

On July 19 it was announced that *The Colorado and New Mexico Railroad* filed their incorporation papers in the Las Animas County clerk's office on July 14. A railroad and telegraph line would operate from Colorado's Las Animas and Bent Counties to Santa Fe, also to Trinidad and Pueblo. The incorporators included the names of *The Atchison Topeka & Santa Fe Railroad*'s officers and directors. The railroad's name was adopted according to the laws of Colorado but was *The Atchison Topeka & Santa Fe* line. No time limits were given in the announcement.[694]

The incumbent, Congressman Don Jose Gallegos, hoped to face his formidable adversary bravely. He began with a challenge from Mora County's Don Vicente Romero, of his own party. The Democrat Convention was held in Albuquerque, a change of venue for the occasion. It was held on July 26. All reports stated that the convention was unusually quiet. No northern counties were

---

[694] Ibid., 7/21/73, p. 1, col. 1.

represented, and no formal account was given to the Republican *Daily New Mexican*. The newspaper was solemnly silent in criticism, but reminded New Mexicans that religion had no place in politics and that any candidate from New Mexico should be able to speak the English language.[695]

The Albuquerque Convention would later be labeled "a burlesque" and the candidate, Gallegos, an "unprecedented deceiver."[696] On August 29 *The Santa Fe New Mexican* published an item from *The Denver Tribune* concerning New Mexico's Delegate campaign. "At Las Vegas the other day the Padre in his speech repeated the charge against Mr. Elkins that he was the friend, protector and encourager of Texas cattle thieves. After he had finished, Mr. Elkins replied that Mr. Hittson employed him as his lawyer to attend to purely professional business. He had simply done his duty to his client in this case as he

---

[695] Ibid., 7/30/73, "The Chronic Howl," p. 1, col. 1.
[696] Ibid., 8/7/73, p. 1, col. 1-2 and 8/16/73, p. 1, cols. 1-2.

would in any other. He went on to explain that he was also counsel for Mr. Gallegos himself. The case involved Mr. Gallegos who stood charged with *having robbed the heirs* of a large estate. He proposed to make the best defense he could."[697]

The Denver paper added that the retort was certainly admirable and gave Elkins a great advantage as far as that one occasion was concerned.

On Saturday evening, September 13, a large public meeting was held in the plaza. Torches and banners were carried while the crowd marched to Delegate Elkins' home, escorting him to the Pagoda which was lighted with Chinese lanterns. Elkins stood before the audience and addressed them in Spanish, thanking them for their support, expressing gratification for the victory, and for their confidence.

---

[697] Ibid., 8/29/73, p. 1, col. 2, [From the Denver *Tribune*], "A Hit, A Hit, A Palpable Hit."

Steve had every reason for confidence. General Grant was now fully established as a popular figure in the Territory. He had won by a large margin in the preceding elections.

Only ten days after the election celebrations in Santa Fe, the announcement of the suspension of the New York banking house of Jay Cooke & Company came to the Territory. The brief message accompanying the statement said, "With no positive reason as to the cause of this unexpected affair, it is attributed to the attempt to float *The Northern Pacific* bonds, and the extensive syndicate behind them. How disastrous the failure may be cannot yet be known, but it is hoped that the suspension will only be temporary."[698]

The joint partnerships made with European banks and syndicates represented in the sales of the Maxwell and Sangre de Cristo Grants was both an achievement and a

---

[698] Ibid., 9/23/73, p. 1, col. 2.

downfall for the American economy. It was intended to unite the country in the use of specie as the medium of exchange rather than "greenbacks." However, the change was made too abruptly.

In Europe, a depression was already under way. The Europeans began to call in American loans. Bonds for railroads were overextended and floating capital was unbalanced. In the United States, there was a failure of currency reform which had deadlocked on the issue of silver. The country's leading bond holder, the Jay Cooke banking firm, was forced to share profits with a syndicate of major European bankers. As a result, the United States joined the depression which also struck European banks in 1873. United States' banks were unprepared to issue enough currency in greenbacks to offset the demands from panicked American investors.

Steve's election on September 1, 1873 was expected. The earliest returns came from the most populous counties, but his majorities were visible in southern counties such as Dona Ana. That county had not been represented at the Republican nominating convention. It was disgraced by its performance in the Mesilla riot which led to Gallegos' election.

Statehood was the issue dividing the public. Many citizens feared taxes to fund public education, construct roads, bridges and public buildings. They sensed the expense was beyond what the local economy could manage. A portion of the public distrusted the federal government, its separation from the Catholic church, especially concerning public education. Rural areas resented the improvements given the more populous towns and wealthier districts.

The issue of Elkins' wealth and his connection to a foreign firm were serious obstacles to overcome. A lawyer's means of income was suspect. Elkins' peculiar knack for establishing corporate structures was incomprehensible in the early era of large enterprise. Elkins' mentors were unknown to New Mexicans, although these men were leaders in St. Louis and Kansas City, familiar cities to most urban territorial residents. Businessmen, like Joab Bernard, bankers like Robert Campbell and William Bernard, mining engineers or geologists like Joab Bernard, and judges like William Bernard were as enigmatic and influential as Kit Carson and Lucien Maxwell.

Made in the USA
Middletown, DE
19 May 2023